SportsWorld

Also by Robert Lipsyte

FICTION

The Contender
Something Going (with Steve Cady)
Liberty Two

NON-FICTION

Nigger, the Autobiography of Dick Gregory
The Masculine Mystique
Assignment: Sports

SportsWorld

AN AMERICAN DREAMLAND

by Robert Lipsyte

Quadrangle Books
Published by Quadrangle/
The New York Times Book Co.

First paperback printing, September 1977

Quadrangle Books are published by Quadrangle/The New
York Times Book Co., Inc., Three Park Avenue, New York,
N.Y. 10016. Published simultaneously in Canada by Fitzhenry
& Whiteside, Ltd., Toronto.

Library of Congress Cataloging in Publication Data

Lipsyte, Robert.
   Sportsworld: an American dreamland.

   Includes index.
    1. Sports—United States. 2. Professional sports—
United States. I. Title.
GV583.L56   796'.0973   75–8299
ISBN 0–8129–6286–9

THIS BOOK is for Jim Roach, who gave me time and space to swing and miss and swing again when he was sports editor of *The New York Times*, and for his assistant and successor, Jim Tuite;

for friends in the sports department who helped me: Gay Talese in the beginning, later Steve Cady, Bill Wallace, Frank Litsky, Neil Amdur, and Pete Bonventre, now at Newsweek; for Sam Goldaper, then of the *Herald Tribune*, who walked me up to my very first press box in 1959;

for two teachers, now gone: James J. Kernan of Forest Hills High School and George Nobbe Sr. of Columbia; for Jonathan Segal, the Quadrangle editor who originally asked me to write this book, and rooted it in,

and, of course, for Marjorie Rubin Lipsyte, my collaborator and best friend.

Contents

Introduction   *ix*

CHAPTER 1   *Welcome to SportsWorld*   3

CHAPTER 2   *Please Rise for Our National Pastime*   23

CHAPTER 3   *Sport of the Sixties: Instant Replay
... Replay ... Replay ...*   50

CHAPTER 4   *The Heavyweight Crown Prince of
the World*   74

CHAPTER 5   *Sport of the Seventies: Sly,
Midnight Moves*   140

CHAPTER 6   *The Back Page*   170

CHAPTER 7   *The Body Biz*   200

CHAPTER 8   *Designated Heroes, Ranking Gods,
All-Star Holy Persons*   217

CHAPTER 9   *The Last American Dream*   276

Index   285

Introduction

FOR THE PAST one hundred years most Americans have believed that playing and watching competitive games are not only healthful activities, but represent a positive force on our national psyche. In sports, they believe, children will learn courage and self-control, old people will find blissful nostalgia, and families will discover new ways to communicate among themselves. Immigrants will find shortcuts to recognition as Americans. Rich and poor, black and white, educated and unskilled, we will all find a unifying language. The melting pot may be a myth, but we will all come together in the ballpark.

This faith in sports has been vigorously promoted by industry, the military, government, the media. The values of the arena and the locker room have been imposed upon our national life. Coaches and sportswriters are speaking for generals and businessmen, too, when they tell us that a man must be physically and psychologically "tough" to succeed, that he must be clean and punctual and honest, that he must bear pain, bad luck, and defeat without whimpering or making excuses. A man must prove his faith in sports and the American Way by whipping himself into shape, playing by the rules, being part of the team, and putting out all the way. If his faith is strong enough, he will triumph. It's his own fault if he loses, fails, remains poor.

Even for ballgames, these values, with their implicit definitions of manhood, courage, and success, are not necessarily in the individual's best interests. But for daily life they tend to create a dangerous and grotesque web of ethics and attitudes, an amorphous infrastructure that acts to contain our energies, divert our passions, and socialize us for work or war or depression.

I call this infrastructure SportsWorld. For most of my adult life, as a professional observer, I've explored SportsWorld and marveled at its incredible power and pervasiveness. SportsWorld touches everyone and everything. We elect our politicians, judge our children, fight our wars, plan our vacations, oppress our minorities by SportsWorld standards that somehow justify our foulest and freakiest deeds, or at least camouflage them with jargon. We get stoned on such SportsWorld spectaculars as the Super Bowl, the space shots, the Kentucky Derby, the presidential conventions, the Indianapolis 500, all of whose absurd excesses reassure us that we're okay.

SportsWorld is a sweaty Oz you'll never find in a geography book, but since the end of the Civil War it has been promoted and sold to us like Rancho real estate, an ultimate sanctuary, a university for the body, a community for the spirit, a place to hide that glows with that time of innocence when we believed that rules and boundaries were honored, that good triumphed over evil, and that the loose ends of experience could be caught and bound and delivered in an explanation as final and as comforting as a goodnight kiss.

Sometime in the last fifty years the sports experience was perverted into a SportsWorld state of mind in which the winner was good because he won; the loser, if not actually bad, was at least reduced, and had to prove himself over again, through competition. As each new immigrant crop was milled through the American system, a pick of the harvest was displayed in the SportsWorld showcase, a male preserve of national athletic entertainment traditionally enacted by the working class for the middle class, much as the performing arts are played by the middle class for the amusement of the upper class.

By the 1950s, when SportsWorld was dominated by what are now called "white ethnics," the black American was perceived as a challenging force and was encouraged to find outlets in the national sports arena. Although most specific laws against black participation had already been erased, it took cautious, humiliating experiments with such superstars as Jackie Robinson and Larry Doby to prove that spectator prejudice could be deconditioned by a winning team. Within a few years, pools of cheap, eager black and dark Latin labor were channeled into mainstream clubs.

So pervasive are the myths of SportsWorld that the recruitment of blacks has been regarded as a gift of true citizenship bestowed upon the Negro when he was ready. It has been conventional wisdom for twenty years that the black exposure in sports has speeded the integration of American society, that white Americans, having seen that blacks are beautiful and strong, became "liberalized."

This is one of the crueler hoaxes of SportsWorld. Sports success probably has been detrimental to black progress. By publicizing the material success of a few hundred athletes, thousands, perhaps millions, of bright young blacks have been swept toward sports when they should have been guided toward careers in medicine or engineering or business. For every black star celebrated in SportsWorld, a thousand of his little brothers were neutralized, kept busy shooting baskets until it was too late for them to qualify beyond marginal work.

The white male spectator who knew few ordinary black men to measure himself against may have had his awareness raised by watching such superior human beings as Frank Robinson, Jim Brown, Bill Russell, O. J. Simpson, and other highly merchandised SportsWorld heroes, but it also doubled his worst fears about blacks: added to the black junkie who would rip out his throat was the black superstud who could replace him as a man —in bed, on the job, as a model for his children.

By the middle of the 1970s it seemed as though the black experience in SportsWorld might be recapitulated by women. SportsWorld seemed on the verge of becoming the arena in which women would discover and exploit their new "equality." It would be a complex test of adaptability for SportsWorld. The major sports were created by men for the superior muscles, size, and endurance of the male body. Those sports in which balance, flexibility, and dexterity are the crucial elements have never been mass-promoted in America. When a woman beats a man at a man's game, she has to play like a man.

There were signs, however, that women may not embrace SportsWorld as eagerly as did the blacks, profiting from that sorry lesson as well as from their own greater leverage in American society. It is no accident that Billie Jean King, while still an active player, became an entrepreneur and an important voice in

American cultural consciousness while Jackie Robinson was a Rockefeller courtier almost to the end of his life.

A great deal of the angry energy generated in America through the coming apart of the 1960s was absorbed by SportsWorld in its various roles as socializer, pacifier, safety valve; as a concentration camp for adolescents and an emotional Disneyland for their parents; as a laboratory for human engineering and a reflector of current moral postures; and as a running commercial for Our Way of Life. SportsWorld is a buffer, a DMZ, between people and the economic and political systems that direct their lives; women, so long denied this particular playland, may just avoid this trap altogether.

But SportsWorld's greatest power has always been its flexibility. Even as we are told of SportsWorld's proud traditions, immutable laws, ultimate security from the capriciousness of "real life," SportsWorld is busy changing its rules, readjusting its alliances, checking the trends. SportsWorld is nothing if not responsive. Hockey interest lagging, how about a little more blood on the ice? Speed up baseball with a designated hitter. Move the football goal posts. A three-point shot in basketball. Women agitating at the college arena gates? Let 'em in. Give 'em athletic scholarships, "jock" dorms, and Minnie Mouse courses. How about a Professional Women's Power Volleyball League?

Stars, teams, leagues, even entire sports may rise or fall or never get off the ground, but SportsWorld as a force in American life orbits on.

Ah, baseball. Our National Pastime. An incredibly complex contrivance that seems to have been created by a chauvinistic mathematician intent upon giving America a game so idiosyncratic that it would be at least a century before any other country could beat us at it. And indeed it was. After a century in which baseball was celebrated as a unique product of the American character, Chinese boys began winning Little League championships, and young men from Latin America and the Caribbean began making a significant impact upon the major leagues. The highly organized Japanese, who had taken up the game during the postwar occupation of their country (perhaps as penance for yelling "To Hell with Babe Ruth" during banzai charges) were almost ready to attack again.

But SportsWorld had spun on. That other peculiarly American game, football, declared itself the New National Pastime. Baseball and God were announced dead at about the same time, but the decision against baseball apparently is taking longer to reverse, thanks in the main to pro football's colossal public relations machine. The National Football League played its scheduled games on Sunday, November 24, 1963, because its historic television deal was pending and Commissioner Pete Rozelle was determined to prove that nothing, *nothing*, could cancel the show. But that winter, NFL sportscasters infiltrated the banquet circuit with the engaging theory—quintessential SportsWorld—that America had been at the brink of a nervous breakdown after President Kennedy's assassination and that only The Sport of the Sixties' business-as-usual attitude had held the country together until Monday's National Day of Mourning unified us all in public grief.

Ten years later, though hopefully still grateful, America had grown bored with the cartoon brutality of pro football. America was boogieing to the magic moves and hip, sly rhythms of basketball, The Sport of the Seventies. We've had enough of pure violence, simulated or otherwise, went the SportsWorld wisdom, now we need something smooooooooth.

There is no end to SportsWorld theories—of the past, the present, the future—especially now that a new generation of commentators, athletes, coaches, and fans feels free to reform and recast sports, to knock it off the pedestal and slide it under the microscope, giving it more importance than ever. SportsWorld newspapermen dare to describe to us action that we have seen more clearly on television than they have from the press box, and SportsWorld telecasters, isolated from the world in their glass booths, dare to explain to us what the players are *really* thinking. SportsWorld analysts were once merely "pigskin prognosticators" predicting the weekend football scores; now they may be as heavy as any RAND Corporation futurist. Is hockey an art form or is it a paradigm of anarchy, in which case are we obligated as concerned citizens to watch it? Is tennis more than just a convenient new market for clothes and building materials and nondurable goods? What will be The Sport of the Eighties? Will no sport ever again have its own decade? Will cable television and government-regulated sports gambling and the institutionalized fragmenting of society balkanize us into dozens of jealous Fandoms?

SportsWorld, once determinedly anti-intellectual, has become a hotbed of psychologists, physicians, and sociologists questioning premises as well as specific techniques. Should lacrosse players really be eating steak before games, or pancakes? Why are the lockers of defensive linemen neater than those of offensive linemen? Does athletic participation truly "build character" or does it merely reinforce otherwise unacceptable traits? Should communities rather than corporations own teams?

But very few people seem to be questioning SportsWorld itself, exploring the possibility that if sports could be separated from SportsWorld we could take a major step toward liberation from the false values, the stereotypes, the idols of the arena that have burdened us all since childhood.

SportsWorld is not a conspiracy in the classic sense, but rather an expression of a community of interest. In the Soviet Union, for example, where world-class athletes are the diplomat-soldiers of ideology, and where factory girls are forced to exercise to reduce fatigue and increase production, the entire athletic apparatus is part of government. Here in America, SportsWorld's insidious power is imposed upon athletics by the banks that decide which arenas and recreational facilities shall be built, by the television networks that decide which sports shall be sponsored and viewed, by the press that decides which individuals and teams shall be celebrated, by the municipal governments that decide which clubs shall be subsidized, and by the federal government, which has, through favorable tax rulings and exemptions from law, allowed sports entertainment to grow until it has become the most influential form of mass culture in America.

SportsWorld is a grotesque distortion of sports. It has limited the pleasures of play for most Americans while concentrating on turning our best athletes into clowns. It has made the finish more important than the race, and extolled the game as that William Jamesian absurdity, a moral equivalent to war, and the hero of the game as that Henry Jamesian absurdity, a "muscular Christian." It has surpassed patriotism and piety as a currency of communication, while exploiting them both. By the end of the

1960s, SportsWorld wisdom had it that religion was a spectator sport while professional and college athletic contests were the only events Americans held sacred.

SportsWorld is neither an American nor a modern phenomenon. Those glorified Olympics of ancient Greece were manipulated for political and commercial purposes; at the end, they held a cracked mirror to a decaying civilization. The modern Olympics were revived at the end of the nineteenth century in an attempt to whip French youth into shape for a battlefield rematch with Germany. Each country of Europe, then the United States, the Soviet Union, the "emerging" nations of Africa and Asia, used the Olympics as political display windows. The 1972 Arab massacre of Israeli athletes was a hideously logical extension of SportsWorld philosophy.

SportsWorld begins in elementary school, where the boys are separated from the girls. In *Sixties Going on Seventies*, Nora Sayre recounts the poignant confrontation of a gay man and a gay woman at a meeting. She is banging the floor with a baseball bat, and he asks her to stop; the bat symbolizes to him the oppression of sports in his childhood. But to her the bat symbolizes liberation from the restraint that had kept her from aggression, from sports, in her childhood.

By puberty, most American children have been classified as failed athletes and assigned to watch and cheer for those who have survived the first of several major "cuts." Those who have been discarded to the grandstands and to the television sets are not necessarily worse off than those tapped for higher levels of competition. SportsWorld heroes exist at sufferance, and the path of glory is often an emotional minefield trapped with pressures to perform and fears of failure. There is no escape from SportsWorld, for player or spectator or even reporter, that watcher in the shadows who pretends to be in the arena but above the fray.

SportsWorld

CHAPTER
1
Welcome to SportsWorld

1

I WAS NEVER an avid spectator sports fan. Although I grew up in New York while there were still three major league baseball teams in town, I didn't attend my first game until I was 13 years old. I was profoundly disappointed. Mel Allen on the radio had prepared me for something grander—lusher outfields, a more imposing spectacle, certainly larger men. I went to only one more game as a paying customer. The third one I covered for *The New York Times.*

I attended few sports events as a child, but there was no escaping SportsWorld. That's in the air. I grew up in Rego Park, in Queens, then a neighborhood of attached houses, six-story apartment buildings, and many vacant jungly lots. We played guns in the lots, Chinese handball against the brick sides of buildings, and just enough stickball in the streets and schoolyard to qualify, years later in midtown bars, as true natives. There was no great sporting tradition in the neighborhood, few organized sports of any kind, and only one sports temple, the West Side Tennis Club in adjacent Forest Hills, which accepted neither Negroes, of whom we saw few; nor Jews, which most of us were. It was an early lesson, although I'm not sure what I learned; I hope that I'm not playing tennis today to compensate for a rejection that at the time merely seemed the way of the world.

Even if they didn't play well, boys growing up in the forties and fifties were expected to talk sports to prove they weren't "fags." Since Queens had no resident team, as did Manhattan, Brooklyn, and the Bronx, we had the luxury of rooting for—or paying lip-service to—the Dodgers, the Giants, or the Yankees. Years later, it would become almost a psychological parlor game to guess who picked which team, since local SportsWorld fake-lore had assigned each a distinct image.

The Dodgers represented beer, sweat, unfiltered cigarettes, raucous laughter, and all joyful animal pleasures. Their "bitter rivals," the Giants, stood for Ivy League cool, pseudo-intellectuals, unlit pipes, and a loyalty based entirely on the current standings. Dodger fanatics were loyal, win or lose; in fact, they were more heroic in defeat, which was their culturally assigned lot. Giant aficionados (cognoscenti?, certainly not fans) were predictably insufferable in victory; in defeat they might weasel, claim that their interests lay with the National League as a whole.

The Yankees were simply professionals, the team for tourists and the rich; much later the Yankees would be depicted as corporate Amerika cranking up.

I was a Yankee fan. If pressed, I would attribute it to my Bronx birth, to the way DiMadge "drifted" under a high fly, or, smart-aleck, that it was a cover for my love for the St. Louis Browns. Actually, I was a Yankee fan because I perceived that sports was based on verifiable achievements, not on pull or hooks or clout, not on how adroitly you brown-nosed the teacher or buttered up the landlord or greased the butcher, but on how well you performed and how often you won. If that was the name of the game, I thought, only a fool wouldn't go with the best.

In 1957, a few days after graduation from Columbia, I answered a classified ad for a copy boy at *The Times*. I wanted a summer job to pay my way out to graduate school in California, but the personnel interviewer assumed I was seeking a career foothold. The job was most coveted, he told me; there were dozens of Rhodes Scholars, Fulbright Scholars, and Ph.D. candidates clawing at his door. Despite my inferior credentials, he said, he would keep my application on file. He was very nice, and he told me I might hear from him in five or six months, with a little luck.

I walked a block south to Forty-Second Street and erased *The Times* with a brace of Republic westerns. I took a subway home to Queens. My mother was perplexed. A man had called a few hours earlier and left a message directing me to report to *The Times* for a pre-employment physical. If I passed it, I would start work next week.

The job was at night, from 7 to 3, and it was in the sports department, filling paste-pots, sharpening pencils, and fetching coffee for the night sports copy desk, the cranky, wretched ground mechanics of sports journalism, a dozen men who sat around an island of wooden desks correcting, shortening, and usually improving the hot dispatches of the Aces and Flying Tigers, the traveling sportswriters whom they envied and hated.

The deskmen rarely saw games and sought their salvation in philately, gardening, and Other Women. Individually they were delightful men—Bourbon raconteurs, ex-managing editors of defunct newspapers, former soldiers of fortune—but as a group they breathed only dyspepsia and disgust. It was a very hard, very unrewarding job, and the pressure was killing. More and more baseball games were being played at night, and at more and more cities with unfavorable time differentials, just as *The Times*, itself expanding, instituted earlier and earlier editions to make suburban and out-of-town deliveries. The stories clattering into the office through telegraph receivers were being written ever more hastily in press boxes around the country. Because *The Times* was The Newspaper of Record, there could be no margin for error, not even in the Toy Department, as we were called by the rest of the paper, which we called Outside. And the ultimate responsibility for getting all the news that fit into the paper, and getting it right, fell upon the deskmen.

Some died with their green eyeshades on, and some simply declared emotional bankruptcy and went crazy. When I started, the head of the desk—or slot man as he was called because traditionally (although not in the Toy Department) he sat on the inside curve or slot of a large horseshoe-shaped table—told me quite proudly that he was too mean to go nuts, as had his three predecessors. They were weaklings, to his way of thinking, not man enough to stand the gaff.

One had run screaming into the night, never to be seen again, the story went. Another had put his head down, minutes to deadline, and cried. He was in a state institution, and every Christmas the deskmen took up a collection to send him a box of cigars. The most recent former slot man had taken his place in the slot one morning, nine hours ahead of schedule, and in the dim quiet sports corner of the block-square city room began begging for copy from his invisible rim men. As janitors warily circled, he tore stories off the wire service machines, edited them, wrote headlines for them, stuffed them into plastic and leather canisters, and fired them through the pneumatic tubes to the silent composing room upstairs where they thumped into a padded well, bounced out, and rolled across the deserted stone floor.

He screamed, "Copy, I need copy, we're on deadline, we'll never make it, we'll never make it." He finally collapsed, exhausted, and was gently led upstairs to Medical. He was transferred to less demanding work in the Sports Department, and performed brilliantly.

The current slot man loved that story, and told it often in his high, needling voice. He was forever digging at the manhood of others, how they had frozen or become hysterical at deadline, how a young reporter "wrote like a quiff," how a deskman's sensitivity to the nuance of a story or headline was proof of his effeminate qualities. The slot man never told the story of the makeup editor who, after warning the slot man to stop harassing him, punched him in the nose and within days was assigned a prime beat on the writing staff. This slot man was vicious and personally inelegant—he could pick his ear, his nose, and his teeth simultaneously, and often did. But could he keep that copy moving, filling the newshole, whipping the philatelists and philanderers into melees of editing, snapping off perfect headlines like chocolate squares, and protecting tomorrow morning's egg eaters from minor upsets due to words. God help the writer who allowed a game to "reach a climax," or a team to "come from behind"; the linotypist who clumsily—puckishly?—made Stan Musial "line a shit to right field" or Phil Rizzuto "start a double lay."

Between editions, needling and picking, the slot man declared all games fixed, all athletes cretins, all reporters on the take, all fans suckers. His expressions of sexism, racism, and anti-Semitism were often ingenious, but no one ever considered his misanthropy specialized. He was a sour man in a sour job, and he was surrounded by *The Times*' version of the Rogues Regiment, drunks from National News and the chronically quarrelsome from For-

eign, and a picture editor who had slipped a cheesecake photo
into a lobster edition and a cityside reporter who had mishandled
an important Communist conspiracy trial and some young
sharpies who had opted for the quicker promotions in Sports
instead of the longer, surer ladders of Outside. It was a rather
traditional sports desk of its day, contemptuous of its subject, of
any reader who took it seriously, and, ultimately, of itself. It was
also a very fearful desk; the slot man fed that insecurity, which
he himself felt. Any word, paragraph, quote, that seemed somehow different, questionable, vaguely provocative, that might
cause someone to ask the Sports Editor the next day, "Say, what
was that all about?," that might elicit a complaint from a local
college athletic director, a local ball club's public relations man,
an executive of Madison Square Garden, or a reader with em-
bossed stationery, was quickly scratched out of stories. Thus the
hunky-dories of SportsWorld bobbed charmingly on placid rivers
of ink, not because of conspiracy or payoff, but because no one in
the Sports Department wanted to rock the boat and no one from
Outside cared.

The aphorism about the best and the worst of newspaper
journalism appearing on the sports page was still true in the late
fifties. The spirit of the so-called Golden Age of the Twenties and
Thirties still clung to the press box like stale smoke, but its greatest excesses were long gone. Newsmen still accepted—sometimes
solicited—meals and gifts, but as far as I knew no one was actually demanding percentages of hot fighters, as had Damon
Runyon and his pals. The most blatant image-spinning and build-
ups had given way to a kind of breezy hackery in which beat
writers accepted the news source's premise, and tried to coat it
with angles and twists. Meanwhile, such stylists as Jimmy Cannon, Joe Palmer, and Red Smith were writing prose as good or
better than anything else on newsprint. But it would take the
skeptical professionalism of the 1960s to finally dispel the stale
smoke and bring the sports pages up to the level of the rest of the
paper.

For a son of the so-called silent generation, too independent to
work for a corporation yet lacking a Beat poet's confidence, journalism was a compromise that seemed like a calling. By the end
of that first paste-pot summer I knew I would stay. It probably
came down to something as romantic as the tremor in my bowels

each night when the great machines in the subbasement roared to life with the start of the press run. I felt emotionally, intellectually, viscerally part of something big and good and even a little daring. I would be a Newslinger, too.

It was a good time to break in. Gay Talese and Howard Tuckner had opened the way for what traditionalists would call "bright, irreverent" sportswriting at *The Times*, and many of the old sacred scribes were about ready to be retired to their halls of fame. Attendance figures, ticket prices, and endorsement fees were climbing as the first American middle-class generation with both leisure and money sought family entertainment. Sports and television discovered each other, and the traditional interface between business and sport, between politics and sport, between education and sport became larger and more complex and more important. This was the period of SportsWorld's greatest growth; Sputnik justified the ruthless crusade to be No. 1.

It was hot times then for a young sportswriter. Bill Russell and Wilt Chamberlain were leading professional basketball out of dank gyms, and Jim Brown's hard black anger was smashing through fat Sundays. The Yankee era was still in flower. Harness racing was being citified by crooked lawyers. College administrators were declaring "whole man" concepts to justify swollen athletic budgets. Sonny Liston and Cassius Clay were inexorably punching their way toward each other. Hank Aaron was hitting home runs, though no one heard them yet. People were playing golf, and even watching it. Tennis was still chic, and would remain so until drip-dry clothing put whites on everyone. Bowling was becoming a big-time sport as automatic pin setters made hangar-sized buildings profitable, and advances in heating and air-conditioning made it possible to build them throughout the country; a growing circuit flourished for touring pro bowlers. Horse racing, auto racing, boat racing. I moved from copy boy to statistician to night rewrite reporter. I wrote high school sports and occasional features, often on my own time, and I was sometimes let out to catch a celebrity passing through town or make a fast grab between editions for a quote to freshen up someone else's limp story. On such an adventure one night at Yankee Stadium, Mickey Mantle avoided my eyes and said, "Go fuck yourself," in answer to a question.

I was 22 and astounded. I read the papers. I knew athletes

didn't always speak in complete sentences, but golly, holy mackerel, they never talked like this. My question, of course, was not entirely innocent, but it was certainly not hostile, or even particularly probing. It had to do with a recent incident in center-field in which Mantle and a fan might have exchanged punches. A public event. In any case, Mantle came out of it with a swollen jaw, and the team had gone on the road for a few days, where *The Times'* regular Yankee writer would no sooner bother the great man than would the White House correspondent try to grill the President. Now the Yankees were back home, and I had been shot uptown to check on Mantle's jaw, and his feelings about turning his back on some bleacherites who might like to use it as a target. But Mantle did not care to discuss the matter, and he had been conditioned by his press claque to disregard questions he did not deign to answer. I didn't know the rules yet; my hands were not long out of the paste-pot. When I persisted, Mantle signaled Yogi Berra, and they began to play catch in front of the dugout, firing the ball back and forth an inch over my head. I sensed that the interview was over.

Mantle was more cooperative later, when the pressure was off, when everyone knew he would never be the new Babe Ruth, not even the new Joe DiMaggio. By then, everyone was climbing over a teammate, Roger Maris, who had the poor grace to hit 61 home runs in 1961, beating Ruth's single-season record of 60. Because Roger was merely a fine ballplayer, nothing mythic about him, and a stiff in public, it was not hard to disqualify his feat in the public mind. SportsWorld can be pathologically protective of its heroes. The asterisk attached to Maris like a scarlet letter reminded all fans that he needed 159 games to tie the Babe, 163 to surpass him. The Babe's 1927 season was only 154 games long.

Lecher, glutton, braggart, the Babe looks better every year. In 1974, when Hank Aaron surpassed Ruth's career total of 714 homers, the Babe's shadow all but eclipsed the new champion. There was a Ruthian renaissance, and a number of serious book-length studies of the man, his legend, and his time that conflicted substantially in theory and interpretation with each other. About Aaron there were the predictable reissues of fan-mag books, and a collection of reportage vignettes by George Plimpton. The black slugger's boast to his trailing press corps, "I'm not

Roger Maris, I can handle you guys," missed the point. Thirteen years earlier, a less sophisticated SportsWorld had to diminish Maris to protect the Babe. Now, it built up Aaron's feat to regild the Babe's statue.

Poor Maris, betrayed by SportsWorld, turning inward for his remaining years with the Yankees. He had believed that an athlete was judged by his achievements; now his life was something of an illusion. At the time, along with everyone else, I thought Maris was a narrow, suspicious bumpkin, quick to anger—what baseball players call a "red ass." But, well, in those days I also wondered why Francis Gary Powers, the U-2 spy pilot, had dishonored Nathan Hale's memory by allowing himself to be captured alive.

Yuri Gagarin first in space, the Bay of Pigs, the Berlin Wall, and I was stuck on night rewrite, engine racing in neutral, waiting to be loosed on that world of benevolent owners and wise old coaches and hopeful rookies and modest heroes. I was not filled with social purpose, I did not see sports as a "microcosm of real life," I wasn't zeroing in on myths to debunk or muck to rake. I just wanted to get out there and see what was going on and write better stories about it than anyone else. A very socially acceptable SportsWorld attitude. I wanted to see what I could do against the heavyweights. I wanted to win.

2

The man who will do anything to win, the great competitor, has seen the locker-room slogans, the official graffiti of SportsWorld, and made them his Sutras and Proverbs.

> —WINNING IS THE SECOND STEP,
>   WANTING TO WIN IS THE FIRST.
>
> —TO EXPLAIN TRIUMPH,
>   START WITH THE FIRST SYLLABLE.
>
> —WHEN THE GOING GETS TOUGH,
>   THE TOUGH GET GOING.

The man who will do anything to win will do nothing to rock the boat. He may lie, break rules, even kill, but his hostile energies are predictable and controllable. He will conform. He will not disrupt the team.

The player who will do anything to win may turn mad dog on the field, but he will not march in campus demonstrations during the season. The coach who will do anything to win may divert antipoverty grants to the athletic department slush fund but he will not disparage the educational standards of the university. The businessman who will do anything to win may steal a rival's formula but he will not expose price-fixing in the industry. And the presidential candidate who will do anything to win may lie, steal, commit unspeakable perversions, but he can be relied upon never to upset the social structure that allowed him to play in the biggest leagues.

Richard Nixon was an extreme example of the SportsWorld politician, a truly great competitor who rose and fell muttering Hustle, Desire, Guts. He won the title because he was a True Believer, and he lost it because he stopped looking up at the locker-room wall.

> —IT TAKES A COOL HEAD
> TO WIN A HOT GAME.

Nixon survived much longer than most the culling-out process of the American sports system. He made the freshman football team at Whittier College, and although he never made the Poets' varsity, he remained on the squad for three years. He participated in practice scrimmages, and he wore a number, 12, as a benchwarmer. He was part of the team although he never played, and he did not receive his varsity letter until 1969, a few days before his first inauguration.

His admirers and his critics agreed that his passion for sports was no mere political expedient, no friendly mask created by imagists. Nixon believed that SportsWorld was the real world, that competition was the only true crucible of the soul, that success was the only true goal of the self.

"The President thinks football is a way of life," said Coach George Allen, an old friend. "He is a competitor. One of the things I admire in the President is not that he came back and won, but came back after being beaten twice. The determination to come back shows he is a competitor and that is why he likes football."

"The Mitchell-Agnew-Nixon mentality is what the game is all about," said Dave Meggyesy, the pro linebacker, when he quit the St. Louis Cardinals in 1969. "Politics and pro football are the most grotesque extremes in the theatric of a dying empire. It's no accident that the most repressive political regime in the history of this country is ruled by a football freak."

Nixon's addiction to spectator sports, particularly football, was no joke. Paul Periot, a former official in a government drug abuse agency, recalled a 1971 White House conference that drew many of the most important researchers and clinicians in the field, along with a garnish of celebrities. There were high hopes that Nixon would lend moral support to the conference's recommended programs. The President walked into the meeting late, spotted Gale Sayers of the Chicago Bears, and took him back to his office to talk football. Nixon never returned to the conference.

And sometimes that addiction was surreal. Here is Nixon speaking at a 1970 Green Bay, Wisconsin reception for Bart Starr, then the Packers' quarterback:

"A word about your Secretary of Defense. I think it is only proper to speak of him in this room where all of us who follow football—and I guess presidents have no secrets but it is no secret that I am a football fan—that we know that the defense is essential if you are going to be able to win the game.

"I remember two Super Bowl games. I think Bart will agree that the defense played as much of a role in winning those games as the offense—the defense against the Chiefs and the Raiders.

"And I think, too, as we look at the United States of America today, we look at the defense of America which Mel Laird, a great son of Wisconsin, now has responsibility for.

"The defense is important. As Mel Laird has said, not because the United States wants a war, but because with that kind of defense we can discourage anyone who might want to engage in an offense."

The metaphor became even more unnerving when Laird announced stepped-up bombings in Vietnam and the mining of

Haiphong. He said, "We have sort of an expansion ball-club that's fighting in Vietnam at the present time. The South Vietnamese will not win every battle or encounter, but they will do a very credible job."

At the Pentagon, the new offense was called Operation Iron Hand. At the White House it was renamed Operation Linebacker. Nixon's code name was Quarterback.

This metaphorical Sportspeak did not originate with Nixon— the ancients "wrestled" with their consciences—but his use of it was subtly different from that of any other contemporary politician. De Gaulle, for example, once used a rugby allusion to deride Prime Minister Wilson's early attempt to push Britain into the Common Market. Said Big Charlie of Harold: "He's a linesman who thinks he's an offensive back."

Hubert Humphrey once used Sportspeak to gracefully disassociate himself from President Johnson's Vietnam policies during the 1968 campaign. Vice-President Humphrey said, "I have not been calling the signals. I have been in the position of a lineman doing some of the downfield blocking. There's a great deal of difference but I make no apology for it. You can't always have it your own way."

Eugene McCarthy, offhand and droll, once said, "We know Nixon's stuff. He's got a slider and he's thrown a spitter so many years he's got seniority rights on it," which cast Nixon into a league with Burleigh Grimes, who was allowed to keep throwing the spitball after the pitch was outlawed because he no longer could throw anything else.

Sportspeak was not reserved for the Establishment. Eldridge Cleaver wrote, "It's necessary for people to take a revolutionary position against everything that exists on the planet earth today. Especially if you're black. You can't wait for them to call you up to bat. You just step up there and say, 'I want to bat, sumbitch.'"

All of them, from de Gaulle to Cleaver, used the language of sports in a derisive or evasive or jocular way. Nixon was serious.

And Nixon, for all his "playing the game" and "helping the team" and "full-court presses" was the least physically active of American presidents since the crippled Franklin Roosevelt, who swam for survival in a White House pool ostensibly built with public contributions. There was some kind of athletic justice in

Nixon's circulatory ailments. After all, this was the man who filled in and sealed *our* pool, who told his Sports Advisory Council, "I really hate exercise for exercise's sake. It is no disgrace if some people prefer their exercise vicariously. There is a tendency with television for people to just sit there with feet up, eating pretzels and drinking and that is their participation in sports. I don't think that is bad."

I found Nixon vaguely sympathetic only once: At a football dinner at the Waldorf he began describing a college game he had seen more than thirty years before, and his voice grew high and light and warm as his hands darted and turned with the memory of two obscure defensive ends bravely rushing, in vain, a nameless quarterback. Nixon was not talking about people, of course, but rather a vicarious experience he had had, much as one might recount with animation a movie that somehow has become real in memory. Nixon had once lost himself in that game, and now, in retelling it, was blissing out again. I felt sorry for him at that moment. He had never gotten over missing the varsity cut, and I suddenly understood that his only goal had been getting his letter, not playing the game. He was more interested in being known as a winner than in playing.

Athletes sensed that Nixon was not one of them grown older, as was Dwight Eisenhower, as is Gerald Ford, but rather he was a groupie, a starballer, what they contemptuously call a "jocksniffer." Many athletes are very sensitive to this, and while they will tolerate—in fact, try to cultivate and exploit—jocksniffers among the press, owners, well-connected businessmen, they have a very special hatred for people who dehumanize them by making them fantasy objects. It was not surprising that with the exception of a few athletes with specific causes to promote—Wilt Chamberlain and his "Black Capitalism," Ted Williams and the threatened extinction of Atlantic salmon, and Jackie Kemp, who was running for Congress—sports personalities carefully avoided Nixon's campaign recruiters.

But athletes flocked to Robert Kennedy in 1968, and not only because he wooed them vigorously, which he did. Kennedy, a third-string Harvard end, may not have been any more accomplished a player than Nixon, but Kennedy was accepted as an athlete himself, a man eager to play so he could win, and to win so he could test himself further, mix it up, grow, close the gap between his reach and his grasp, rewrite the record book. It is important to remember that in SportsWorld the so-called jock mentality is not limited to superior athletes. While it would be highly unusual to find an active champion in a competitive sport who did not have a jock mentality, there are thousands of go-getters, top dogs, whiz kids, captains of industry, academic commandoes, self-starters, and kings of the hill who never made a grammar school team, yet, in their fields, play as cock-jock a game as Joe Namath or Jimmy Connors or Muhammad Ali. Robert Kennedy might have turned out to be even more of a macho politician than his brother, whose friendly biographers leave the impression that JFK played one-on-one against Khruschev with all our lives during the so-called Cuban missile crisis.

But Nixon was always more jocksniffer than jock, more manipulator than gladiator. It was no surprise that his closest friend in sports was the Washington Redskins coach, George Allen, who often said, "Winning is living. Every time you win, you're reborn, when you lose you die a little." Their interrelation is instructive.

Allen and Nixon met in 1952, at a sports banquet in California. Allen, then 30, was the Whittier coach, and he had just won a championship for Nixon's alma mater. Nixon was 39, a senator with a national reputation. They recognized each other immediately as tough, opportunistic soul brothers, secret sharers of the belief that anyone not on the team is an enemy, that any act can be justified as long as it is in the interest of a seemingly righteous goal.

Allen's climb was as spectacular and rough as Nixon's. He undercut the authority of Coach George Halas while his assistant at Chicago, then committed breach of contract to become head coach of the Los Angeles Rams. The owner fired him for unethical conduct, but the Rams players, never before so successful, threatened to leave with Allen, and the owner backed off.

Allen players are known for using the "crackback," a legal block in which a lighter player, usually a wide receiver, cuts toward the linebacker at a severe angle and takes him out at the knees, on his blind side. There is little risk to the blocker, but crackbacks have interrupted or ended the careers of quite a few players. Allen does not have to specifically order his players to cripple the opposition. He merely has to remind them that 'cnly winners are truly alive." And remain on the team.

A constant and masterful trader, Allen has even traded players he didn't own. Once the NFL fined him $5,000 for trading a future draft choice he did not have the rights to for a veteran player who could help him win immediately. The trade was allowed to stand because it would have been awkward for the league to force Allen to return a player to a club that had just publicly discarded him. Allen defenders say it was all a book-keeping error. Allen critics say that he counted on such a wrist-slap judgment from the start: In modern pro football economics, a $5,000 fine is a parking ticket, especially if you don't get towed away.

Allen came to Washington in 1971, replacing the late Vince Lombardi, and quickly revived a team dubbed "the Deadskins." President Ford, who has written that "George Allen's principles are consistent with mine," has said that Washington rallied around the new Redskins because a winning team can "galvanize an en-tire Metropolitan area."

Allen did it by creating a climate of paranoia on the club that rivaled Nixon's at the White House. The key to Allen's prepara-tion for a game was the painstaking accumulation of intelligence data. He sent spies to other teams' practice sessions, and it was rumored that he tapped phones and bugged offices; this was gen-erally discounted, but some teams routinely increased security in the weeks before playing Allen. His own practices were held in an isolated training complex with padlocks and guards.

Allen made it clear to the local press that he expected them to be a propaganda arm of the team, parroting his lines and avoid-ing stories that could be distracting to Redskins or psychologi-cally useful to the enemy. Allen covered his own locker-room bulletin board with out-of-town newspaper stories selected to in-furiate and "psyche-up" his players, a common practice that many players find demeaning to their intelligence and maturity, although there is evidence that it can prod a player into a more aggressive performance.

Such practices, along with the demand that religion, home life, personal pleasures, other businesses or hobbies, be deferred to football during the season, is a warm and comforting discipline for many players. They can avoid making complex decisions, they can narrow the focus of their lives, they can avoid their responsibilities as husbands, lovers, fathers, sons, citizens, and all the while they can believe that what they are doing is truly important. Athletes, even seemingly sophisticated athletes, are at least as susceptible to SportsWorld as anyone else.

The Redskins got off to a slow start that first season under Coach Allen, and so President Nixon made a supposedly unannounced—although well-recorded—visit to the team's practice field. There he told the players, "I've always said that in life, as well as in sports, politics, and business, what really makes a team or a country is when it has lost one, it doesn't lose its spirit. I think this team has the spirit it takes. I think this government has it. You're going to go on and win."

It took longer for Nixon to be proven wrong about the government than about the team. The Redskins lost their Conference championship game that season, and there are those who think that the turning point of the game was a Washington flanker reverse that was so quickly perceived by the San Francisco defense that it resulted in a 13-yard loss instead of an 8-yard touchdown. Washington lost the game by only 4 points. One of its linemen later revealed that Nixon had specifically asked Allen to run that play.

"He's really hurting us," said Washington quarterback, Billy Kilmer, of Nixon. "He calls us all the time. I think I'm going to ask George Allen to tell the President not to talk about the game until after we've played it."

Larry Csonka, who was still with the Miami Dolphins when Nixon called Coach Don Shula at 1:30 A.M. with a down-and-in play he wanted used, had this to say in *Always On the Run*, his joint autobiography with Jim Kiick, written with Dave Anderson: "By his position, when the President advocates football, he's implying it's great. He makes it an apple pie thing. The danger is that some people then think everything is right with football. They push little kids into organized football without realizing that when there's too much organization by grownups, it's the grownups' game, not the kids' game."

Football, says Dave Meggyesy, "is an attempt to sell a blown out, smacked out people, fighting inflation, the exploitation of their work, of their earth, of Vietnamese and American Indians, that our system is still socially, economically and politically viable. Pro football keeps telling them you can't be second-rate, you have to be winners. No matter who you victimize, no matter how hard you work or who you sacrifice, it's all worth it to be No. 1."

Coach Allen's first big chance to be No. 1 came in 1973 when the Redskins played in the Super Bowl. In the first series of plays, the Miami Dolphins had the ball on their own 27-yard line. It was fourth down, seven to go. Miami moved into punt formation. The Miami center, Howard Kindig, preparing to snap the ball, adjusted it in his hands.

Suddenly, the Washington middle guard, Harold McClinton, reached across the line of scrimmage and smacked the ball out of Kindig's grip. The ball bounced back a yard and McClinton burst forward and fell on it. Officials ruled it a fumble recovered by Washington, who now had the ball only 26 yards from the Miami goal line, a fine starting point for a touchdown drive, an almost certain field goal.

But the decision was challenged by Miami's Coach Shula, every bit as ambitious and smart as Allen. A rules conference was held. The decision was reversed. Upon proper reflection, it was decided that since Kindig had not actually snapped the ball, that in fact it had never left his hands until McClinton batted it out, McClinton's act was illegal. Washington was penalized 5 yards for interference, the ball was returned to Miami, now on its 32-yard line.

Miami went on to win the game, 14–7. Had McClinton's little crime gone unrecognized and unpunished, Washington might well have won. It was certainly a worthwhile gamble, which is exactly what it was: Earlier in the season, Allen had carefully checked out the play with the NFL office, and he had been specifically informed that a defensive player may not touch the center or the ball until the snap is completed.

Paul Zimmerman, the *New York Post* football writer who uncovered the incident, later recalled, "I once asked Allen how he would like to be remembered. He screwed up his face and thought very seriously. It would be like an epitaph, you know. Finally, Allen said, 'That I want to win so bad I'd give a year off my life.' "

It doesn't seem likely that Nixon, once he was no longer President, got encouraging calls from Coach Allen. He was now a loser, as good as dead.

SportsWorld has no time or place for losers, except as foils for winners; a Billy Conn is trotted out in Joe Louis' shadow, a Ralph Branca helps Bobby Thomson explain the 1951 Miracle of Coogan's Bluff. But there was no victory to balance Nixon's defeat. SportsWorld understood immediately that Nixon had blown it all by himself, he choked in the clutch. When he said he was toughing it out, he was actually freezing at the plate. He had swallowed the apple, not bitten the bullet. He had lost control, gone for the desperation shot when cool, percentage control play was called for. He should have dumped his team and built for the future. But Nixon was running without realizing he had already dropped the ball. SportsWorld knew right away it was just a matter of time before Nixon would be fired by the owners. That's what coaches are for.

The bench jockeys turned it on. Politics is like sports, explained Sam Dash, majority counsel of the Senate's Watergate committee: "When you play a game you have to play by the rules. Otherwise there can be no game."

In 1969, when Nixon declared Texas the country's No. 1 college team over Penn State, Coach Joe Paterno of Penn State challenged the President's football expertise but still went to the White House a few weeks later to help his coaches' association honor Nixon as the man who had done the most for college football that year.

It was four years before Coach Paterno told a Penn State commencement audience, "I can't understand how the President can know so little about Watergate in 1973 and so much about college football in 1969." Paterno, a perennial winner, is one of SportsWorld's institutionalized "radicals," men once considered dangerously subversive until it was understood that they were merely winners ahead of their time. In the midst of the economic and spiritual depression of 1975, Paterno suggested such radical measures as limiting to twenty-five the number of football scholarships any coach could give in any one year (the limit at the time was thirty), and cutting down the number of recruiting visits, by coaches and by prospects, an enormous money-saver for the college.

Nixon's replacement had something that Nixon desperately wanted but could never have—jock chic. Ford's brief presidential "honeymoon" with the media was based entirely on his jock chic, the graceful presence of the true athlete as he faces life physically. The man or woman possessed of jock chic walks proudly naked, sure of the responses, the skills, the beauty, the acceptability of his or her body, even long after that body is no longer reliable or attractive. It's a life-long gift, jock chic. A sagging Johnny Weissmuller can rise out of the water posturing for the camera into his seventies; and old dancers, beauty queens, astronauts, middle-weight champs, will never need to undress in the dark.

Jock chic is absolute comfort within one's flesh, the ability to walk through a crowd as if it were a kindergarten class, to face interviewers, cameras, life, without blinking or trying to hide hands in a pocket. Jock chic makes all clothes appropriate and becoming; jock chic is sexy and enviable and sometimes awe-inspiring. It has nothing, however, to do with intelligence or morality. As the media found out quickly enough about Ford.

It was not as if he was a SportsWorld unknown. President Johnson's comment that Ford played football too long without a helmet while at Michigan obscured a far more interesting exchange. Johnson, a cock-jock politician supreme and a physically compelling presence, was no sports fan. When the Laotian prince and princess visited Palo Alto in 1967, Johnson warned them off the Stanford game. He said, "College football is a great spectacle, but I am not sure that it gives an accurate picture of America. To see some of our best-educated boys spending an afternoon knocking each other down—while thousands cheer them on—hardly gives a picture of a peace-loving nation."

Ford, then House minority leader, responded the next day. He rebuked Johnson for belittling the game, and added, "Personally, I am glad that thousands of fine Americans can spend this Saturday afternoon 'knocking each other down' in a spirit of clean sportsmanship and keen competition instead of assaulting Pentagon soldiers or policemen with 'peace' placards and filthy words."

The same day, Johnson was visiting three continental military bases, pressing the flesh of the young Americans who did not have the choice between demonstrating or playing. Johnson took up the metaphor. He criticized those who "debate the war from the comfort of some distant sidelines."

As Vice-President, Ford had this to say: "We have been asked to swallow a lot of home-cooked psychology in recent years that winning isn't all that important anymore, whether on the athletic field or in any other field, national and international. I don't buy that for a minute. It is not enough to just compete. Winning is very important. Maybe more important than ever."

As President, he seemed never to forget that football had been his ticket out of Grand Rapids and into the big time. He was always centering footballs, as if the feel of them as blood rushed to his head was reassuring. He asked to be judged in a Sports-World context, and, of course, he was. Martin Peretz, editorial director of the *New Republic*, wrote, "It troubles me that he played center. . . . He can only consider options for 20 yards in either direction and . . . he has spent a good deal of his life looking at the world upside down through his legs."

Pete Gent, the former Dallas Cowboy who wrote the novel *North Dallas Forty*, said he was glad Ford had been an offensive lineman, a position that gets "very little glory except what he does for the team in general." Gent told sports columnist Vinny DiTrani that an offensive lineman is "not a prima donna, like a running back or a quarterback—or receiver. He's primarily working for the good of the team, which is the way I hope the President works, too."

Nixon was by now out of the league, for the good of the game, to restore public confidence in the integrity of the contest. The coup de grace was a cheap shot, a crackback. Ford's pardon of Nixon amounted to an unanswerable accusation of guilt without a trial. The pardon cancelled Nixon's next, and biggest, match, the trial itself. Now there were no more contests for Nixon to win. There was no longer a chance for him to be reborn. He was finished.

The SportsWorld metaphor is so rich in possibility, one must simply stop. There is no ending. The cycle is self-renewable. Sports touches every other aspect of American life, and in return is touched. Sports sells television sets, and television finances the growth of sports to provide more television entertainment at higher rates to finance the continuing expansion of sports.

The language of sports, its organization, its values, its class system, its discipline, its energies, are used by politics, by business, by all the factors that engineer our daily life, to justify, vivify, enhance, sometimes obscure nonsports activities, and then these words and concepts and values reenter sports, changed, and insidiously they affect our games: The teaching of self-discipline and responsibility becomes authoritarianism; the search for good health becomes getting fit to win; and sheer sweaty fun becomes highs and lows, rushes and nods.

The specialness of sports, that joyous, yes, ennobling, quality that can lift us out of our lives toward new standards of excellence, that can inspire us to stretch our bodies and spirits, has been co-opted and cheapened and can no longer be trusted.

The sports boom of the fifties, sixties, and early seventies may be over, although, like the death of a sun or the interruption of a narcotics shipment, it will be some time before the event is fully realized on the street. And even then, the pushers of SportsWorld will find something to deal—handi-myth and oldie-goldie nostalgia and instant heroes adulterating the grains of breathtaking beauty that keep us hooked on hopes of future delight.

CHAPTER
2

Please Rise for Our
National Pastime

1

IT WOULD TAKE at least a grand jury to get at the origins of the
New York Mets, but we can assume that the SportsWorld coalition that conceived and executed the plot was basically the same
as the groups that saddled other cities with new teams predi-
cated on new stadiums and new parkways built with public
funds. Those in the city concerned with property values, labor
supply, and public relations wanted a major league team to replace the Dodgers and Giants, who had left after the 1957 season.
Major college teams and professional basketball, hockey, and
football are of no great public relations value to a city unless they
are winners. But a big league baseball team is a station on the
Good News Network. Since 1953, when the Boston Braves moved
to Milwaukee, new datelines have appeared almost every year on
the sports page, those glad rags that Chief Justice Earl Warren
turned to first because "the sports page records people's accomplishments. The front page usually records nothing but man's
failures."

Accomplishment after accomplishment, Baltimore, Kansas
City, Los Angeles, each franchised for Good News; Houston,
Atlanta, Seattle (temporary), Oakland, certified Major League
no matter the quality of its educational, criminal justice, or
health care systems. San Diego. Voila! The stars even fell on
Montreal.

Within twenty years the mental map most Americans carried spread from seven states to fourteen, from one coast to three, from 1200 miles, the distance between Boston and St. Louis, to 3000 miles, and included mountains and savannahs and lifestyles that had always seemed somehow foreign.

Baseball, transmitted by newspaper and radio and television, gave America access to itself. After all, the jet routes were for only a fraction of Americans. The rest sent just their minds traveling—to Florida or Arizona for spring training, to Wisconsin for the All-Star game, to California or New York for the World Series.

After the first twenty years of expansion, only two of the top twenty-three marketing areas in North America—Miami and Toronto—were still waiting for their first major league baseball franchise to boost civic pride and stimulate construction and sales. Those that had lost teams to other cities—Boston, Philadelphia, Washington, Milwaukee, St. Louis, Kansas City, Seattle, New York—were ridiculed and pitied as cuckolds. New York, the No. 1 marketing area, a city whose white middle class was, like baseball, fleeing to the suburbs, seemed to have put more energy into getting a new team than improving municipal services; the priorities rated cosmetics over nutrition.

The New York sportswriters were as enthusiastic as the power brokers. Bright careers had stalled when the Dodgers and Giants left town. The sports job market shrank. There was a frenzy of reevaluation, new layouts, and experimental feature writing in the city's sports departments. The Dodgers and Giants had left gaping newsholes behind them; their departures had severely disrupted old patterns on seven daily newspapers. In sports departments where the start-up question, "What are we going to do?" traditionally had been answered by "What did we do last year at this time?," the space was clear for clever press agents and ambitious young writers and quick-witted editors to pour whimsy and personality sketches and neglected sports into the hole.

The football Jets, then called the Titans, got much of their early publicity because the Hot Stove League—the baseball gossip, rehash, and speculation that sports pages used to feature all winter—was suddenly suffering a fuel crisis. Basketball, horse racing, and all the filler sports like fencing and professional tennis and dinghy racing profited, too. It was no coincidence that some significant changes occurred during that period. Jimmy Cannon was hired off the *Post* by the Hearst syndicate, for the *Journal-American*. The *Herald Tribune* called back Stanley Woodward, the most influential sports editor of his day, and the top paper, *The Times*, broke custom to appoint a working sportswriter, James Roach, as editor.

When the National League's Second Coming was imminent, it was not only the baseball writers who rooted it in. Political columnists and editorialists found symbols of hope and renascence for the city, nay, the entire Western world, in a new franchise on The Big Apple. The National Pastime was back with its implications of rural America at play, a simpler, greener, whiter time.

The baseball writers needed no historical justification to write up a snowstorm. The baseball writer was still prince of the press box then, second only in prestige to the columnist on his own paper. If you can't be a millionaire, they said, you might as well be a baseball writer and live like one. It was an amiable, if pathetic, fiction. The golden age of leisurely train travel, day games, and midnight deadlines lay ruined in the contrails of red-eye jets en route to twilight-night doubleheaders. And an increasing adversary relationship was developing between the press and the baseball bureaucracy.

The writers had come to realize—and by and large accept—that the players, managers, owners, and administrators they were committed to report on regarded the press as a device with which to communicate among themselves, as well as with their customers. As the interoffice memo writers of sports, the press kept everyone up to date on employee performances and business dealings while whipping up the interest of ticket buyers with daily reports of games, which, however critically or literarily written, were still free daily ads.

When the sportswriter fulfilled the industry's expectations he was granted the gifts and favors of the "house man," but generally treated without respect because his price was so low—free tickets for his friends and family, ashtrays and tumblers bearing the team's logo, a pat on the back from the current star with a cheery, "Man, you're getting fat. Better lay off them free sandwiches."

Baseball writer Barney Kremenko recalls a compliment from

Gen. William D. Eckert, who served an undistinguished hitch as Baseball Commissioner in the late 1960s. One day, three months after Kremenko's last paper, the *World-Journal*, had folded, the men met and Eckert said, "You had an excellent story today, you've really been writing fine stuff lately."

If the sportswriter played D.A. or started reporting the frequent jealousies and conflicts within a team, he would be considered hostile and treated as an outsider. He would be alone in a group of men he had to interview every day, travel with, eat with, kill time with in strange cities.

In the late 1950s the pressure on the sportswriter to be more than a reporter of athletic details no longer could be ignored. Television was offering his reader a better seat at the game than he had, as well as play-by-play and interpretation by insiders who were hired and paid by the ballclub. At the least, the sportswriter had to offer his reader fact and opinion unavailable elsewhere, and that meant controversy, bold speculation, and outspoken second-guessing. Dick Young of the *Daily News* was among the first to realize what he had to do to survive; he appointed himself as champion of the "new breed" of fans against the "lords of baseball," a straw-man cabal of owners and top executives. He also spiced his stories with flag-waving diatribes, sexual innuendoes, and specific criticisms of managerial tactics and players' skills. He was hard-working, knowledgeable, a gifted writer, and personally tough; Young can still be seen throwing punches at television cameramen who try to block his view at news conferences. Winners always know who their enemies are.

SportsWorld adjusted to the new coverage; if spectator sports were to maintain credibility, they would have to prove they contained the same grit and juice and musk that Americans were getting in such other popular entertainments as politics and war.

The first few years of the Mets, however, were an undeclared moratorium on the new Roto-Rooter sportswriting. Joy in Mudville. Nothing was too good, or even enough, for the Mets. Park land was rezoned for commercial purposes by a Robert Moses juggernaut (his biographer, Robert A. Caro, describes the resulting stadium as Moses' "answer to the Colosseum of the Caesars") and a contract was negotiated that gave almost absolute control of the "public" facility to the Mets' owner. As if she couldn't have built her own ballpark.

Mrs. Joan Whitney Payson has been lovingly characterized by the sports press as "an elegant anachronism" and "the Mother Dumpling of the Mets." As one of the world's richest women from one of the country's most powerful families, it was assumed that Mrs. Payson was not in baseball for personal publicity or tax advantages, as were most all other owners. Now here was a real down-to-earth fan, a patron of the arts, thoroughbred horse racing, and the Republican Party, who grew so heartsick over the loss of Willie Mays and the Giants (she owned 10 percent of that team and later bought Willie for the Mets) that she just simply had to have a local team all her own.

Mother Met installed her stockbroker, M. Donald Grant, as Chairman of the Board of the Metropolitan Baseball Club, Inc. She hired George Weiss, late of the Yankees, as general manager, to ensure baseball orthodoxy, and Casey Stengel, also late of the Yankees, as field manager, to ensure a friendly press. Indirectly, she also brought Jimmy Breslin into the major leagues. Then a free-lance sportswriter, Breslin wrote a short, slipshod, but cozy book about the Mets that so pleased Mrs. Payson's brother, Jock Whitney, that he installed him as a columnist on his *Herald Tribune* and launched one of contemporary journalism's most significant careers.

That spring, Mrs. Payson, warm and dotty, a sixtyish society dame from Central Casting in floppy hats, blonde curls, and shapeless dresses, appeared briefly for ceremonial occasions, mincing and trilling. She was guarded jealously by Grant, her Minister for Baseball, who otherwise was seen only when he came to the trainer's room for his morning rubdown. I once described him as "tallish, pouchy, gray, well turned out," and the next time he saw me he said, "Pouchy, eh?," and never spoke with me again.

(A routine lesson. Years later, I wrote that a handsome, flashily dressed stranger seen in the company of several former heavyweight champions was a known gambler barred from most racetracks and should be barred from fight camps as well. We bumped into each other one night in the dimly lit parking lot of a Las Vegas motel, and while I sucked for air he threw me a wink and said, "Handsome, eh?")

We could write anything we wanted about Casey Stengel that spring, the sillier the better. That's what he was there for, to

decoy the press away from the politics of the new stadium being
built in Queens, away from the business deals of Weiss, who was
busy stocking the club with established, burned-out ballplayers,
"anesthetic" ballplayers, Branch Rickey called them; their names
were big enough to anesthetize press and public to their loss of
skills.

Casey Stengel talked nonstop from the practice ballfield
through dinner to the closing of the hotel bar and out into the
lobby, making absolute sense, sometimes brilliant points, so long
as you listened carefully, caught the subject's name early in the
monologue, then followed him through detours and changes of
place and era. Stengel was 71 that first Mets' spring training, but
he looked older; the skin of his face was extravagantly pleated,
his hair was white except at the crown where it was stained
yellow from cigarette smoke, and he walked like an arthritic
chimpanzee, a shuffling sidestep on permanently bowed legs. He
made it easy for lazy and insecure writers to continue the stereotype of him as a kind of senile savant babbling "Stengelese,"
which had been invented by columnists whose schedules did not
permit a long day's listening. They dashed in and out of marathon monologues and filed paragraphs of double-talk intercut
with cute references to the "Ol' Perfesser" still "spry" despite his
advanced years, his mind still "remarkably active." Disposability
has always been important in SportsWorld. New shipments of
fresh young bodies and banal middle-aged minds are required
every season, and contributing old people are always regarded as
phenomena or buffoons, or both. Avery Brundage, the dominant
Olympic politician of the twentieth century, was always depicted
as a rigid defender of outworn ideals, when, in fact, he was a
cunning manipulator of the latest ideological fads. Stengel, a
tactical innovator until he retired, always tinkering with teaching
methods and line-ups, was treated as a clown and a breathing
museum piece. He was neither. The very first time I interviewed
him (speaking a little too loudly and enunciating a little too
clearly), I asked him if it was true he had put the motel pool off
limits to the Mets.

"Thass right," he snapped. "And I told 'em they couldn't screw
either. All season. Now print that."

He was unfailingly true to himself. He thought the Mets were "horseshit" (a favorite baseball epithet for incompetence) and that "Mrs. Payson and the attendance got robbed" every time they played. This was treated as a charming eccentricity by the press rather than honest appraisal, which they were not used to. On the other hand, he had no qualms about trotting out his two worst rookies and telling the press that the Mets' future hopes rested on their sloping shoulders. When the youngsters soon disappeared from camp, most writers refused to acknowledge the joke, a harsh one on the boys and a subtle one on them. Some writers attributed it to Casey's failing faculties.

Casey worked hard diverting the writers for the Mets, but he soon lost interest in the team itself. For him, baseball was a chance to manipulate young athletes, to make them perform above their abilities, to impose his will through their bodies, and win. This was impossible with the tired veterans Weiss kept hiring, so Stengel concentrated on entertainment, and the size of the crowd never determined the energy of the show. He was even better, it seemed, with one blue-haired old lady in a hotel lobby, or two little kids by the pool, than an entire Kiwanis convention.

He was capable of foul-mouthed nastiness, especially toward ballplayers who messed up or dogged it, and he could be incredibly kind. I remember one muggy, mosquito-ridden night in Houston, his Mets falling apart and his eyes red-rimmed from fatigue, Stengel was leaning against the railing in old Colts Stadium, an open ballpark, watching his infield practice. He cursed softly. A middle-aged man leaned over the railing and touched his arm.

"I wonder if you remember me, Case," said the man, mentioning his name. "I pitched against you in Kankakee."

Stengel snorted at me, and turned. The man, over 60, his clothes shabby but clean and pressed, was holding the wrist of a big, surly-looking teenage boy, who seemed to be straining away out of embarrassment.

"Why, sure," said Casey, clapping the man on the shoulder. "The old fireballer himself, why I was sure glad when you quit that league, did you make me look bad, why, I never could hit you a-tall."

Stengel reached over the railing and grabbed the man's sleeve in one lumpy hand and the boy's in the other. He began to talk, faster and faster, about Kankakee, about the minors, about old ballplayers, and as the life force flowed from his body into theirs, welding them all together, the man straightened and loosened his grip on the boy, and the boy smiled and moved closer to the man.

"Wooooops, gotta go now, thees a-mazin' Mets gonna play, could use you right now, send that boy around if he can throw like you, I'll give him a bonus." Casey shambled away, and the man and the boy, bumping shoulders lightly, walked back up to their seats. When I caught up with Casey, he just shrugged at the question before I even asked it. I'm still not sure if he knew the man, if he didn't know the man, if it mattered to him at all whether he knew him or not.

Stengel was particularly sensitive to the needs of the handicapped; patient and unselfconscious around the crippled and blind, offering up his seamed face to questioning fingertips, dogtrotting up stadium steps so a quadraplegic would not have to be wheeled down. Another reporter to whom I once mentioned this suggested that Stengel, master of public relations that he was, paid particular attention to the handicapped when I was around; he knew I'd shorten my game detail to squeeze in a little kindness. It was a preposterous suggestion, but if he really thought it was true, I asked the reporter, how could he go on day after day writing about Stengel as a court jester without a fold in his brain? "People think he's a nutty old fart; they like to read about him," he said. "Besides, my editors wouldn't believe anything else."

While the press was rediscovering Stengel that first year, and exhorting New Yorkers to support "their" team, Mrs. Payson was often photographed at the racetrack, a transistor radio clapped to her ear, presumably receiving the Mets game a few miles away. There were detailed accounts of the expense Mrs. Payson incurred having scores transmitted to her various island homes. By amplified telephone she once told an assembly of reporters that "all of New York is pleased" with the appointment of Gil Hodges as manager. She was in London at the time.

Even disembodied, Mrs. Payson's enthusiasm was never doubted. Nor was her right to impose a baseball team on New York. Suppose the people really didn't want one? Or would have preferred that the money spent to build her a stadium be used for housing or mass transit or recreational facilities or even a new arm for the Statue of Liberty? And if it was "their" team playing in a "public" stadium, why did *she* have the power to charge admission? Or sell the team? Or move it to another city?

In 1962, had we even thought of such questions, they would have been drowned in the mantra, "Let's go, METS!, Let's go, METS!," a hopeful, senseless racket that levitated the Giants' old Polo Grounds, a condemned ballpark the Mets used for the two seasons that Shea Stadium (named for the political lawyer who cooked up the basic deals that brought New York a new team) was under construction. Besides, we were all too busy supplying answers to be much bothered with questions.

It was smart and streety Dick Young who first promoted the Mets as a people's team, a bastard child of the Dodgers, and a vehicle for his own flowering as a sporting Vox Pop. Young's new breed fans were youthful, vocal, active, obviously hostile to security guards. They came out to participate, to assert themselves, and Young was their champion. He protested when management had the early banner wavers ejected. Within a year, the spontaneous demonstrations had been institutionalized as Banner Day. With prizes.

Young's sidekick, Jack Lang of the *Long Island Press*, compiled and maintained for all newsmen a voluminous schedule of "negative" statistics recording the Mets' failures and mistakes. Management refused to keep such statistics, despite the sportswriters' insistence that they would someday be historically important.

Young and Lang were certainly not "house men." But their playful stories, their "neggies," their coverage of the young, pre-rock crowds as part of the show, set the line for other newsmen on Mets coverage: This was not just a bad expansion team, this was the worst in history!

Fantastic!

It was just this interest and enthusiasm that moved tickets and attracted the New York-based national media, which is always looking for an important trend story only a cab-ride away. The newsmagazines discovered the Mets, the radio and television networks discovered the Mets, the monthly magazines discovered them. They refined the original Young-Lang framework, following the lead of Roger Angell, the *New Yorker*'s fan-in-residence, who heard in the cries of the fans "a new recognition that perfection is admirable but a trifle inhuman, and that a stumbling kind of semi-success can be much more warming." Angell wrote this after the Mets entertained the Dodgers and Giants in their first return to New York. The Mets lost all seven games, at a fantastic profit.

I don't deny my own contribution. Two weeks after the second season began, I picked up an obligatory quote from Margaret Mead about the rowdy fans: "It's something like tribal rites," said Dr. Mead. Then I went into practice for myself.

"The Metophile is a dreamer," quoth Lipsyte. "He believes that one day he will punch that arrogant foreman in the plant square on his fat nose; that he will get in the last word with his wife; that he will win the Irish Sweepstakes; that the Mets will start a winning streak.

"The Metophile syndrome, say psychologists, is defiance of authority. It is present in almost every ego that is not involved in the higher echelons of General Motors, the Seventh Fleet, or Washington Affairs. Translated into pure Metophilian, this means that life beats us nine games out of ten, but the tenth game is a beautiful blue-eyed creation worth waiting through a losing streak for."

Entranced by our own prose, we left no symbol unturned. Out of a clumsy first-baseman named Throneberry, Len Shecter of the *Post* and Stan Isaacs of *Newsday* created Marvelous Marv, the Lovable Inept. They wrote that his initials (M.E.T.) had sealed his fate at birth. Isaacs started a fan club for Throneberry. In one inning, Throneberry was charged with an interference that let in four runs, then hit a triple that drove in two. But he was called out because he forgot to touch first base. The excuse was classic: How could he be expected to remember where the bases were, he got on so infrequently? There was no end to Marvelous jokes—how the Mets had thrown him a birthday party and he dropped it, how he purposely missed pegs from third so the ball would hit hecklers behind him.

A controversy flared. There were those who thought Shecter and Isaacs had no right making fun of a ball player who was merely trying to earn a living, and there were others who saw something antisport and ultimately subversive in the diminishing of heroes: If you can't find something positive to write about an athlete, go find another athlete to write about, but don't hold up incompetence as a model for children.

Throneberry, like most Mets, like most big league players, had been a superstar at 12; he had carried the fantasies of a family, a neighborhood, all the way up to the major leagues. He had been a high school football hero in Memphis, he had married a local beauty queen, he had turned down a dozen college football scholarships to sign for a bonus with the Yankees. The New York Yankees. He had roamed the outfield with Mickey Mantle, and pinch-hit in the 1958 World Series. He had dreamed of batting titles and his glove in a glass case at Cooperstown and big endorsement contracts, and, if he imagined reporters at all, they were asking him deferentially what he had eaten for breakfast and when he knew it was going out of the park. And here they were mocking him.

"It was no joking matter," Throneberry told me years later. "Now, I enjoyed that year with the Mets, after all, I was in the major leagues. Some things that happened then might have been funny the next day, but not when they happened.

"I hate to lose. I hated to lose as much as anybody, maybe more. But I realized you can't bring back what you've done. You can't live a day that's gone. I tried to start every ballgame like a brand new day."

Then Throneberry's voice dropped. "You know, I kind of think of myself as a former Yankee, not a Met. A man is always sentimental about his first team."

Throneberry adjusted that year as a Met. He hit sixteen home runs, which is respectable, and his batting percentage, .244, was higher than his career average. He learned to swallow his anger at the writers who padded around him, laughter in their eyes. Richie Ashburn, a teammate with experience in politics and broadcasting, helped Throneberry understand that he might as well go along with the gag. It was making him a celebrity, it could be worth a buck. When Frank Thomas, a team star, made two errors on one ground ball, Throneberry asked him, "What are you trying to do, take my fans away from me?"

Of course Throneberry adjusted. After all, he had always been an object, he had always acted out other people's fantasies. This

was just another vicarious trip, with condescension instead of
deification, pratfalls instead of heroics. At the end of each World
Series game, two players are unofficially named the Hero and the
Goat, and there is no finer story than yesterday's Goat (he
dropped a fly, he struck out with the bases loaded) becoming
today's Hero (this time he caught the fly and nailed the runner at
the plate, he hit a grand-slam homer). Throneberry was made to
personify Goat for a whole team of Goats, just as Mantle was
supposed to be Hero for a Yankee team of Heroes. Clever sportswriters can be more dangerous than known gamblers, who can
only ruin an athlete's career. The athlete who believes his press
risks living a life that may have been fantasized by someone who
worships athletes or despises them or isn't sure from day to day.
Angell points out the "simultaneous adulation and bitter patronizing of the young and lucky that reveals how out of it we reporters are, how second-hand." In the coverage of the early Mets
add the desperate need on the part of reporters that this team
should prosper and never abandon them.

The fans, psychological teenagers all gland and stomach, took
their signals from the press. Ahead of their time they "let it all
hang out" and "did their thing." The press, in turn, received its
signals back, its theories now confirmed and anecdotalized and
made *newsworthy*.

We attributed the behavior of the fans to the magical power of
the Mets to create love, which I no longer think was the case.
Rather, the Mets projected a wounded animal vulnerability that
unlatched the repressions that fans normally carry to the ballpark
and only let go when they are not awed by the players and the
game.

From an isolated press box, we watched the fans through bin-
oculars; the distance lent a certain anthropological charm to their
bedsheet messages, their incessant marching up and down the
aisles, their booing and cheering (which was as often for each
other as for anything happening in the game), and their endless
posturings for the television cameras once they began panning
the crowd. Many fans came to the ballpark to be seen back home.

We were very heavily into interpretation. One early banner,
"Is Kranepool over the hill?," was seen as a form of black or
gallows humor, rather than a blunt needle into one 18-year-old

first-baseman's ego. We were foolish enough to laugh one Father's Day when a father in the upper deck reached for and missed a foul and his son punched him in the face. That is, the young, childless reporters laughed.

The sexual revolution may have started that year in the Polo Grounds. One chilly afternoon, a woman sitting behind home plate spread a blanket across her male companion's knees and ducked her head beneath it. When special policemen disconnected them and began hustling them out of the park, they protested, "But it's okay, we're married," and then the clincher, "Hey, we're Mets fans."

The 1962 Mets were hyped into a national moral extravaganza, a Job team flogged into the record book. As bad as they were—and they were the worst—they might have been buried without so many witty epitaphs had they died in, say, Pittsburgh or Milwaukee or Minneapolis, cities that do not even rate full-time bureaus of the national media. But in New York the Mets were on the platform to be launched into the skies of SportsWorld Eternal where dwell only two other baseball teams—the 1919 Chicago White Sox, who had to dump the World Series to become immortal, and the 1947 Brooklyn Dodgers, who had to play a Negro. (The trials of Larry Doby in Cleveland that same year were never as well covered as Robinson's in New York.)

The immortalization of a whole baseball team is no small matter because baseball's appeal is basically regional. Even the great teams, the turn-of-the-century Philadelphia A's, the St. Louis Cardinals' Gas House Gang, the New York Yankees' Murderers' Row, wormed their way into the public consciousness as opponents to local teams, not as entities themselves. The national telecasting of baseball games did not change this pattern at all. Recent Baltimore Oriole teams, considered on a par with the great old teams, received little national recognition, and, in fact, had difficulty promoting themselves within their own area. The Oakland A's, after three straight world championships, were still best known for owner Charles O. Finley's ducal hi-jinks. An insurance multimillionaire in his late 50s, Finley made up nicknames for his ballplayers (Catfish, Blue Moon), hired and fired on whim, squabbled with the press, and carried on in a feudal style that lacked only blood duels and prima nocte.

But the Mets were a running joke, a live sitcom, and in 1962 America could still take a joke. It might have been the last year. We had gotten through 1961 without going to war with the Soviet Union over the Berlin Wall, and 1962 looked good. The Mets were at spring training when John Glenn went into space. The New Frontier, Camelot, the Peace Corps, the Green Berets, all were shots of speed into the American psyche. We sensed energy and purpose, muscles coming to life beneath the fifties flab. We could laugh at the hopeless, hapless Mets, destiny's doormats, because we still felt good about ourselves. For all the talk about underdogs and blue collars and the powerless, the average baseball fan, a white, middle-America workingman, did not then see himself as oppressed; in fact, he was living more comfortably, buying more luxuries, and affording his children more opportunities than ever before.

New York's feelings for the Mets were more complex, and included gratitude for bringing the Giants and the Dodgers back, at least a few times a year. For the sportswriters, the Mets became less fun to cover once they left the intimate, ramshackle Polo Grounds for the sterile, stone Shea Stadium. With the fans growing brutish, demanding victory now, and the players turning surly and selfish with no hope in sight, it was difficult to write about the Mets without sounding silly or snide. The one-joke joke was over; Dick Young and Red Smith soon began writing columns demanding that the team grow up and take its place in the standings. During their first seven years, the Mets finished last five times and next-to-last twice.

After covering the first two years fairly regularly, I was spared most of the next sour five. As an "expert" on so-called lovable losers, I had been assigned to cover the dismemberment of Cassius Clay in 1964. It was understood that the regular boxing writer would reclaim his beat once Sonny Liston buttoned the Louisville Lip. The instructions telegraphed to me in Miami Beach said to check the locations of area hospitals so I would waste no deadline time following Cassius to intensive care. The instructions proved useful. I followed Liston to the hospital, and then I followed Muhammad Ali until the fall of 1967, when I began writing a general sports column and plugging into the seasonal cycle, which, in the coming years, would be personal-

ized by Joe Namath, Vince Lombardi, Dave Meggyesy, Kareem
Abdul-Jabbar, Bill Bradley, Howard Cosell, Jim Bouton, Bowie
Kuhn, Denny McLain, Billie Jean King, Joe Namath, Vince Lom-
bardi, Dave Meggyesy, Kareem Abdul-Jabbar, Bill . . .

Ah, the music of the spheres, be they round or oval, never
changes. Only the lyrics. And then only gradually. For the fan
there is a kind of security in this, supportive, even therapeutic,
but for the sportswriter it can be deadening. In the late sixties
and early seventies, when the turmoil in sports could no longer
be ignored or pinned on a few athletes "misguided" by Karl
Marx, Jack Scott, Ho, Che, Benjamin Spock, Ralph Nader (pick
one, any one), many sportswriters—not necessarily just the older
ones—trembled in print for the future of the Republic. Is nothing
sacred? Where are our values? Who will be our heroes? What of
the children?

SportsWorld was merely adjusting on its axis, and those com-
mentators who recognized this, like Howard Cosell, Sandy
Padwe, Ira Berkow, Isaacs, Shecter, Larry Merchant, Jack Mann,
Dave Burgin, Wells Twombly, were considered "controversial."

Many of the others were off beating shadows and railing at
thunder. They attacked Joe Namath, who was everything they
always wanted in a sports subject, and they refused to understand that Curt Flood could indeed be a slave, even at $90,000 a
year. Were they stupid, were they fastened too tightly to the old-
line Establishment tit, were they overloaded with emotional baggage? Were they so blinded by racism and religious prejudice
that they overlooked Muhammad Ali's right to be protected by
the Constitution?

Or were they simply trapped in their own paper cages? A
sportswriter learns early that his readers are primarily interested
in the affirmation of their faiths and their prejudices, which are
invariably based on previous erroneous reports. They do not
want facts that conflict with preconceptions.

The business writer and philosopher, Hy Maidenberg, once described the journalists' learning process thusly. A man walks into a
room wearing a red hat and is punched in the face without explanation. He returns the next day wearing a red hat and is punched
again. The third day he wears a green hat and is treated cordially.
Without ever having been told, he never wears a red hat again.

The beauty of sports, an otherwise intelligent friend has told me, is that it's all black and white, precise regulations, definable goals; and, again unlike life, there is always a definite conclusion. My friend always loves to hear about the drizzly, raw day that Joe DiMaggio, then a batting coach, saw me shivering and sent a rookie pitcher to the Yankee clubhouse for a spare warm-up jacket. My friend always knew the Clipper had class. But my friend hates to hear what Yogi Berra yelled from the Yankee team bus the night it was trapped in a crowd of friendly fans at the Kansas City airport. Yogi yelled, "Go home, you little cock-suckers."

Friends and readers are not the only parties interested in keeping the sportswriter the jongleur of the Happy Pages. In the middle sixties, when I began suggesting that there would be fewer riots at Madison Square Garden if its boxing department stopped promoting its matches as race wars, a Garden official called Jim Roach, *The Times* sports editor, to suggest that Lipsyte had "gone sour" on boxing and might be happier if he got a "change of scene." Implicit in the suggestion was the faint possibility that the Times-Garden pipeline of free tickets and "hot scoops" might be pinched.

Had I been working for many other papers at that time, I would have gotten a change of scene. The threat alone would have worked. But *The Times* sports pages more than paid for their tickets and scoops with free Garden publicity presented as news. Most newspapers are not willing to provide the time, the money, even the moral support necessary to cover sports as something more than a series of carefully staged pseudo-events. *The Times* itself has a tendency to treat sports as "fun and games," a kind of balance to the unrelieved grimness up front, but it is not, as far as I could ever see, as hooked into the sports establishment as it is into the social and political establishment. Other newspapers, particularly those that allow ballclubs to pay the travel and living expenses of sportswriters covering the team, are more responsive to pressure from news sources, even if the individual sportswriter tries hard to forget which corporation is making his job possible.

As it is, the sportswriter must make a conscious effort to remember for whom he is working, and to whom he is responsible. The sportswriter entering the cocoon of a big league ballclub shares many of the same problems with a foreign correspondent in a friendly country or a political reporter on the campaign plane of a candidate with whom he sympathizes. The home office is far away, and reality is with people who work for the news source or for other news-gathering agencies. Manager Ralph Houk used to tell new Yankee reporters, partly in welcome, partly in warning, "We are all in this together."

A pitcher's racial slur, decides the baseball writer, was a drunken reaction to the pressure of the pennant race, and to report it might cause unnecessary dissension on the team; of course, he is too good a reporter to think, even subconsciously, that if this team goes all the way, I get to cover the World Series.

A candidate's tantrum, decides the political reporter, was aberrational, a product of the campaign's killing pace, and to report it would blow it all out of proportion; of course, he is too good a reporter to think, even subconsciously, that if this man becomes President I become the White House correspondent.

Reporters make decisions every day about what their readers will or will not know. Most decisions are trivial, a few have been literally earth-shattering. Most sports reporters think they sleep better than political reporters because no lives are involved in their being right or wrong. But in the long run, the infectious values and myths transmitted by bad sportswriters may be the deadliest words in the paper.

2

In the fall of baseball's centennial year, 1969, during a bitter mayoralty campaign and a hot National League pennant race, a sociologist stood on a midtown New York streetcorner and asked 150 passersby, "Who is going to win?"

One hundred and three answered, "The Mets."

It was hardly a scientific survey. And given the local mindset, many interviewees might have preferred not to discuss politics with a man so large and black as the sociologist, the 6-foot 8-inch fiercely bearded Harry Edwards.

But Dr. Edwards' conclusion—that more New Yorkers were thinking about sports than about politics, that more were enthralled by Tom Seaver than by John Lindsay—was hardly a shock.

Why shouldn't they be? All their lives they had been told that politics was dirty, that baseball was beautiful; that politicians were connivers, that ballplayers had the hearts of children; that a smoke-filled caucus room was the hellish furnace of democracy and that a sunny ballpark was its shrine and reward. In 1969 people were just beginning to realize that they had been given sunny ballparks to keep them out of smoke-filled rooms, that politics was more exciting than any spectator sport, that the meanest little elected official had more direct impact on his times than all but a handful of the best-known athletes.

It turned out that 1969 was a critical year for baseball. The new President was a rabid football fan. Even worse, anti-Nixon elements had been alienated by the refusal of most baseball clubs to rearrange their schedules around the days of mourning for the Rev. King and Senator Kennedy. Many players resented having to play, and this feeling of powerlessness would be translated into a militant guild spirit against the owners for years to come. Worst of all, the National League had hastily expanded, to Montreal and San Diego, to keep up with the American League, and for the first time both leagues were split into East and West Divisions, with playoffs leading to World Series. So much for tradition in the 100th Year.

But the game had not changed. Unlike football, which is so crude a game it can be played in rain and snow, baseball is wondrously precise and ordered, yet it requires only as much as a fan wants to give, be that a casual, dozing inattention in front of a televised game as gentle as a low fire, or a mental and emotional involvement so intense it spills into madness and murder.

Time stands still in baseball. The play, not the clock, determines the length of the game. Theoretically, innings may follow innings until we all die on the bases; we have the power to keep the rally alive. No wonder baseball is the richest in language and symbol of all our sports; no wonder the sportswriters who approach it as professionally as they would an election or a four-alarm fire are called "irreverent" and "iconoclastic," as if they were carving their by-lines on a cathedral wall or discovering Made in Hong Kong labels on saints' relics.

Everyone has played baseball. Even most girls have the feel of bats and gloves, and all boys know there were fat, skinny, short, crippled, one-legged, and one-armed major leaguers. Generations learned how to find percentages by figuring out batting averages, and how to read and imagine by deciphering box scores.

That baseball is male soap opera, at its best a serial *Billy Budd* or *Mr. Roberts*, is not exactly friendly commentary. And to lump it with the franchises, fast foods, day care, nursing homes, motels, might be construed as an abuse of freedom of the press by most fans, certainly by Bowie Kuhn, who arrived in 1969 to be host of the 100th birthday party.

Commissioner Kuhn was 42 at the time, but seemed older. His hair was graying, and he was 6 feet 5 inches tall, a man who moved and spoke deliberately. A lawyer, he supposedly halved his income to $100,000 because he loved the game and wanted to save the republic. He exuded the moral righteousness of a Princeton/Wall Street/WASP whose ancestors had arrived before there was even a nation for the Pastime. Once, "shocked" at a column I had written speculating that his decision to suspend the pitcher Denny McLain for associating with gamblers might be construed as clamping the lid on widespread gambling and game fixing within baseball, he summoned me to an evening meeting in his Fifth Avenue office. I went for the drama and for the certain second column that would come out of it. We talked for more than an hour, during which he was as vague and evasive as usual. When I pointed this out, he said, "I make clear what I want to make clear."

I asked, "Then why should I believe you?"

Kuhn's stiff-necked, hammer-handed, uncompromising Hollywood posture of integrity suddenly sagged into sadness. He looked at me with compassion, perhaps pity, and softly said, "I have a very simple faith in people, I can't help it, I was brought up that way."

I tried not to laugh in his face while I wrote that down. I'll bet you were. Lucky Bowie. And lucky baseball. The pirates' brotherhood of club owners had found the perfect front man for a game that had the arrogance to call its climax the World Series instead of the North American Professional Baseball Championships for Men.

Commissioner Kuhn had a good rookie year. He got credit for the All-Star game reception at the White House (reuniting church and state?) in which Nixon accepted a trophy and said, "It took a lot of years, but I finally made the team."

Responded Kuhn, "Mr. President, you have made the team."

The President then told everybody about Connie Mack's decision to start Howard Ehmke in the 1929 World Series and Babe Ruth's "called shot" homer off Charlie Root. Nixon said, "I like the job I have now, but if I had my life to live over again, I'd have ended up as a sportswriter."

Jim Bouton and Len Shecter were writing *Ball Four* in 1969, and Curt Flood was preparing to file suit against the reserve clause, but the dark clouds were small in the distance. Baseball's birthday present to the country was the Mets, hyped as a moral extravaganza, the sporting equivalent of those two other scheduled and ballyhooed Summer Games of '69, the First Moon Landing and the Woodstock Music Festival. There would be spoilsports to claim that Armstrong's giant leap was toward Doomsday, that a generation had left its future in the mud of Bethel, N.Y., but everyone seemed to love the idea of the Mets. Losers shall become winners, the last shall be first, the meek shall inherit the earth. There were few spoilsports to point out that from the beginning the Mets had been one of the most profitable clubs in baseball, that no matter how the cash-flow charts were mickied the city was losing $300,000 a year on Shea Stadium, and that linking Casey Stengel and Marv Throneberry to this slick young 1969 team was, in the words of Los Angeles columnist Mel Durslag, like congratulating Orville Wright on the success of the Boeing 727.

Like Throneberry, I was sentimental about my first team. I found myself drifting back to baseball that year, but except for the newspapermen there were few familiar faces. Yogi Berra, having been canned as manager of the Yankees, was now a Mets coach and promiscuously friendly. He had finally grown comfortable with the personality that Joe Garagiola had fashioned for him at a thousand father-and-son Communion breakfasts and Little League trophy nights and network television shows. Garagiola had Americanized himself through sports so thoroughly that his charming eccentricity was his bald head, while Berra had been left behind as the Italian peasant shrewdie, Life with Luigi, not-so-dumb-as-he-sounds, if you listen real close, folks— "Nobody goes to that restaurant anymore," says Yogi, "because it's overcrowded all the time"—you can tell he's really smart even if he hasn't got the language down pat yet.

The other familiar face was Gil Hodges'. As a player the first year of the Mets he had been hampered by injuries. I remembered him standing on the practice ballfield in 1962, posing for a cigarette ad. A man from the company was explaining to me, "We want to have our product associated with symbols of acceptance. Quality men use quality products. If Hodges smokes Viceroys, it might do something for you, too."

In 1969, when other sportswriters called him Gilly and repeated stories about his strength—"Hodges could tear your earbrows off," Stengel once said—I kept thinking of him as a recent heart attack victim who couldn't stop smoking. Thus, his physical strength and his put-down trick of gazing steadily and silently at a man until he left or surrendered or began babbling, seemed much less imposing. Like Stengel and Berra and most over-observed sports figures, Hodges had been tagged—strong, silent, religious, a family man—and released. That awful calm of his was just a lid, and his dryness was masking a running private joke with himself. One morning at spring training, after two Mets had been sidelined with flu, a newspaperman asked, "Do you think the fellas got sick because you had them run in the rain?"

Hodges replied, "I don't know, but if you think so, write it. I couldn't care less." His steady gaze then pushed the reporter across the room.

Late that afternoon, he announced the next day's schedule to the press and a different reporter asked, "Gilly, what happens if it rains again?"

Hodges' gaze flicked to the morning interviewer and he casually said, "Oh, I guess we'll just have two more men out sick."

It is difficult to convey that sense of a man in a daily story, and it is the cumulative weight of daily stories that creates the sports figure's public image. Brief appearances on television merely confirm or alter the image. Hodges was thought to be a rock, a fine fellow, and a good baseball mind, and this all lent serious purpose to the 1969 Mets. Tom Seaver, the top pitcher, was a determined middle-brow, sincere, cautious, optimistic, who has listed James Reston and Barbra Streisand as the two people he most admired outside baseball. Once, over breakfast, he told me, "I hate to do things on the spur of the moment. You can make a mistake if you react totally emotionally to something. That's how a lot of women get into trouble, letting their mouths get ahead of their minds."

Physically energetic, friendly, exuberant, Seaver was merchandised as the All-American Boy of the 1970s—a verbal, seeking, open-minded, profit-motivated son of the suburban California middle class. And well-adjusted. When Mets wives were asked if they worried about their husbands "cheating" on the road, they expressed confidence that Tom's moral influence would get the Mets to bed early and alone. Tom's agent told me that Tom "combines the modern thinking and old-fashioned values that America wants now." He thought Tom would be dynamite box office for years to come.

Tom Seaver never did become a national hero, partly because of baseball's regionalism, partly because the public sensed that this slightly overweight, smooth-skinned son of an amateur golfing champion had no dark hungers in his soul. Seaver's stomach was bigger than his eyes. The public likes to anoint those who pant for fame, not those who advertise. Seaver's agent placed this ad in various publications: "Now available, Tom Seaver, America's top athlete and sports personality, plus Nancy Seaver, Tom's lovely wife, for those situations that call for young Mrs. America or husband and wife sales appeal."

That ad drew little more than obscene phone calls. Within baseball, the ad was regarded as bush-league and demeaning to Tom's image. In his defense it should be said that he was honestly trying to include his wife in his successes. But macho athletes and writers preferred to view him as greedy and dominated. In fact, several players later suggested that the Mets' decline after 1969 actually began that October when Seaver insisted on taking Nancy to Las Vegas, where comedian Phil Foster had organized an "act" for a number of Mets. Most Mets arrived in Vega stag. They resented the presence of a wife; men in groups, particularly athletic teams, always feel threatened by an outside relationship one of them might have that supersedes loyalty to the group. Also, Nancy's presence sustained rumors that Seaver was being slipped more money than the others for the engagement.

After the 1970 season, when the Mets dropped to third in the East, several writers seized on the Tom and Nancy theory to explain the Mets' "collapse." In the minds of most sportswriters, money and women are the termites of athletes' souls. If a greedy wife or a sex-crazed girl friend doesn't wreck Youngstud, then a scheming agent will. Year after year, fresh new Youngstuds appear before the aging writer, whose own problems with money and women are only getting more complicated. As he gets older, the sportswriter is more likely to begin identifying with the owner of the team, and carrying his messages. In 1969, two of the wealthiest owners in baseball, beer baron August A. Busch of the St. Louis Cardinals and chewing gum tycoon Philip Wrigley of the Chicago Cubs, accused their players of thinking about money all the time, of having too many outside interests, and of falling out of touch with the common people. They were careful to make their charges in front of friendly writers who not only would not fall down laughing, but would seriously write how "fat-catism" among players lost more pennants than overconfidence.

Owners and writers are never really satisfied until athletes are impotent and broke. Much of the public shares this feeling. One of the reasons for the success of Roger Kahn's *The Boys of Summer* was its theme of ruination; most of the "boys" were sick or bitter or dead.

The 1969 Mets were too new to be fat cats and young enough to respond eagerly to the press. They were good copy. The "Lodge Brothers," as *New York Times* columnist Arthur Daley referred to his colleagues on the baseball beat, went after the Mets like they go after ice cream in the press box. They felt they deserved the Mets; 1968 had been a bad year for sportswriters, too. The New York Athletic Club boycott, the black-power demonstration at the Mexico City Olympics, polarizing racial tensions on many college varsities, organized political activism among pro athletes, and the beginnings of what would surely be annual management-labor confrontations hinted at stormy, confusing seasons ahead. The handwriting was on the locker-room wall. Sports would be a battlefield upon which we would all be

consumed. Wait, yon scribbler, tarry awhile. One last feast before your pen runs dry. The Mets.

New York City apparently felt the same way about the Mets,
and made of them a kind of sporting Last Hurrah. Earlier in
1969, Joe Namath and the Jets had won the Super Bowl, but that
triumph was not New York's. It had been transmogrified into a
triumph for Youth and Hair and Machismo and Long-shot Odds.
Besides, a dying city never pins its false hopes on football. Only
baseball, the National Pastime, can administer the cardiac thump.

There is a great deal of baseball urban sociology, and some of
it is fairly serious. A case was made, for example, that St. Louis
suffered no major riot during the long hot summer of 1967 because the pennant-bound Cardinals were led by three blacks,
Lou Brock, Curt Flood, and Bob Gibson. Detroit blew, despite
the Tigers' stretch run, because the team's only black star, Willie
Horton, was hurt.

In New York in 1969, the whites were simmering. The Lindsay
administration seemed more responsive to blacks than to middle-
class ethnic whites, to Manhattan than to the other four boroughs, to theatrical liberalism than to day-to-day services.

Lindsay, campaigning for reelection with what sounded like a
Banner Day slogan, "I Made Mistakes," came to baseball late.
But he stayed. He would course into the locker room behind a
flying wedge of aides, remote, stone-faced. When the television
camera's red light glowed, he would snap on a smile and stride
up to congratulate the game's hero. The Mets were image-
conscious, and none of them ever turned a naked back on
Lindsay as I had once seen a Los Angeles Dodger do to the then
Vice-President, Hubert Humphrey, with a loud, "Take a hike,
Pinky."

Lindsay was taller than most of the Mets, and handsomer.
He materialized on television as somehow having been involved
in the pennant race. Manager Hodges reportedly refused to endorse Lindsay. But when pitcher Jerry Koosman poured cham-
pagne on the Mayor's classic head during a stagey televised
locker-room party, he was also bestowing what was construed by
the fans as an endorsement from the whole team. By the time the
Mets won it all, got their ticker-tape parade and the keys to the
city, it seemed as if the ballclub had actually pounded a few

more beats into New York's sick old heart. Anyway, that's what the editorialists and the political columnists told us.

Hey, everything's gonna be all right. If the Mets can do it, so can we. We're No. 1.

That a baseball team still had this power in 1969 was a tribute to the pervasive force of SportsWorld. People in New York, as elsewhere, were rehyphenating themselves—Italian-Americans, Polish-Americans. Once, for those who had wanted to be Americans quickly, baseball had been a giant step. King Kelly and John McGraw, then Honus Wagner and Lou Gehrig, then Joe Di-Maggio, Stan Musial, Ralph Kiner, then Mays and Clemente. The game never disappointed; America did. So much of the anti-baseball rap of the 1960s was actually disaffection with traditional institutions. Walter O'Malley, who moved the Dodgers from Brooklyn for a chunk of downtown Los Angeles, thus securing his niche in the Sages' Hall of Fame, said in 1969, "Is baseball on the spot? I would say yes, but then religion is on the spot, government is on the spot, the integrity of treaties is on the spot.

"These are times when people spit on the flag, when priests go over the fence. You have to understand the pattern of things today. There is rebellion against the establishment and baseball is linked to the establishment."

The team that brought baseball back for an encore, for one more season in the sun, was one of the whitest in the major leagues. Of the twenty-five Mets on the World Series roster, there were only four blacks—the outfield stars, Jones and Agee; the part-timers, Charles and Clendenon—and no Latins. The team was young but aggressively clean-cut, the kind of boys who died in Vietnam. The next-to-last World Series game fell on October 15, Moratorium Day, and Seaver was pressed to take the antiwar stand he had long promised, and Lindsay was pressed to order the Shea Stadium flags to half-staff.

But when you're hot you're hot. The sportswriters let Seaver off the hook when he weakly pleaded to be allowed to concentrate on his starting assignment: The immediate problem was the Baltimore Orioles; the war would still be there tomorrow. And Lindsay deferred to Commissioner Kuhn, who stepped in to order Old Glory to the top of the flagpole, much to Lindsay's relief.

Seaver won, the Mets won, Lindsay won.

Baseball won.

Ah, baseball. The Giving Tree of American sport, the game that offers History . . .

"My grandpa fought off Indians, rustlers, and varmints back in Hornsby's Bend, Texas," the late Rogers Hornsby, a Hall of Fame batter, coach, and manager once told me. "I like television westerns because these are real guys, not your city phonies and big-promising politicians and foreigners. All red-blooded Americans, like me, and they're not going to let anybody spit on the flag while they're around."

. . . and Passion . . .

"I loved the game, Babe, not success," said Bo Belinsky to Pat Jordan in *The Suitors of Spring*. "Man, you can't stash baseball. If you're lucky, you capture it awhile, you go through it at some point in your life, and then it goes away and you go on to something else. Some guys try to live off it forever. Babe, it's a sin to live off 'sport.' "

. . . and Common Sense . . .

Tom Seaver, discussing high baseball salaries in his book *Inside Corner*, edited by Joel H. Cohen: "It's difficult to rationalize. How about the guy who's selling dope and making half-a-million dollars? Nothing's been done about him. He's certainly not doing a single thing that's constructive for society at all. What's the criterion? How do you judge things? The inventor who comes up with a faster repeating rifle. Is he to be rewarded? Should he be highly paid? That's difficult to understand. So even though doctors may make X amounts of dollars and athletes may make three times that amount in a shorter period of time, I, as an athlete, wouldn't approach it in that sense. Rather, I would approach it in terms of the economic world I live in. In other words, how important am I economically to the people I work for?"

. . . and Ecstasy . . .

"Baseball is beautiful," announced Commissioner Bowie Kuhn. "To me it is the supreme performing art. It combines in perfect harmony the magnificent features of ballet, drama, art, and theater, along with continuous action and suspense."

. . . and Ingenuity . . .

Charles O. Finley recounting to Ron Fimrite of *Sports Illus-*

trated an early success: "I went to all the merchants in town asking them each to give $25 to pay for our uniforms. In return I assured them we'd have the names of their firms on the backs of our shirts. What I did then was to go out and buy 98¢ sweat shirts and just have the names stenciled on. The full uniforms didn't cost more than $15 apiece. The rest was gravy."

... and Verities ...

"What Maury Wills did in 1962 was history, what I'm doing in 1974 is news," said Lou Brock after stealing 105 bases to surpass Wills' record by one. "Ten years from now, I'll be history and some other kid will be news."

In 1974, editorialists thanked baseball for "a glorious divertissement" in a "troubled and uncertain time." But never again would a baseball team be able to rub rouge on the cheeks of a dying city and fool people into thinking vitality had returned, as it did in 1969. Seaver won, the Mets won, Lindsay won, and nothing changed at all for those poor dummies who cheered them all in, thinking they were cheering for themselves, too.

As it turned out, Mets fans celebrated their moment of triumph in the only way they knew: They ripped up and carried off from the ground of "their" ballpark 6,500 square feet of sod, and they scattered 2,020,000 pounds of trash over the streets of "their" city.

CHAPTER
3
Sport of the Sixties: Instant Replay... Replay... Replay...

KING FOOTBALL came on as The Sport of the Sixties, riding a wondrous hype that included such dynamite concepts as relevance, ethnicity, professionalism, and violence. All things to all men, and some women. Side by side, in the stadium or in front of the Big Window, could sit Charlie Lumpenfan, getting off his rocks in approved lower-class visceral reaction, and George Stade of the Columbia English Department, who could write, "Who else but a people grown sedentary on profits from the violence that continues to be their national habit are likely to feel the psychosocial relevance of football with any sort of poignancy?"

Or so we were led to believe. The National Football League itself, in an official press release, once modestly referred to itself as "vicarious warfare nurtured by the technology that is this land's hallmark." It was not a very large jump then, for a philosophy professor, John McMurtry, who had once played professionally in Canada, to attack the game for glorifying "the property-seizing principle, . . . struggle and competition, . . . victory and the powerful."

There were Marxist interpretations, Freudian interpretations, and many socioreligious interpretations of football. While the NFL was careful never to expropriate college football's claim to preparing the youth for war (who else but West Point's "lonely end," Bill Carpenter, could have called for a napalm strike on his own position in Vietnam?), it did promote all that tough jargon like bomb and blitz and power sweep, and it did produce two of sports' most articulate radical spokesmen, Dave Meggyesy and George Sauer Jr., the former Jet wide receiver, who equated the game with Social Darwinism in a tract that said, "I think the values of football as it is now played reflect a segment of thought, a particular kind of thought, that is pretty prevalent in our society. The way to do anything in the world, the way to get ahead, is to aggress against somebody, try to dominate, try to overcome, work your way up the ladder and in so doing you have to judge and be judged as what you want to be in relation to somebody else all the time."

Michael Novak saw football as a kind of live diorama of professionalism, which he defined as "the remaking of human beings in the image of machines." In *The Rise of the Unmeltable Ethnics*, Novak wrote, "If professional football were forbidden to use special units and each man had to play several facets of the game well instead of one, we would have a game more in human scale, less destructive of knees, legs, cartilage, muscle and bone. In its present form, however, pro football is almost a perfect symbol of our professional classes."

But young professionals watching their lives being dramatized were not the only people allowing television games to alter their Sunday habits and later their Monday night habits, too. Addiction to the sport, as much as the contest itself, became a currency of communication on every level of American life; ritual manchat at water coolers and in car pools, interclass howdy-do, a way for fathers and sons to discuss loyalty, love, sacrifice, dedication, discipline, success, failure, pain, in detached and nonthreatening symbols. When women talked about football, it was often with exasperation, for the shrewdest realized that many men used it as a socially acceptable way of avoiding their wives and mothers on the longest day of the week.

It was not in the game—repetitive, mindless, banal, best remembered for its few breathtaking moments—that we learned about ourselves, but in the hype and money and the trappings. It took Nixon and the seventies for us to realize that both American capitalism and American football were elaborate hoaxes, and that not only were they contradictory to each other, but each was self-contradictory.

Here was football demanding that gratification be deferred until a specific goal was reached, while capitalism urged us to desire and consume without purpose, or selectively sacrifice so we could desire and consume again.

Here was football demanding collective spirit within each team and total antagonism among all opposing teams, while opposing owners operated jointly to keep their costs down, their prices up, and their employees indentured. If there was a larger lesson in that, perhaps it was that in capitalism, as in football, the regulations to balance growth and power were actually conspiracies to control the workers. And just as football was mock war, contained and regulated, so had war become mock war, contained and regulated. But shoulders and knees still popped, and young men still came home in rubber bags.

Football flourished in a decade when all sports flourished because of money, leisure, energy, color television, and a social climate of racial, political, and sexual conflict that made so many traditional patterns of living unpleasant, even dangerous. It was a loud, brassy, ethnic sport that could challenge baseball without coming face-to-face with its deeply rooted political influence or its nostalgia: Football is not, after all, a summer game. The NFL Commissioner, Pete Rozelle, and many of the owners, white players, and press seemed to come from that emerging middle-management class of non-WASPs, as did the two most important culture heroes that football imposed upon us in the sixties, Vince Lombardi and Joe Namath, both sons of immigrants, both hardworking, loyal, talented products of Americanization, and both willfully misunderstood.

Lombardi was always celebrated in the extreme. His saintly dedication to winning was hailed as a beacon on the path toward America's renewal. His diabolical dedication to winning was denounced as an example of creeping fascism.

Namath had few moral advocates. Lombardi's assessment of Namath—he once called him "the perfect quarterback" but expressed revulsion at "some of the things he stands for"—seemed to echo SportsWorld's more traditional wing. SportsWorld's "mod" or "swinging" faction made excuses for Namath's lifestyle —it was "today." Actually, Namath's lifestyle was yesterday, a kind of Drugstore Cowboy Cool clothed as Sixties Singlestud Chic.

The two men complemented each other. Lombardi was football's front man while it was promoting itself as a sadomasochistic weekly adventure show written by Robert Ardrey, Konrad Lorenz, and Lionel Tiger. By mid-decade, when territoriality, aggression, and male bonding were slipping, Joe Namath arrived with that outrageous price tag on his arm: He was "the $400,000 quarterback." Flash. Zap. Pizzazz. He forced the merging of the leagues and pumped up the game again.

By the end of the sixties, Lombardi was firmly established as the Father and Namath the Son while football was being packaged and sold as psychodrama: America working out its problems on Sunday in an orderly fashion, blacks and whites and hunkies and WASPSs subordinating themselves to the commonweal. Violently.

Poor Lombardi, a decent man, compared, both seriously and facetiously, by both boosters and rippers, to Patton, Mussolini, and God. He was criticized and praised for his support of the antiballistic missile, his support of gun-control legislation, his friendship with the Kennedy family, and the rumor that Attorney General John Mitchell once considered him as a possible running mate for Nixon.

Lombardi was called politically naive. He was called Machiavellian. He was convincingly portrayed as both a football idiot savant and as a cloistered academic who pleasured himself with word games in Latin. He was held up as an example of the truly inner-directed man. He was characterized as a coach who was uneasy around his players' wives because he was never sure what the men said about him at home.

Lombardi was sold as a teacher of life, a prophet of piety and patriotism, and a social engineer who could control the most vicious forces on earth (Ray Nitschke, the middle linebacker) and the most undisciplined artists (Paul Hornung, the Golden Boy from the Golden Dome) and harness them to productivity (141 victories, only 39 losses and 4 ties in 9 years as Green Bay's head coach). Lombardi's monumental vanity never allowed him to derail the runaway jock pop that extrapolated his football cliches into pep-rally social theories.

Lombardi looked right. Powerfully built without being particularly large, Lombardi was so aggressively unattractive that handsome coaches like Bud Wilkinson and Ara Parseghian seemed insincere beside him. The son of a Brooklyn butcher, Lombardi had chosen to live in the Midwest. He had a heritage of hard work: He had been a hod carrier of a lineman at Fordham, he held a full-time job as an insurance investigator while attending law school, he coached three sports and taught physics, chemistry, algebra, and Latin in a New Jersey Catholic school.

Success had come relatively late for his field; he often suspected that his ethnicity, his lack of glamour, his bluntness—all later "attributes"—had held him back in the company of soldiers, priests, and athletes. His run in the stratosphere of SportsWorld was relatively brief; he was an assistant at West Point and at the Giants before he arrived in Green Bay at the age of 46, and he died in Washington at 57.

The Lombardi legend, as it has been packaged in glossy coffee table books by NFL Properties, Inc., in sentimental TV documentaries and dramatizations, in the self-serving reminiscences of newspapermen, is harmless enough and even amusing. Coach was so pure in his vision, we are told, that he not only had the strength of ten, but could lumber through life spraying unintentionally rude remarks and shameless tears.

But the Lombardi legacy, as usurped and abused by school and college coaches, is dangerous. It becomes the subordination of self to group, of group to authority, of authority to goal. All to win a football game.

In 1974, a suburban high school coach could publicly mourn, "This is a new breed of kid; they won't go through a wall for you," as if he had naturally inherited or even deserved such power over others. So many deaths and injuries, physical and psychic, are caused by pseudo-Lombardis whom Coach Himself immediately would have spotted as emotionally insecure and mentally unprepared.

Coach did not demand obedience to inflate his ego. He did not impose discipline to ensure his control. He did not attack those who disagreed with him because he was defensive.

He had a vision for success and he demanded and imposed and attacked to keep that vision clear. Once, I asked him to comment on a statement made by Jerry Kramer that the Packers were a little flat this particular season because a new league alignment had brought them less challenging competition.

"Kramer who?" snapped Lombardi.

"Your guard."

Lombardi glared at me. "He didn't say that."

"But I heard him on the radio."

"Don't come in here and tell me things like that," snarled Lombardi.

It was typical, and if ever a man snapped and glared and snarled, it was Lombardi. He was also capable of sighs and grunts and guffaws and snorts and rasping and bawling and stompings out and whirlings around that somehow made the fashionable Ivy League cool of the fifties and early sixties seem effete. In *The Decline of The Wasp*, Peter Schrag writes, "The uncouth boor has taken over. He controls the imagination while the rest of us watch from a safe distance and send our man Plimpton to report back on how it feels . . . in those precincts of action which seem forever beyond our reach."

It is an engaging thought, George Plimpton as WASP voyeur coming out to watch the ethnics' roughneck play, according to Schrag, "because life on the inside is too empty and dull to sustain without some help from beyond." In any case, whether he was spying or slumming, Plimpton's superbly crafted reports turned out to be major definers of the experience he infiltrated. Lombardi was not a character in Plimpton's *Paper Lion*, the first truly mass-appeal book about football, but he was central to Kramer's *Instant Replay*, edited by Dick Schaap, the best-selling diary that helped establish Lombardi as a public name. Implicit in both books was the basic swinishness of the game; but rather than being brutalized by it, the players are exalted, they trade lumps, suffer and sweat, but retain their personalities and find joy in commonality. It is interesting to compare the best of the football books with the best of the baseball books, which exalt the game itself, which is basically beautiful, and survives the men who play it.

One wonders if Lombardi could have been so successful as a baseball manager, much less a political leader, fine-tuning the more precise actions and reactions required in games of individual, disconnected performances. Lombardi had incredible suc-

cess with players who had all but given up their dreams. He
promised them the opportunity to be the best, and he proved to
them he was capable of leading them to victory. With the same
driving personality, but a lesser intelligence, Lombardi would
never have been able to persuade his players that they had better
be "fired with enthusiasm or you'll be fired with enthusiasm."
They would have dogged their grass drills and been happy to be
traded away; it is always easier to start again, where no one
knows your bag of tricks.

Lombardi's secret was no secret at all. Lombardi was intelligent, but not intellectual. He had a strong, supple mind; and he
used it like a tool to isolate problems and solve them. He did not
spend time questioning the suppositions that cause the problems.
He was smarter than most football coaches, and he proved this
by reducing the game to its basic techniques, and then concentrating on drilling his players on those techniques.

Once he said, "Some people try to find things in this game that
don't exist. Football is two things. It's blocking and tackling."
This was very bold at a time when other coaches were flim-
flamming the audience and confusing their players with elaborate plays that could be explained only in elaborate jargon. But
this also made for some dull Packer football games. Green Bay
teams, especially at the beginning of Lombardi's reign, ground
out their yardage in short, methodical blasts.

Players understood immediately that he was basically a
teacher, their teacher, not a flashy show-off. And Lombardi understood that while they would all say they were in the game for
money—anything else might sound tacky—they were motivated
by a need to be recognized as the best. Athletes generally get
lower salaries than the public is led to believe (and athletes go
along with the deception because many of them are ashamed of
their salaries compared to those of other entertainers), but their
big payoffs are in the records and titles and championships that
proclaim to the world that this man or that team is the very best.
There are few other ways to win that kind of absolute recognition.

Lombardi offered them the chance to be the best. His ranting
and his tears, his approval and abuse and smiles and fines, his
vicarious kicks from the bedroom-barroom escapades of Hornung

and Max McGee, his pragmatic benchings and trades, could all
be tolerated because even when they were whimsical or experimental, they were still part of his master vision to make this team
the best it could be. The true goal is to be the best; in football,
this can be attained only by winning.

Lombardi's most famous aphorism, "Winning isn't everything,
it's the only thing," is a self-evident truth. In pro football. To
transpose this aphorism, to make America the Green Bay Packers
and the NFL the planet Earth, is fascist rhetoric. A football team
has a specific collective objective, a democratic country must not.
Lombardi never actually transposed the aphorism. In fact, he did
not originate it and I never heard him say it.

But Lombardi understood power. When his chance finally
came after years of being a high school coach or an assistant for
such well-known coaches as Earl Blaik and Jim Lee Howell, he
demanded absolute control. By taking charge of Green Bay's
business affairs, he made sure there was no one above him to hear
a player's appeal. He was the final authority. He believed that
athletes, like children, respond best to absolute power used rea-
sonably and fairly. Once they are sure they will be judged by
their achievements, they can concentrate on their game. The
enormous improvement at Green Bay during Lombardi's first
season proved all his canons: Hard work wins, fundamental football wins, motivation wins, finding and starting your best players
wins. He proved it was simple.

In Green Bay, his influence was immense. Well-to-do businessmen, his so-called trained seals, followed him to guffaw at his
jokes and perform small chores. Kings have always had courts.
Lombardi often treated his imperiously. The local newspaper
was his personal house organ. While he flaunted out-of-town
writers who came to interview him, he could turn off the tours
and hospitality and become nasty if the questions were disagree-
able. "Why dontcha learn something about the game?" he'd bark.
A street was named for him in Green Bay. Free cars were pressed
on him. He rarely bothered to meet with the rubber-stamp board
of directors of the municipally owned team. It was in Green Bay
that the Lombardi jokes were spawned. "When he says 'sit
down,'" said one player, "I don't even bother to look for a chair."
And another: "He's very fair. Lombardi treats us all like dogs."

His lack of sympathy for other men's hurts was well known; however, no one has yet come forward with a permanent disability caused by Lombardi's diagnosis that a fracture was all in the mind.

For such an ostentatiously religious man, some of the jokes seemed irreverent. Lombardi shouts at the sky, "How many times do I have to tell you, NO SNOW!" or, after his wife told him in bed one night, "God, your feet are cold," Lombardi replies, "Around the house, dear, you may call me Vince."

People seized upon these jokes, retold them threadbare, simultaneously acknowledging and mocking their need for strength and order, for protective and inspirational leadership, for the example of a man who entertained no doubts about either the righteousness of his cause or the best strategy to reach his objectives.

Although it was not until he was dying that SportsWorld retroactively painted every lily along his life's path, Lombardi was obviously aware during his last years that pro football was peddling him as Professor Vince, St. Vince, and General Vince, a hat, halo, or helmet for every occasion. He was not always comfortable in these roles, and they increased his fear of being financially exploited. He had been underpaid most of his life, and from Green Bay on he played catch-up. His harsh treatment of players who tried to negotiate through agents, who played out their options or jumped leagues seems hypocritical beside his own move to Washington with several years remaining on his Green Bay contract. Suddenly a stockholder, he urged his fellow owners to stand firm against rising player demands. "Gentlemen," he said, "don't give your game away to a bunch of 20-year-old kids."

Commissioner Rozelle helped settle the summer 1970 strike-lockout by warning the Players Association that Coach was within forty-eight hours of death, and the wave of irrationality that would follow this crushing loss would obliterate any hopes for a settlement. The players, resentful of this manipulation and distrustful of Rozelle's deadline, nonetheless settled. Snookered again. It was a month before Lombardi died.

Once safely dead, incapable of embarrassing, Lombardi became the subject of a thousand plastic eulogies, all anthologized by the NFL. One by one, players stepped forward to make personal witness of Lombardi's power to change men's lives, and most of them said they "loved" Lombardi. This one had been turned from barroom brawling and set on the path of righteousness, that one had been cured of boils by a mere touch of the Lombardi scorn. Commissioner Rozelle recalled how he had agonized over the proper punishment for Lombardi after Coach, screaming, had pursued officials into their dressing room after a game. Another coach might have been heavily fined, but it was enough to send Lombardi a scolding letter, said the pious Rozelle, to make him feel "sheepish."

Lombardi died just before the start of the 1970 season. By then, Namath had completed five seasons and by virtue of his 1969 Super Bowl triumph was no longer considered a mere "celebrity"—in Daniel J. Boorstin's classic definition "a person who is known for his well-knownness"—but a genuine "hero," a person "distinguished by his achievements."

By then, his label, "the $400,000 quarterback," sounded as quaint as "the It Girl," and our sophistication was such that we knew the figure included so many deferred payments, no-interest loans, insurance premiums, stock options, retainers for relatives, bonus clauses, and depreciation allowances that no one actually paid or received that much money. But had Namath been handed it all in a boodle bag he would still have come cheap at the price.

By the middle of the sixties there was only one true measure, and that was price. Crowds meant nothing anymore. Thousands upon thousands were showing up for a cause or a concert, and even extreme expressions of belief were suspect.

Price. What's it worth? If the price is high enough it must be worth something, and I want a piece of it, too.

The merchandising of football through Namath actually began in 1960 when, unable to buy into the NFL, several sons of Texas oil, most notably Lamar Hunt, created the American Football League. It is axiomatic that a new sports league needs a New York showcase, and the AFL had the Titans, owned in front by Harry Wismer, one of the country's most popular football broadcasters, and coached by Sammy Baugh, one of the country's most famous old quarterbacks. It was a disaster from the start.

The Titans could not give their tickets away. Literally. Their tickets arrived in fat decks at every sports department in town, where, following custom, editors used them to try to bribe printers to set type quickly and accurately, and to lock it into the pages before going to lunch or holding an impromptu union meeting. But even the printers looked disdainfully upon Titan tickets, a gloomy prognosis.

It was all cultural conditioning. The more "responsible" the newspaper, the more wary the editor of anything new "until it proves itself." The Establishment ends up dictating coverage and emphasis because it is "reliable." Football coverage in cities with NFL teams was dictated by the Irish Catholic clans that had started the pro sport forty years earlier, nursing it through hard times when responsible newspapers were using their space to glorify such reliable establishments as the football factories at Notre Dame, Pittsburgh, Wisconsin, Purdue, Michigan, Ohio State, Southern Cal. With the fifties came prosperity for the NFL, and a turning of the wheel. In New York, the Mara family, which had bought the franchise for $500 in 1925, dismissed the Titans as sandlot and Wismer as an irresponsible fool. It was true that Wismer's payroll checks often bounced, that Slingin' Sammy called him a "man you can't trust around the corner," that his quarterback and a defensive lineman moonlighted by phoning corporation presidents and trying to bully or flatter them into buying season tickets.

Meanwhile, Giant tickets were often mentioned in wills and divorce settlements, and Giant players were active in New York brokerage houses, advertising agencies, and broadcasting studios. The national media became aware of the football mother lode through the Giants, and, in return, made national heroes of Frank Gifford, Sam Huff, Y. A. Tittle, and others who might never have reached such heights playing in St. Louis.

The Giants' PR man had an unlisted number; after all, when he wanted a newsbreak he could have it leaked at Toots Shor's or the bar at Manuche's, or call Jack Mara's best friend, Arthur Daley of *The New York Times*. As a matter of fact, one previous Giants' PR man, before he went on to a notable career as a foreign correspondent and novelist, was Daley's eldest son, Robert.

The Maras' limited vision—shared by most other NFL families

—saw football as a series of Mom-and-Pop outlets with diehard fans, grateful players, and a housebroken press. Either they could not imagine the game's potential for growth, or they were unsure of their capacity to grow with it. The Titans were a threat to be laughed out of town. *The Times*, like most papers, followed the Mara line in the early sixties. After all, they were reputable businessmen. The AFL upstarts had no tradition, no class, and no quarterbacks. Just some of that funny Texas money.

Predictably, Wismer's Titans went bankrupt, but the league floated the franchise until a group headed by David A. (Sonny) Werblin, the president of the Music Corporation of America, picked it up and renamed it the Jets. Werblin could turn it on—spectacular parties, glitter and noise. He came out of an industry that played newspapermen like drums, got them high, got them laid, even got them exclusive stories if they were bent that way. By now, the AFL and the NFL were competing for some of the same players. Stories of wild bidding, midnight plane charters, and "babysitters" who kept prospects cached in motel rooms with gin and girls until it was time to sign contracts generated lively publicity and didn't hurt anyone's attendance. But the new league had yet to come up with that one college superstar whose choice of the AFL over the NFL would influence sponsors, fans, the press, and other college players.

And then Werblin, the starmaker, the man from Pop, presented Namath, $400,000 worth of ink alone.

I came to football late. I had written a few Titan features, covered a few college games, but personal preference and other assignments had kept me away for most of the sixties. I never enjoyed football as much as I did baseball, and, later, basketball. The game is too remote, unreal, the players too anonymous, their movements obscured. Now, watching at home on a good color set, the game has more appeal than it ever had from the press box, although the game I am now watching is one framed and edited for me by the network technicians.

For all I know it is an anthology of film clips or the state of the art of Japanese special effects. Some of Howard Cosell's popularity must have to do with his credibility; Howard would never lie, there really is a game on down there.

Or is there? Plugged into Super Bowl Sunday, 1975, my eyes

are washed with autumn leaves and O. J. Simpson's nipples, my head is filled with "the glory of one bright afternoon" by a *Prose Edda* voice over *The Minstrel Boy*, first as a march, then as a dirge. "Pro football is a game, not a war . . . for win or lose, not death. . . . Say that in the summer, for winter brings the playoffs. . . ." Crunch. Behemoths rose out of the mist. And it would be more than an hour before the Pittsburgh Steelers played the Minnesota Vikings.

Super Bowl IX was promoted as "Art Rooney's Super Bowl." Rooney, nearly 74, was the only old-line owner who had never won a championship, and sportswriters installed the Steelers as "sentimental" favorites. Somehow it was good for the game if Pittsburgh won. I looked up a paragraph in *They Call It a Game*, a 1971 book by former Cleveland cornerback Bernie Parrish concerning the Jets' 1969 Super Bowl triumph: "Namath and his teammates' performance secured the two leagues at the very least $100,000,000 in future TV revenue. The game was almost too good to be true. Considering other devices imposed by TV's needs to lift fan interest and raise the advertiser's prices, perhaps it *was* too good to be true. What troubles me is that TV looks at the game pragmatically, as an infinite number of unique program scripts. A Colt slaughter of the Jets would have confirmed the public's suspicions of a gross imbalance between the two leagues."

Elsewhere in the book Parrish suggests a number of ways to fix games, most of them simple and believable. My own favorite was the theoretical example of a Jets' offensive coach, who had been fed the Colts' sideline defensive signals, relaying them to Namath before each play.

Speaking of the devil. Namath himself appears on my Big Window, accompanied by Dandy Don Meredith, strolling down Bourbon Street dispensing local color. Cokes are selling for $3.85, limousine rental is $600 a day. Sometime around a "Don't Be Fuelish" announcement we learn that thousands of private planes are coming in for the game. We already know that commercial time during this five-hour NBC package costs $214,000 per minute, more than Super Bowl VIII, but still No. 2 to the first television showing of *The Godfather*, $225,000 per minute. Now that's putting points on the scoreboard.

New Orleans is filled with sportswriters, we are told, who are drinking "NFL booze" and, "all in all," having a "pretty soft week."

But not as soft as they deserve, I thought. They paid for that trip all season long, turning tricks for the NFL publicity machine, wading through pounds of press releases, writing their game stories off quarter-by-quarter mimeographed play-by-plays rushed to them in the press box, shedding SportsWorld tears for the knees of Namath and all our crippled heroes playing through agony to teach us courage. What a cruel joke. That season Jacqueline Susann and Cornelius Ryan were writing through agony for us, dying of cancer. And sportswriters were defining success, failure, manhood, femininity, cowardice, and courage on the actions of athletes pumped with amphetamines, Butazolidin, cortisone; taped, braced, splinted; attended by doctors, trainers, coaches; carted in and out of games for minutes, seconds, at a time.

By the time the Pittsburgh–Minnesota game started I was itchy to get out of the house. I lasted less than a quarter. Coming home in the late afternoon we ran into unusually heavy traffic, men leaving Super Bowl parties. I wonder if it would really matter to them in the long run to find out these games were fixed; after all, it was clearly in the national interest for Namath and then Rooney to have their days. Also, the sum of the parts of a football game, the final score, seems less and less important than the single moments of spectacular execution now that television can show us a balletic catch or a thunderous block over and over again, slow, actual, fast, set to varying music that signals us to laugh or weep or mutter "Way to go, sumbitch" as we sink deeper into cushions and let Csonka and Kiick do our running.

As columnist, I covered Giant games and Jet games and title games and Super Bowl games more out of duty than choice. Actually, the conceit implicit in that "duty" was squelched by Namath in the middle of the 1967 season, the first time I ever spoke to him alone.

"People don't know what they're seeing, reporters don't know what's happening in a game," he said pleasantly. "I throw a pass that's intercepted and people blame me when it was the fault of someone who wasn't where he should have been. I throw a touchdown pass and I get the credit when it was underthrown, and only a great catch made the play.

"Look, we're not always sure what happened till we study the films. And you don't have access to the information we do."

Trivial incidents become symbolic monuments in retrospect for journalists, often for no better reason than to prove they were there, when the candidate cursed, when the sharecropper spat, when Namath took down a gift-wrapped box from the top of his open wooden locker. We chatted while he unwrapped it with a great deal more interest than one would expect from a 24-year-old with a white llama rug on the floor of his Manhattan penthouse.

The gift was a pair of white drawers. A helmet and the Jets insignia had been stitched in green on one thigh. Namath seemed pleased with it until he held it against his naked body. The drawers were at least two sizes too wide. He shrugged, replaced the drawers and tossed the box to the dressing room attendant. He was disappointed.

I don't remember what we talked about after that. But I remember thinking that Out There, the "people we fly over," as network executives refer to so-called Middle Americans, think Joe Namath is larger than life. Why? Because we told them so. And now, no matter what happens, even if the press changes its mind, we're stuck with our monster. We'll have to either keep him pumped up, or blow him to pieces; no one will ever believe he's basically a tall, dark, friendly neighborhood wise guy who loves his mother, clings to old friends, and happens to throw a football as well as most anyone ever has.

He was just another worker, after all. So many football players are the sons or grandsons of men who came to America from eastern and south-central Europe and fertilized the Promised Land with their fingers, feet, pieces of scalp, whose bodies might be buried in the foundation of a skyscraper, a mine, in the water beneath a bridge. Like their fathers and grandfathers, the players understand using their bodies as investment capital. Even a generation or two after citizenship it is still their only capital. But now they want a higher return.

Namath's father had come from Hungary as a boy, settled in Beaver Falls, Pennsylvania, a steel-mill town, and steered his four sons into baseball and football, the American sports. Not his native soccer, the sport Nelson Rockefeller played at Dartmouth, but the high-risk, low-residue games that could get an unscholastic Hunky local recognition, free clothes downtown, a municipal summer job, a free college education, a white collar, a one-way ticket out of town.

In return, Namath became an object, the way every athlete becomes an object: property for the owner, copy for the media, dream-actor for the fan. This is true in every sport, but most vivid in football, which has the largest number of players on a team, and the most pronounced caste system; the glory of the stars and the obscurity of the rest is usually out of proportion to their actual contributions to the result of the game. On the field, padded, performing as "animals" in the pit, committing simulated murders, protecting or attacking smaller, faster men, running with the ball, kicking or standing alone near the goal line the last hope to stop a touchdown, every player fulfills somebody's projection of his own personality. Away from the arena, reshaped by street clothes into scaled-up models of average men, they are, generally, nice, intelligent, usually gentle, young family men. It is in the steamy meat rack of a dressing room after a game, seventy, eighty, ninety bodies, most of them naked, pushing, milling, puking, grab-assing, parading back and forth from the showers, the sauna, the trainer's room, that the peck order of SportsWorld shakes down into its rightful places.

The newsmen, dwarfed, sweating, jostle to interview the coach, the quarterback, a linebacker, a receiver, who may be flush with victory or personal success, or surly with defeat. The politic players answer clearly, win or lose, in voices loud enough so pencil reporters and radio mike-pointers don't have to scramble for the cast pearls; over the long haul, these players are rewarded for their common decency with a "good press." Other players, their west Texas farms already paid for, perfunctorily consider the repetitious questions as they peel off bandages, read fan mail, shout at teammates, call for cokes, examine toes, walk away; they will pay for these indulgences at 34, 35, fighting for their jobs, when reporters describe with relish their "loss of a step" or their nervous tendency to "hear footsteps." In corners, reporters and anonymous linemen who have cultivated each other, inside facts exchanged for helpful mentions, whisper, heads together, and avoid the snapping towels and flying tape cutters and self-conscious profanity of the totally ignored.

The congestion in front of a star quarterback is literally suffocating. Namath, for example, sat in front of his open wooden stall, answering questions in a low voice, his head usually a few inches above his knees. During periods in his career when he was moody and refused to speak to certain reporters who had "ripped" him in print, interviewing Namath could be an exercise in the journalistic equivalent of Tomming. There would be a lot of standing around, shifting from foot to foot, grinning through long pauses while the quarterback tended to his body or received friends who weren't on deadline.

A reporter would clear his throat, very obviously, almost a comic turn, and say, "Nice screen in the fourth quarter, Joe."

"Cup?" replies Namath. Feet shuffle as the pack moves.

"Joe, why did you go with Boozer on the third down when Maynard was open?"

"I put it down over here," says Namath, the words driving the pack back another step.

"How's the knees feel, Joe?"

"Oh, man." Joe laughs, we all laugh, even before we find out what has happened. His paper cup, a make-do snuff spitoon, has been crushed beneath a newsman's foot and brown juice has squirted over a magazine writer's English suede shoes. It's worth it to everyone else—now Joe will answer a few questions.

One wire service reporter, a strawberry blond young man, used to lie down between Namath's feet and look up at him; those of us whose jobs did not depend on grabbing a few hot quotes and flinging them into the airwaves or onto the wires could afford to be superior to the scramble and mock such a decadent scene, but we were ultimately kidding ourselves. The strawberry blond heard and recorded everything Namath said, got up, dusted himself off, filed his story and went home to his family having completed an honest day's work in a lunatic asylum while those of us on the fringes of earshot, pretending not to strain to hear, merely compounded the lunacy.

Behind us, the keepers of this particular asylum, the owners of the team, were leading into their locker room two state legislators, a U.S. Senator-elect, the president of a Fortune-500 corporation, and an otherwise unnotable man who had been captain of one of the owners' high school football team. They weave among the flesh clumps, the piles of stinking underclothes, the benches, the TV cameras, the owners' scampering grandchildren, to find wall space against which to flatten themselves.

Then they gape at the meat. Their meat.

Since an athlete can be exchanged for money, goods, services, or another athlete, a trade that may be designed merely to start a new series of depreciation allowances on his market value, the goals of the athlete and the goals of his owner may not only be dissimilar, they may be in conflict.

The athlete wants the recognition and added income of victory right away, or at least while he is still on the team.

The owner may have a longer-range scheme. Perhaps, as is usually the case, he is using the club as a tax shelter for his primary, nonsports business. Perhaps he would prefer a terrible season to a mediocre one, thus gaining a higher priority in the next draft of college players in which clubs pick over the new crop in reverse order of success, worst first. With his new, young player, the owner is a little stronger at next season's salary bargaining time, reminding the veteran not only how poorly the team did last year, but that with Youngstud in the wings he should be grateful for any contract at all.

But beyond that, the owner instinctively understands that the athlete represents celebrity without power. The athlete's role is the traditionally "female" role. He is selected and rewarded for beauty and performing skills. He is used to satisfy others and taught to define himself by the quantity and quality of that satisfaction. He is chattel; he is allowed no major decisions. When he grows too old to please he can be discarded; at worst, he might have to be paid off, but he cannot force the owner to keep him on the team, or play him.

The athlete can use his "wiles," even withhold his "services" to get what he thinks he deserves (an individual player "holds out," players' lawyers call mass striking "going all the way"), but his rights and resources are few. He is basically powerless beyond giving or withholding his services, which if given with enthusiasm is called "really putting out." Ultimately, whatever he does get for himself is at the sufferance of his master.

The term "jock," when used by the owners and administrators

of SportsWorld, is roughly analogous to the term "broad." Dumb jock (broad). What do you expect from a jock (broad)? Jocks (broads) are all the same.

It is not easy to consider Namath in this submissive role. He is better known than anyone who has ever owned or managed or represented him; he even survived Werblin, who was bought out by his partners. Yet, for all his fame, Namath has no real power within sport. The best he has been able to do is use his athlete's wages and celebrity to help him become a capitalist elsewhere. His grandest venture was a sleazy, poorly managed fast-food chain, Broadway Joe's, Inc., which turned out to be less a hamburger than a stock hustle. He rented his name, and he bailed out as soon as he could, exactly eight months after he told a Senate subcommittee he was in the franchising business to stay.

But then, not all that much is available, even for superstars. Hank Aaron is paid to endorse Magnavox, but he was not offered voting stock, an executive suite, and a seat on the board. And why should he be? He never paid his dues. While those men we left flattened against the Jets' dressing room wall were competing for grades and student offices and junior jobs, the Namaths and the Aarons went straight from school into protected pockets of SportsWorld, like broads into HouseWorld, insulated—for a while, at least—from identity crises, moral dilemmas, bewildering choices.

The men against the wall will never outgrow their envy and contempt for the jocks, even though many were fine athletes themselves. It is apparent in their stares, so hot-eyed one might wonder if they are sexually aroused. But it transcends sex. It has to do with romantic, obsolete definitions of masculinity, an ironic joke. The "ethnics" and the blacks were told that to be a man here they must run faster, throw farther, jump higher, hit harder. But when they do, when their grace and strength bursts the psychic bars of their SportsWorld cages, their owners and keepers feel soft and small. They can reassure themselves only by visiting their locker rooms, by reminding themselves how controllable is this meat, how vulnerable and perishable it is, how sooner or later it will be so much dead weight. Advertising men love working with athletes because they respond to orders unquestioningly and will suffer retakes without tantrum. Sharp salesmen, those street psychologists who have everyone's number, invariably cuff athletes on the gut and tell them how great they look, only slightly louder and more profanely than they tell the same thing to receptionists and secretaries and whores.

Athletes are encouraged to display little idiosyncracies, dabs of style like paste-on beauty marks to give them "color" and help distinguish one from another. This monster tackle paints in oils, this killer spade sews his own clothes, this brutal linebacker teaches Bible school, this running back eats glass at parties, Joe Namath is an "individualist" who insists on wearing white shoes.

Joe Namath's white shoes became his symbol because, like most young men just starting out after college, there was not yet very much to know about him. If the shoes had any meaning at all beyond fashion, perhaps they were warning signals to opposition linemen: Break these legs at your peril, they're carrying the entire league. Namath's own explanation, that in college he had wound white tape for added support around his black football shoes inspiring a Jets official, perhaps Werblin, to present him with special-order white shoes before his first game, rings with the banality of truth. But it wasn't good enough. Better if those white shoes were a personal statement, symbols of rebelliousness, a finger up the Power Structure's nose, a Yeah, Yeah, Yeah, to the Beatles, a Right On to the Youth Movement, an It's What's Happenin', Baby. The white shoes were inflated and floated down the newshole.

Namath was only superficially a man of his times; unlike Ali, a shaper of his times, or Seaver, a product of his times, Namath adopted hip fashions and current argot and the Playboy Philosophy and draped them over the same old bones. By the time Namath was wearing long hair, long hair was no longer a reliable badge of political conviction. When he grew a beard, provoking sportswriters and coaches to predict the breakdown of discipline in America, Namath could only say, "The Only Perfect Man who ever lived had a beard and long hair and didn't wear shoes and slept in barns and didn't hold a regular job and never put on a tie. I'm not comparing myself to Him—I'm in enough trouble trying to stack up against Bart Starr—but I'm just saying that you don't judge a man by the way he cuts his hair."

High school and college coaches, men who are paid to make

boys work for free, had apparently decided by some mysterious conjugation to stand tough on hair. The new coach at enlightened Columbia University could say, "We don't have time to grow hair, to be sidetracked. Long hair and beards lead to other things, to lying under trees and singing songs." Other coaches, more direct, made it very clear they felt that students were challenging them on this issue, macho à macho, and they simply needed to win, even if professors and deans were letting their hair grow.

And Namath made a fool of them all. With enough outside offers and deferred income to give his aching knees a permanent rest, Namath worked as hard at football as anyone in the game. The Columbia coach was eventually shipped back to the boondocks a loser, and the crew cut became a symbol of rebellious middle age.

Namath moved on to beards, fur coats, whiskey, endorsements for casual sex, and the ownership of an alleged Mafia hangout. He began making his greatest contribution to sports, the introduction of open talk about what Dick Schaap has called "the three silent B's of the sports world, broads, booze, and betting." Yet Namath as any symbol of the New Athlete, as a leader of Jock Lib, is a pathetic joke.

When the Commissioner ruled in 1969 that Namath either quit football or sell his interest in Bachelors III, Joe cried. He said it was unfair. And he sold out.

The moustache. That liberating Fu Manchu was shaved on a television commercial for a reported $10,000. The mink coat was a publicity stunt for the so-called Peacock Revolution (remember that one?) worth a reported $5,000, plus the fur. And just when everyone else was sniffing, smoking, and shooting up, Namath came out for Johnny Walker Red, in moderation, as a pregame tranquilizer and a postgame pain killer.

The National Anthem. According to Dave Anderson in *The New York Times*, Namath said, "I like it played. Every time I hear it before a game, it reminds me of where we are in the world, in life. I kind of thank God that we're in this country. When I hear it I get a chill. It's a thrill to me. I can't understand why people are thinking about not playing it." (Some months later he appeared on the White House "enemies list" as "Joe

Namath, New York Giants; businessman, actor," proving to me, in retrospect, how absolute was Nixon's loss of control of his players. Whittier's No. 12 would never have put the Jets' No. 12 on the wrong team.)

The ladies. Perhaps 1000 by now (he claimed 300 while still in college). Not one celebrity among them, no starlet, model, club singer, recognizable name or face, just a body count, perhaps phantom, certainly questionable.

If Namath were gay, for example, afraid that coming out would embarrass his friends and family, void his endorsement contracts, and complicate his playing career, it would have been simple to arrange a tidy little marriage of convenience.

If he were a deviant—an exhibitionist or sadist—it would probably be public knowledge by now, as in the cases of other famous athletes.

If the Superstud image were merely early Werblin, a glamorous option on the 1965 SportsWorld Model Male, Namath would have been able to drop it after his Cock Jock triumph in the 1969 Super Bowl.

If he's submerging a fear or playing leading man in his own fantasy, one can only wish him the best of luck and a good therapist, and hope that new generations of young athletes have the intelligence and counseling to come to terms with that old-fashioned grotesque, sexual "scoring."

If there is any answer at all, Namath may not have a glimmer either. If there ever was a "real" Namath, a core personality substantially different from his public posture, it is long gone, and was only partially formed anyway. He has been responding too long to all the people who want a piece of him, an autograph, a hot quote, a deal, a speech, a lay, a long naked look in the locker room, a chance to speculate and theorize like this. He happened to be available just when SportsWorld needed a pop star, a big, dark, sexy-looking quarterback who could lift a league and a network into position to challenge the early settlers, break open the territory, spread the gold. He succeeded beyond their wildest hopes, primarily because of his electrifying talent. But the fact that he was white, a first-generation native-born "ethnic" at that, and could be merchandised as a "rebel" when he was actually a throwback to those mythic athletes of the so-called Golden Age whose dedication to the team, whose sense of responsibility to performance, whose loyalty to family and home have been preached as sports' standards, made Namath one of the most salable sports commodities of his time.

His time, of course, was the sixties. I think I sensed his time was up one summer night after the Super Bowl extravaganza, sitting in Bachelors III with Howard Cosell and O. J. Simpson, who was holding out for more money on his rookie contract. The bar was packed, and O. J., a warm, stylish man, looked it over with amused eyes.

"It's a better crowd since last time I was here," he said. "It was kind of slummy then, come as you are, but now it's more shirt and tie. Not real class, but comfortable.

"It's nice for Joe to have a place of his own, where he can come and relax and people won't bother him. Just look at him."

I asked, "Are you going to open a bar, O. J.?"

"I've never considered it," he said. "I don't even think there's real money in it."

There was a stir near the door, signaling the entrance of Namath. O. J. did not rise or crane his neck, he just stiffened ever so slightly. Cosell sensed the change, and said, "I'll tell Joe you're here."

"No, Howard," said O. J., firmly, "you don't rush the great ones."

"Hmmmmmph," said Cosell. "It's after 1 A.M., I've got an hour's drive home, and I have to be up at six o'clock in the morning."

"The same way people don't rush you, Howard."

"I understand," said Cosell, smiling. "O. J., you're beginning to show me something."

Namath's head bobbed up and down along the bar as he moved through clumps of customers. Each time he made a circuit of the bar he came closer to our back corner table. There was no question that he knew we were in his place. Toward 1:30, Cosell picked up our bill and went home.

Toward 2 A.M. I began to get restless. I had another stop before driving home. But I wanted to watch the great meeting. Namath swept past, six or seven feet away this time, and O. J. looked away, but smiled. "He's playing his little game, but that's all right, we all have our little games, everybody's got to do his thing. Even me, I got my little game."

They understood each other. They had understood each other since childhood, O. J. running with whites in San Francisco, Namath playing with blacks in Beaver Falls. Advertising men always marveled at O. J.'s ease with whites, men and women, his obvious pleasure in meeting people, making them like him; so many black athletes on the underground railroad from the ghetto to the pros have desperately little social contact with whites.

The lack of overt racial tension on the Jets was usually attributed to Namath's "understanding" of blacks, his willingness to "treat them as equals"—Northern liberalism at work, along with a dose of patronage. Namath had known enough blacks to like and hate them as individuals, and he had no physical fear of blacks; he had grown up with them and his own childhood had been as violent as theirs.

Being white was no longer enough. An O. J. Simpson, married, a father, articulate, aware, smooth and bland as butter, a more impressive envoy from SportsWorld, was ready to take his turn.

A few minutes after 2 there was a sudden scuffle near the table, and O. J. looked up. Cool and sweet, he said, "Hey. Joe."

Namath glided forward and slid into the banquette. "Oooooo-oooooooooo Jayyyyyy," he said, as if surprised to find him.

CHAPTER
4

The Heavyweight Crown Prince
of the World

1

SWEET-NATURED KILLERS like Jack Dempsey, Joe Louis, and Rocky Marciano traditionally have been considered the model heavyweight champions. They were accommodating and controllable. They were capable of murderous rages in the ring, paroxysms of schooled brutality that could bring a crowd to its feet, turn its stomach upside down, flush out its soul, and send it out weak and gibbering. And they were also capable of toe-scraping humility, elaborate displays of soft courtesy to influential men, carefully unsexed chit-chat with rich women, and incredibly modest preachments to interviewers and fans. As symbols of masculinity, they were SportsWorld's most cynical hoaxes.

Poor, tough boys, Dempsey and Louis and Marciano could earnestly explain that splitting open another man's face, perhaps killing him, was purely a piece of work, a paid job, nothing personal. And their lives exemplified the dogma that winning the heavyweight championship of the world was the culmination of a man's life; nothing much seemed to happen to them afterward.

Dempsey would sit by the hour in the window of his Broadway restaurant, endlessly delighted to throw back kisses to student beauticians on a break, to shake fists at passing delivery boys, to bob his head and wave to the nods of prosperously portly men in velvet-collared Chesterfields. On his seventy-fifth birthday, when a man should be able to say anything he truly believes unless he no longer remembers what it might be, he looked down at his highly polished black shoes and said: "A champion owes everybody something. He can never pay back for all the help he got, for making him an idol." I had been asking him about Muhammad Ali, and he had been clumsily dodging my questions. As much as he may have envied or hated or admired Ali, he was too cautious to express an opinion. He finally told me that he had once expressed an opinion: He had endorsed one of the hundreds of political candidates who asked for his support, and he was still sorry because now there were people "on the other side," who probably disliked him for it. The candidate had been Gene Tunney's son.

Unlike Dempsey, who owed his popularity to longevity, Joe Louis was a champion who truly stirred people; he was a mainstream hero for Negroes when they needed one and he became a hero for all Americans. Jimmy Cannon's description of the young champion Louis as "a credit to his race, the human race" may seem corny, even condescending now, but in its time the phrase proved Cannon's perception and Louis' power. He was physically appealing, awesome at work, a kind, generous, gentle man who was not entirely capable of functioning without guidance. He became a sad case, addicted to cocaine, gambling on golf and young women, and something of a joke; Dick Gregory used to describe President Eisenhower at a news conference as "the white Joe Louis," a bit he dropped from his act one night when Louis walked into the nightclub. Gregory could not bring himself to hurt Joe Louis.

Louis was offended by Muhammad Ali, or at least Louis was told that Ali should offend him, and the old champ turned up in the opposition camp nearly every time Ali was preparing for a title bout. Louis was paid what is known as "walking around money," and could be trusted not to give out a coherent interview. At least once a week, for the benefit of photographers, a "spy" from Ali's camp would be found in the gym watching Liston or Patterson or Whoever train, and Louis would be dispatched to bum rush him out. The spectators and the photographers and even the spy seemed to enjoy the flurry, but I always thought Louis sweated and took it seriously.

Marciano, youngest and least mythic of the three, was outspoken about Ali. The new champ was bad for business. Marciano made many speeches and appearances, and he once told me that Ali demeaned the grandeur of the title. "It's a very bad situation now," he said, "because there is a lack of respect for the present champion and that creates a lack of respect for all past champions. Nobody questions my fights, they were all tough ones, but people just don't treat you the same way since he came along. And just look around these days, where are all the books and movies about boxing? I got interested myself because of colorful writing, Hype Igoe and Jack London, and all those Johnny Garfield movies."

Marciano, with his unkempt toupee and his belly bursting through shirts with missing buttons, was not exactly a walking ad for the dignity of ex-kings. He scuffled for a buck to the end. He had tricks, from getting other men to retrieve his coat from the checkroom to showing up in a city the morning of a banquet without some article of clothing—his hosts would gladly treat him to a tie or a suit and sometimes matched luggage to put it in. He died in the crash of a small plane carrying him to an engagement.

Ali, in turn, expressed contempt for all three of them—they were too small, too slow, too ugly—although I sometimes sensed Ali's disappointment that Louis never gave him his due as a boxer. Ali, after all, or at least Cassius Clay, sprouted from the soil of SportsWorld as surely as anyone else who read Jimmy Cannon or went to Johnny Garfield movies.

Yet Cassius Clay was different in ways it took a white, middle-class sports press steeped in its own fakelore too long to find out and understand. Our frames of reference were the hardscrabble field hands—Jack Johnson, The Great Black Threat, and Louis, son of a Georgia sharecropper who migrated to Detroit; the southern seekers and the northern ghetto-breds—Sugar Ray, Sonny Liston, Floyd Patterson, all redeemed in the Shadow of the Ring. It would have been difficult enough for us to separate this latest black boy from all the others; it was virtually impossible to perceive that he considered himself socially superior to white men, to a Colorado roustabout like Dempsey or the son of an Italian shoemaker like Marciano or even a purebred Aryan like the Swede Johansson.

After all, his great-great-grandfather, according to his family, was Henry Clay, "Gallant Harry of the West," bold schemer and five-time presidential aspirant until he was finally locked away in the history books as "The Great Compromiser." A kinsman of Henry Clay's, an historical figure in his own right, Cassius Marcellus Clay, known as "The Lion of White Hall," a Kentucky abolitionist and Lincoln's Ambassador to Russia, owned a son or grandson of Gallant Harry's, whom he set free well before Emancipation. The freedman took his former master's name, and passed it down. The first white reporter to prospect deeply in Muhammad Ali's background, Jack Olsen of *Sports Illustrated*, found the present black Clays of Louisville an accomplished, active family of teachers, musicians, artists, and craftsmen. Cassius Marcellus Clay, Sr., the boxer's father, was a handsome, unstable, smart, frustrated dreamer who filled his sons' heads with grandiose visions and earthly dreads. But, he also gave them the gift of time. Cassius, Jr. never worked a day in his life outside the ring. His mother, Odessa, granddaughter of an Irishman named Grady, touched her toes to trim her waist like any other nonworking suburban housewife. When Cassius began boxing at 12, he was no sickly lad building his body for revenge against bullies, no street-boy channeled by a sympathetic social worker. Someone had stolen his brand-new $60 bicycle, an expensive toy in 1954. Cassius, righteously angry, went looking for a policeman.

Had that policeman spent his off-duty hours coaching rock singers or teaching water colors or giving a course in hotel administration instead of managing amateur fighters, SportsWorld might have been spared its Frankenstein monster. The boy was bright, confident, ambitious, extroverted, and bursting with energy. Education would fail him—years later, his high school reported his IQ as 78, his only satisfactory subjects art and gym; yet still he was graduated. Except for tennis, he did not seem to like too many other sports. I asked him once if he had ever played football, and he said, "Just once, that's all. They gave me the ball and tackled me. My helmet hit the ground. POW. No, sir. You got to get hit in that game, too rough. You don't have to get hit in boxing, people don't understand that." Our conversation wandered on, and somehow we began talking about ice hockey, a game he considered very violent. He seemed fascinated but physically uncomfortable when I told him about goalies skating off to get their faces stitched, then returning to play, and how players sometimes switch all the paper cups containing a team's dentures, then watch laughing as they try to fit the wrong ones in. He made a face. "Why do people let theirselves get done like that?" I was a little surprised at the naivete of the question. I said that most hockey players were poor, rural Canadians with no other chance for money and fame. He said he could understand that, but he kept shaking his head and saying, "Games is just for a little while, your face and teeth is all your life."

In boxing, Clay found a perfect expression for his narcissism, his need for constant recognition, and his enormous physical energy. Yet he would never have stayed with it if he hadn't been able to develop a style based on speed and conditioning; from the beginning, he was rarely hit hard, and almost never hit often.

In boxing, too, he found the kind of stable male guidance he missed at home. The truly dedicated boxer, at least early in his career, delivers his body and soul to his trainer. For six years, Joe Martin, the policeman, directed Clay along the main path of his life, 100-odd amateur bouts. Martin's last act for Clay was to persuade him to "gamble your life" and go to Rome with the U.S. Olympic team. Clay had an almost pathological fear of flying, but he also knew that a boxing gold medalist comes home a ranked contender.

The Olympics is the international kingdom and power of SportsWorld. Because winning armies are expensive to assemble and risky to maintain, a country's best propaganda tool—pound-for-pound and dollar-for-dollar—is a successful world-class athletic team: an example of socialism in action or a testament to the vitality of democracy or living proof the people love the junta. Such a team, the theory holds, bolsters the will of the home folk, increases the respect of allies and uncommitted nations, and demoralizes the opposition. For smaller countries, the Olympics is a spectacular showcase; a handful of Turkish wrestlers and Ethiopian marathon runners and Hungarian fencers, for example, grab headlines out of all proportion to the political importance of their countries. The aging oligarchs who run the Games for their own amusement and cartels have been steadfastly unprincipled in their bending of Olympic rules. Their bleakest chapter was the 1936 Nazi Games, when they closed their eyes to the systematic exclusion of Jewish athletes from German sports clubs, a direct violation of Olympic rules. Later violations, such as the governmental subsidization of Soviet and other so-called Communist-bloc nations, racial discrimination against black South African and Rhodesian athletes, and the blatant commercialism of the skiers, were invariably handled in such a way as to set no binding precedents for the good of the Games.

For American sports fans, the Olympics is a mildly interesting diversion that conflicts every four years with the start of the football season and the climax of the baseball season; the fact that the sports we really care about—football, baseball, professional basketball and hockey, auto and horse racing—are not involved, makes it difficult for anyone outside the press and television corps to care very much about final results, those "national point standings" that each country manipulates to make itself a winner.

But for American international politicians, the Olympics is an important summit convention, a kind of staging area for sports diplomacy on all its levels, from a high school basketball coach's mission to Israel, to Arthur Ashe's tennis tour of Africa, to a Ping-Pong team to China and a volleyball team to Cuba. And weak American teams in such "minor" sports as weightlifting and gymnastics make good foreign relations: A defeat is no great embarrassment for the United States, and creates a bond of friendship with all those who have competed more successfully.

Furthermore, the increasing number of black American athletes gave the impression, sports diplomats hoped, of an integrated country that could deal fairly with its African and Asian friends.

In 1960, in Rome, Cassius Clay was everything the sports diplomats could have hoped for—a big, beautiful, brown, youthful, exuberant glad-hander who not only won the light-heavyweight medal but answered a Russian reporter's questions about racial prejudice with what sounded to me at the time like a press agent's quote: "Tell your readers we got qualified people working on that, and I'm not worried about the outcome. To me, the U.S.A. is still the best country in the world, counting yours. It may be hard to get something to eat sometimes, but anyhow I ain't fighting alligators and living in a mud hut." Very neat in 1960, first year of the sit-ins. And when Clay returned with his gold medal and signed with the Louisville Sponsoring Group, a C. Wright Millsian power elite of whiskey, steel, tobacco, oil, newspaper, television, advertising, and real estate millionaires, Cassius seemed plugged into the SportsWorld establishment for as long as he could knock men down. He was coming out of glorious tradition.

The original professional athletes in America were blacks—prizefighters, oarsmen, and jockeys. As soon as money, prestige, and mythic symbolism were offered to sports heroes, the blacks were squeezed out. They have yet to regain their places in rowing and at the racetrack. Zachary Molineaux and his sons, eighteenth-century Virginia slaves, are often credited with founding professional boxing in America, but for most of the next 100 years American black fighters went to England, where they found mainstream acceptance, and often opened successful gentlemen's gyms when they retired from the ring. America had a succession of "colored champions," and some suspiciously dark boxers who fought as Indians and Arabs, but that twentieth-century bogeyman, Jack Johnson, was the first Negro cut into the substantial heavyweight pie, and his storied persecution was motivated as much by economics as by prejudice.

The custom of rich men running young fighters and good race horses grew easily out of that early slave tradition. Cassius Clay's southern masters had, as Cassius would put it, "the complexions and the connections to give me good directions." They turned him over to Angelo Dundee, an excellent trainer with booking and match-making connections, and let the media hype their boy into a star.

Since freedom of the press guarantees open season on criminals and athletes, Clay's buildup was, in its way, as shameful a process as the wrecking job a few years later. A few observers like Dick Schaap found dark portents among the early laughs, but most writers, perhaps assuming Clay wouldn't be around long anyway, went for the easy copy, the outrageous doggerel, the boasting, the predictions. Early in 1963, Cassius was on the cover of *Time* magazine, which hee-hawed, "Cassius Clay is Hercules, struggling through the twelve labors. He is Jason, chasing the Golden Fleece. He is Galahad, Cyrano, D'Artagnan. When he scowls strong men shudder and when he smiles, women swoon. The mysteries of the universe are his Tinker Toys."

Early in 1964, after only nineteen professional fights, he arrived in Miami to fight for the heavyweight championship of the world. The boxing commissioners and the sporting press expected him to be beaten badly, but no one raised too strong an objection to the mismatch, which was flowering into another in a newly profitable string of closed-circuit television spectaculars. Po' ol' Cash, but everybody gonna have himself a payday.

Me, too.

2

The Beatles were standing in the center of the Fifth Street Gym in Miami Beach, a large, dingy, smoky room, waiting for Cassius Clay to show up for his daily work-out. They seemed to be as impatient as I was. None of us had yet met Clay. The Beatles were surprisingly small, and their white, terry-cloth cabana jackets gave them a bunny-rabbit softness. The $1-a-head crowd in the gym were no music fans; they glanced over the group, on their first American tour, and dismissed them as girls. One of the Beatles asked me, "Where th' fuck's Clay?," and after I said I had no idea, I introduced myself. We shook hands, and the Beatle politely said his name was John Lennon. I knew from photographs he was Ringo Starr, but his little joke made no impact on my self-importance—I was Robert Lipsyte of *The New York Times*, in jacket and tie, representative and conduit of The People's Right to Know. Ringo introduced me to the others, jumbling the names. The game palled quickly. The real John Lennon said, "Let's get the fuck out of here," but two massive state troopers blocked their way, and actually herded them into a small dressing room, where they were imprisoned for another six or seven minutes until Clay burst into the gym, brandishing a cane, and roared, "Hello there, Beatles. We oughta do some road shows together, we'll get rich." I gaped, and so did the Beatles.

The first beholding of Cassius Clay, perhaps the first half-dozen, especially in 1964, were startling. The exaggeration of the size of SportsWorld heroes, of almost all male performing celebrities, has prepared us for disappointment. But Clay was much larger than we had been led to believe, far more of a sheer physical presence. It would be something of a shock a few days later to see him actually towering over Liston at their fight. And Clay's healthy, shining good looks were somehow an insult to those who were willing to accept him as a sly braggart boosting the box office. He *was* beautiful, and if we had been taught anything, it was to be modest about talent and beauty; the monologues of Clay had been written for a jockey who looked like Yogi Berra.

Although they had never met before, Cassius and the Beatles fell into a routine as soon as the cameras were in place. He knocked them all out with one domino punch, they formed a pyramid to get at his jaw, they prayed he would stop beating them. Clay was just 22 then, the Beatles' contemporary, and they shared the future. They began to laugh so hard that their quick little set pieces lost their precision and collapsed into broad slapstick. They were inside the ropes, performing like monkeys in a cage, and they were laughing at the rest of us; of course, what a trick! Outside the ropes, getting it all down in my 25¢ spiral-wired notebook, I wondered briefly if I was part of the trick, too, the Mets again, but, no, this was happening, and I was here to report it. An out-of-town assignment is no time to recall all-night college debates on whether a toppling tree makes noise if no one is there to hear it, and so I pushed the thought away. The Beatles finally had to be herded out by the troopers, and Clay skipped rope and hit the bags and sparred and went into the dressing room for his rubdown where he babbled on about his beauty, his speed, his future, for any reporter who had missed earlier versions. I found a corner of the room and took notes and waited, thinking I might outlast the other reporters and get some information they would miss. There were only a few of us left, the steam from open shower stalls curling the pages of our notebooks, when a columnist from Los Angeles asked, "But what if you lose, Cassius, what happens then?"

"So beautiful," he murmured at a fogged mirror. "Your publicity has overshadowed your talent. You are the double-greatest."

"Let's be serious for a minute," insisted a sportswriter from

Boston, which seems to breed tough and testy sportswriters. "What if the champ beats you?"

Clay, on the rubbing table, laughed into the fists propping his chin. "I won't feel bad. I'll have tricked all the people into coming to the fight, to pay $250 for a ticket when they wouldn't have paid $100 without my talk."

"So this whole act," said the Boston man, "is just a con job, eh?"

"People ain't gonna give you nothing no way, you gotta go get it." He pushed up on the table, and his eyes sparkled. "I'm making money, the popcorn man making money, and the beer man, and you got something to write about," his eyes danced over us, "your papers let you come down to Miami Beach where it's warm."

The Los Angeles columnist winked at me, but the Boston man got angry. "Exactly what are you going to do when Sonny Liston beats you after all your big talk?"

"If Liston beats me, the next day I'll be on the sidewalk hollering 'No man ever beat me twice.' I'll be screaming for a rematch." The big brown body relaxed and seemed to melt into the rubbing table. The voice dropped to a whisper. "Or maybe I'll quit the ring for good. I'm 22 years old now." He dismissed us by closing his eyes. "I think I'm getting tired of fighting."

We found ourselves tip-toeing out.

I appreciated Clay that very first day. I was in the middle of writing Dick Gregory's autobiography, *Nigger*, and the insights I gained from that project helped me get a sense of Clay that would be refined over the years. He was a fiercely dedicated boxer with a showman's flair that did, as he said, overshadow his ability; he shared with Hemingway and Dali the knack of melding art and publicity to the advantage of both.

Liston was something else entirely. Clay, at least in the sixties, before he became a federal case, might have been pegged to the American comic-hero tradition of Davy Crockett, but Sonny had been spun out of all bad dreams since the beginning of fear, the Soulless Black Destroyer, the Bogeyman. Liston's camp was filled with people claiming that Sonny was sweet and loving with them while vile to the rest of the world because he was a natural man responding to the vibrations around him. Such explanations came from his trainer, whom he sometimes kicked in public, and from Martha Malone, his Beverly Hills criminal lawyer, who was married to Joe Louis. (When I asked her once what Louis' function was in Liston's camp, she raised an eyebrow and said, "Joe's with me.")

The press had laid brick upon brick of hyperbole until Sonny was The Invincible Thug. He was an excellent fighter with a powerful punch. His high ranking in the late fifties was justified, he had certainly been a logical challenger to Champion Floyd Patterson. But Patterson was SportsWorld's Model Negro and sometimes Honorary White Man, an NAACP integrationist who had risen from "juvenile delinquency" to walk with Kennedys and Kings, and there was no better way to boost Floyd than create a straw monster for him to tear apart.

When Sonny easily beat Floyd twice, SportsWorld was stuck with the image it had created. "I'm sorry for Liston," Cassius would say, infuriating reporters, "you people put too much load on him, you built him up too big and now he has such a long way to fall."

Liston had no store of compassion for Clay, in fact, just beneath his streetcorner wit—"You say Clay fast, huh? He didn't kiss no bullet, did he?, he didn't run through hell in no gasoline sport coat, huh?"—was a jailhouse rap we didn't always grasp right away. "Naaah," said Sonny, "his goading don't get behind me. He's a fag and I'm a man."

The days building toward any one-shot sports spectacular, Kentucky Derby, Indianapolis 500, Super Bowl, are seductive and enflaming for the press, but the week before a major heavyweight championship match has a unique rhythm and madness that spills through a young reporter like hot wine. He begins to reel from sparring sessions to press conference to cocktail party to secret meeting with characters left over from old movies who will, for the price of a cheap dinner, reveal information about fixes and dumps and satchels of betting money coming in from Venezuela by diplomatic courier.

The Scene is all; it covers the week like a striped tent. The Scene becomes the World, and if Diem and JFK and the little black Birmingham girls were still dead, if Baldwin's *The Fire Next Time* and Friedan's *The Feminine Mystique* and Dylan's

"Blowin' in the Wind" were recent early warnings of the coming turbulence, we did not know and could not have cared as the hours pounded on toward showdown.

There were bit players on the Beach that week from the same cosmic repertory company as the principals: Budd Schulberg, astounded perhaps at life following his art—who was to say that Cassius had not been created of scraps from *What Makes Sammy Run?* and *The Harder They Fall* and *A Face in the Crowd?*; Norman Mailer, constantly torn between observation and participation, following a tradition of writers who sensed that their solitary creations and public judgments made them secret sharers to all prizefighters; and, tucked into a corner of the tent, Malcolm X, Cassius' spiritual adviser and potentially the most powerful individual black man in the world. I never saw him that week, although his presence hung threateningly over the Scene; the promoters of the live gate, when they realized they had scaled the price of tickets too high, demanded that Clay publicly deny the rumors he was a so-called Black Muslim. It was a ploy to shift blame for a box office bust from their mistake to the vague excuse that vacationing Jews were boycotting the fight because of the Muslims. Clay refused, the promoters threatened to cancel the fight, Clay called their bluff, and the matter was dropped. As far as the promoters were concerned, it was a sharp business tactic that had failed. To Clay, however, it was the first inkling of what he would consider Muslim power. Malcolm helped him feed on it.

I had met Malcolm the summer before, on the afternoon of the second Patterson-Liston fight, on a streetcorner in Brooklyn. He was watching, contemptuously, I thought, as more than a thousand blacks and whites picketed the Downstate Medical Center to protest bias in the construction industry. I had been assigned to write a feature sidebar to complement the fight story out of Las Vegas, a nice soft human interest piece with a local angle. Talk to Patterson's wife or some juvenile delinquents from his old school or one of those handy old pugs who used to hang out in bars around Madison Square Garden with an outstretched empty glass and a bag of marbles for a tongue. I just couldn't hack it that day—those stories were getting to be my song—so I headed to Brooklyn where blacks on the picket line told me that the fight was nothing anymore when men and women were lying down in front of bulldozers. A lawyer said, "They'll always give us opportunities to act like animals," and another man said he felt good whenever a black man beat a white man in sports, but the stakes were much higher now. I felt I still needed something stronger to tie the story together, to save me from Patterson's wife or marble-mouth, and when I recognized Malcolm from newspaper photos, I rushed across the street and asked him what the Liston-Patterson fight meant to him.

"That's a stupid question," he said, and three neatly dressed men with shaven skulls, Fruits of Islam, I later learned, formed a wall with their chests and walked me into the gutter.

I shouted at his back, "The only stupid question is an unasked question," and Malcolm turned, smiled, and nodded at his bodyguard to let me through.

"I'm pleased to see that the two best men in the sport are black," he said, "But they'll be exploited, of course, and the promoters will get all the bread. They let a Negro excel if it's going to make money for them."

I was delighted, but at the time all it meant to me was that I was saved from having to write another soft dumb feature.

A few months later, Malcolm characterized President Kennedy's assassination as an example of violent white America's "chickens coming home to roost," an advanced observation. Elijah Muhammad, leader of the Nation of Islam, used the remark as an excuse to forbid Malcolm further public utterance. Nevertheless, Clay left his Miami Beach training camp several weeks before the fight to accompany Malcolm to a Muslim rally in Manhattan and he invited Malcolm and his family to be his guests in Miami the week before the fight. After the fight the new heavyweight champion and the ascetic, ironic prime minister of Islam celebrated with vanilla ice cream.

The fight itself was a fit finale to the bizarre buildup. Liston on his stool, unable or unwilling to come out for the seventh round, was as marvelously inconclusive as Evel Knievel—ten years later —parachuting into the Snake River Canyon. Both times we were promised a finite package, an end to uncertainty, an uninterrupted dream, and both times we were cheated of orgasm and left a little more hung up than when we started.

By 1974 we were almost used to such open ends, but in 1964 we still thought we had the right to know at least who won.

Sonny Liston on his stool was bleeding, obviously exhausted, perhaps hurt, but SportsWorld had taught us that it was death before dishonor in a heavyweight title fight, and it was inconceivable that a champion would just *quit*. It had to be a fix. The films would soon remind us how Clay dominated the fight, stood flat-footed and banged his jab into Sonny's face, dodged his heavy hooks and sliced open his cheek, but in the stunned moments after the bell for the seventh round went unanswered the freshest memories were of Clay's madman turn at the afternoon weigh-in—pure hysterical fear, according to official medical opinion—and of Clay's own attempt to strip off his gloves and quit when he was temporarily blinded by sweat and rosin before the start of the fifth round. Had to be a fix, the people said. Sonny would never just give up.

Terrible Sonny. At a press conference the next morning, an amiable, even charming Liston passed off the loss of his title as "one of those little things that can happen to you." Journalists milling beneath his platform, obviously no longer in fear of his glare, finally prodded him into saying, smiling, that the loss made him "feel like when the President got shot." The medical reports on his injured left shoulder were vague, something between a tennis elbow and torn muscles. Sonny claimed to have thrown out the arm in the very first round. The press exchanged homemade rumors—the Muslims had threatened to kill Liston if he didn't dump, Liston had bet his purse on Clay at 7–1, Liston had dumped because a return-bout clause in the contract assured him a rematch and second payday with Clay. None seemed so wild when Liston ended the session with a cheery, "Thanks, fellas" and the suggestion of a wave with the slung arm.

Clay's press conference was also out of recent character. He spoke so softly we had to strain to hear him, and he pleased his audience with a gentle, "I'm through talking, all I have to do is be a nice, clean gentleman." He recapitulated the fight, said he would defend against all ranking contenders, and displayed such an even, mild temperament that hundreds left the hall to catch planes home or file stories on "a new Clay molded to the championship throne" before someone asked him if he was a "card-

carrying member of the Black Muslims." In newspack journalism
there is a tendency for reporters to stay at the water hole only
long enough to fill up for the next story or broadcast, and so only
a small percentage of the fight's 500-man press corps heard Clay
shout: "Card-carrying, what does that mean? I go to a Black
Muslim meeting and what do I see? I see that there's no smoking
and no drinking and no fornicating and their women wear dresses
down to the floor. And then I come out on the street and you tell
me I shouldn't go in there. Well, there must be something in
there if you don't want me to go in there."

It quickly escalated, primarily because the reporters who had
remained tended to be the younger, more vigorous, socially conscious liberals of the newspack who felt comfortable talking nonsports and wanted to challenge Clay on the Muslims' separatist
dogma.

"In the jungle," said Clay, in a rote we would all become very
familiar with in the years to come, "lions are with lions and tigers
with tigers and redbirds stay with redbirds and bluebirds with
bluebirds. That's human nature, too, to be with your own kind. I
don't want to go where I'm not wanted."

And then, as arguments were trotted out, civil rights arguments and citizenship arguments and sports idol arguments, Clay
suddenly said: "I don't have to be what you want me to be, I'm
free to be who I want."

It was very simple, but at that time, coming from a brand-new
heavyweight champion of the world, it was profound and revolutionary. A declaration of independence from SportsWorld. *I don't
have to be what you want me to be, I'm free to be who I want.*

It would be another three years before SportsWorld got the
message, before sportswriters and officials and fans and, most
important, other athletes, were convinced that Clay was "sincere." That became a very important word. Editors and readers
always asked me if I thought Clay was really "sincere" about the
Muslims, as if that was a piece of intelligence we could act upon,
use to guide our coverage of him, or our caring about him. I
always answered that I thought Clay had been sincere about
what he was saying the last time I heard him say it. As time went
on, I became less ostentatiously politic: it really didn't matter if
he was sincere or not, he was giving the Muslims national public-

ity and community clout beyond Elijah's capabilities to control it.

A few weeks after the fight, I went to Harlem with Gregory and we visited first Malcolm, then Cassius. On the street Malcolm had been stiff and cold, but lounging in the backroom of Michaux's Bookstore he talked about Clay warmly, less like his guru than an older brother or uncle, and surprised me with a brief flurry of jabs as we discussed some technical aspect of the fight. He said he thought Clay was very smart, and he was continually impressed at the way Cassius recharged himself with the energy of crowds. I asked him if he had tried to take Clay with him when he publicly broke with the Muslims a few weeks earlier, and he shook his head. Cassius would have to make his own decisions in his own good time. Later, as I was leaving, he told me that my fight coverage had been among the fairest: I took that as heady praise until a *Times* editor, to whom I foolishly recounted it, said sourly, "That's just great, we'll put it up on the trucks, 'Malcolm X Loves Lipsyte.' "

Clay was in a three-room suite at the Hotel Theresa surrounded by young black men and round yellow cardboard containers from the Chock Full O' Nuts luncheonette downstairs. Some still contained orange juice. We chatted for a while, then he answered the phone with a theatrically deepened voice: "This is the heavyweight champion of the world, Muhammad Ali . . . Ahleee . . ." annoyance creased his brow, and the voice rose, "Yes, I used to be Cassius Clay."

He spoke for a few minutes, then clapped a hand over the mouthpiece and looked around. "They want a message," he said to one of the neatly dressed, shaven-skulled young men, "they want a message for Africa."

Dick Gregory responded first. "Tell them to look to the East and pray."

Clay nodded gratefully. "Tell them to look to the East and pray to . . ."

"No, man," said Greg, "they *know* who to pray *to*. Just give them that and they'll take it from there."

Greg wandered out after a while, and I spent the next three hours in the suite. It would be the first of many times I was the only white man in Clay's presence, and the first of many times I listened through his states-of-the-dogma addresses. I tended to prefer to be the only white with Muslims; first of all, it seemed to imply a guest status of protection; second, it meant there would be no wasted time and anger over the pointlessly insulting questions of reporters who seemed challenged to defend the white race. As for the dogmatics, I learned to listen to them for subtle shifts in policy and emphasis; I'm not sure I ever really caught any of significance, but I was impressed at how Clay shaped and polished and refined his Muslim commentary over the years until the early rote had been so thoroughly filtered through his quick brain that it was his, much as the predictions and the doggerel and the mock bombast, which could not have been all his at the start, eventually became his through absorption and reconstitution.

That day he told me he was first introduced to Islam in Atlanta, when he was 17, "fished" off a street corner, and that he eventually came back to it when he found that civil rights, for which he had briefly marched in 1960, had brought no equality to the black man, and that traditional religion's "spooks and ghosts" were merely white man's tricks to enslave the black man on earth with a promise of "pie in the sky when you die by and by." He wanted his "down on the ground while I'm still around."

The talk turned, twisted, drifted, was interrupted a dozen times, visitors, callers, the sudden need to jump up, shadowbox, flex muscles, shout. He ran through roles; sage, clown, athlete, preacher, revolutionary, conservative, mime, king. Once he ran through the entire weigh-in scene, screaming "Hey, sucker, you a chump" at one Muslim brother playing Liston while another carefully held him back as had Bundini Brown, an assistant trainer, that morning in Miami Beach. "I was tired after the weigh-in," he finally said, blowing hard, "and I thought I might have burned up too much energy acting the fool."

When I reminded Clay that he had staged a similar weigh-in mad scene, a kind of warm-up, for the Charlie Powell fight the previous January in Pittsburgh, he laughed and bounded up, and started over again, "Sucker, I'm the champ, I'm the real champ," then suddenly sat down again. "For thirty-five minutes I put that on, and Liston was searching my face for fear. He saw none. This is what destroyed him."

When I asked him about Floyd Patterson, already trumpeted as his next opponent in a match between the Crescent and the Cross, he shook his head. "It wouldn't be fair for a man of his abilities—such a puny, light man who can't take a punch—to stand up for all the Catholics in the world. Besides I don't want no religious wars." With five quick jabs and one uppercut, he knocked Floyd out in the Hotel Theresa, then begged, "Come on, you chump, get on up, you sissy."

But Floyd wisely stayed on the floor, and Clay raised his arms. "Winn-ah, and still champ-peen of the wor-old, Muhammad AH-LEE."

He dropped his arms. "It's funny. If I changed my name to Jimmy Jones or Calvin Washington nobody would say nothing. Muhammad Ali. Worthy of all praise most high. They wouldn't introduce me in Madison Square Garden the other night."

He sat down. "My dream and love is boxing. That's all I want to do. But people keep coming to me, like you, and they want to talk about the Muslims. I would never talk about my religion if people didn't keep asking me. And I try to be nice and helpful.

"Well, one good thing about America, you stand up for your rights and people will eventually adjust to it. Like my name."

3

The movie, record, and endorsement contracts offered to Cassius Clay if he should somehow survive the fight with Liston were not fulfilled by the Champion Muhammad Ali. In some cases the entertainment companies and the advertising agencies were reflecting white America's distress over a Muslim champion, in others the product or vehicle was no longer appropriate. In any case, Ali's continued membership in the sect was costing him a great deal of money. The editors and the readers were beginning to realize he was "sincere." And they felt threatened.

The Muslims were hard, healthy, disciplined, devout, separatist, and violent. Those whites flabby with "guilt" could visualize Elijah galvanizing black America into a Super Mau-Mau. Those whites masquerading their racism as "backlash" instinctively understood that the Muslims were not unlike the fierce secret European sects of their own not-so-distant history. There were rumors that the Nation of Islam was financed by, variously, the Ku Klux Klan, Texas oil, the Arab Legion, the CIA. Between black civil rights activitists who presented themselves to "the white power structure" as the lesser of two evils in regard to the Muslims, and black writers and academics who were busy creating for themselves areas of expertise, Elijah's influence and membership were blown up beyond the little old man's wildest dreams.

By the time Ali was in training for his November 16, 1964, rematch with Liston in Boston, he was the heavyweight hero-king on ghetto streets and a usurping pretender in Middle America. He had run smack into history. In that summer of the Harlem riots, the Mississippi murders of Chaney, Goodman, and Schwerner, and the Gulf of Tonkin "retaliation," he had come back from triumphant visits with Nassar and Nkrumah to announce, "I'm not no American, I'm a black man."

The Muslim presence around Ali, once no larger than the shadow of Malcolm X, was now a tangible, sometimes intimidating force. The Muslims marched Ali in phalanx along those narrow, twilight Boston streets, they guarded his hotel, they physically inserted themselves between the champion and the press. One of them, Clarence X Gill, the military chief of the Boston mosque, a thickset, yellow-complexioned man, seemed to take particular pleasure shouldering and elbowing journalists aside as he led the champion's entourage. More than one outraged complaint from the press was coldly, challengingly stared down.

Another Muslim prominent in that retinue was Leon 4X Ameer, who acted as Ali's press secretary and, until he was advised that it was not customary, tried to charge reporters for interviews with Ali. Ameer was a small, officious, humorless man who had served as Malcolm's bodyguard before his apostasy and was now chief East Coast karate instructor for the Fruit of Islam. Ameer and I had taken an instant dislike to each other the summer before when Ali was in New York to tape a TV show and the three of us and several other Muslims had spent an afternoon tooling around Harlem listening to Marvin Gaye records on a

Cadillac limousine's phonograph and gorging on lamb shank and Navy bean pie at the Temple No. 7 Muslim Restaurant. Hung up in Elijah's "white devil" rhetoric, Ameer could not understand how Ali could compromise himself by traveling so openly and amiably with a white man, though we all' tacitly understood it was distant drum beating for the next fight. By Boston, Ameer and I barely spoke except to order each other out of the way.

This time, the promotional tent that covered buildup week was dark, eerie, depressing, filled with secret corners and ugly rumors. There had been a Senate investigation into the contractual ramifications of the last fight. The results were routinely inconclusive but the hearings had raised so many unanswered questions about Liston's underworld relationships that old prejudices against boxing were easily revived and flogged by politicians and editorial writers. Robert F. Kennedy, then Attorney General, was said to be looking for an eleventh-hour way to run the fight out of Boston. The World Boxing Association, the chaotic sport's only national or international governing body, had recently stripped Ali of his title on the grounds that by complying with a return-bout clause in the original contract he was flouting one of its most important safeguards against fixed fights. Except for the fact that the WBA, a coalition of many state and foreign boxing commissions, was as flexible and self-serving as any Olympic committee, one would be tempted to agree with its ruling; Liston's financial backers were promoting this rematch and Ali was theoretically a Liston employee for the night. But since the Massachusetts Boxing Commission was not a WBA member, it seemed useless to press the issue.

Less significant but far more fun were the rumors to be floated. The Muslims had threatened to kill Sonny if he tried to win this fight. The Muslims were ready to drop Ali if he lost this fight. Win or lose, Ali was leaving the country to become an Egyptian. The presence of foreign newsmen at these prefight sparring sessions and cocktail parties, particularly the British wolfpack upon whom the Bostonians had modeled themselves, guaranteed every rumor its day in print. The British, hampered by restrictive libel laws at home, were at liberty in America, and they justified the expense of their trips with scandalous headlines. Once published abroad, the rumor became a "report" returned to the United

States via United Press or Associated Press or Reuters, and American newsmen would then have to write stories qualifying or denying "foreign press dispatches." It became a convoluted game. Harold Conrad, a former Hollywood scriptwriter who was head publicist, sowed irresistible innuendoes he asked the Englishmen not to print. Eventually, American newsmen used the Englishmen to notarize their own favorite rumors. The Englishmen, of course, were hardly innocents to be manipulated—every one of them, it seemed, had narrow brushes with Black Muslim death squads, particularly the ones who carried sword canes and bore titles like "World's Greatest Sportswriter" beneath their by-lines, won years before swimming past crocodiles in burning rivers to file the first results of the Pan-African cricket finals.

But the press wasn't piping smoke out of thin air. There was a strained stridency to Ali's voice these days, and we variously ascribed it to religious hysteria, Liston-dread, and the conjugal demands of Sonji Roi, the sexy Chicago barmaid he had married suddenly, and mysteriously, the previous August. Just two months before that marriage, between mouthfuls of Navy bean pie, Ali had eyed the Muslim waitresses in their long gowns, nudged me and whispered that he was looking for "a virgin girl ain't no one touched" to be his wife. Sonji, divorced, a mother, a few years older than Ali, was not even a Muslim.

But there was another glaring inconsistency about Ali in Boston that disturbed American newsmen far more. During workouts, Lincoln Perry, the black movie comedian whose screen name, Stepin Fetchit, had come into the language to characterize the lazy, dumb, cowardly black stereotype, lounged on the ring apron in a rubber skullcap and white turtleneck sweater. American reporters were offended, and sat stony-faced through the 72-year-old Fetchit's old jokes and occasional comic mimes. Once, when the phrase "Uncle Tom" was brought up at a press conference by a reporter, Fetchit began yelling, "Uncle Tom was not an inferior Negro. He was a white man's child. His real name was MacPherson and he lived near Harriet Beecher Stowe. Tom was the first of the Negro social reformers and integrationists. The inferior Negro was Sambo."

While we muttered among ourselves, Ali suddenly shouted. "Whatsa matter, write it down, your pencils paralyzed?"

The Muslims around us clapped and stamped their feet on the wooden flooring until the gym shook. "You tell it, brother," they chanted, "Oh, make it plain." It was the first time I saw them smile.

Leon 4X jumped up on a chair. "Thank you, champ, thank you, champ," as if he were ending a presidential news conference, and Captain Clarence signaled his phalanx of Fruit to form their protective pocket for Ali and bulldoze through us to the street.

My own relationship with Ali was going through what would become a cyclical apogee. I tended to have few, if any, private interviews with him while there was a heavy concentration of press, preferring to lay back and cover the overall scene. He was far more open and relaxed between fights than during the weeks immediately preceding one; also, any fresh areas I opened up would quickly become pack property in the mad fact-picking of the buildup. It was in Boston, professionally irked at being surprised by Sonji, Fetchit, and Ali's rejection of Malcolm, that I began to seriously consider that what seemed like inconsistencies in Ali might really be examples of long-term patterns. Once an observer was willing to grant that Ali was sincere about his religion, dedicated to his boxing, and burdened by various anxieties, that all three were sometimes interrelated, and that all three were nourishing a monumental egocentricity, the observer had a basic scaffolding from which to start building his own useful theories about Ali. Or at least do better than call him a misguided youth or an enigma.

Covering Ali for *The Times* offered the advantage of allowing, even demanding, the kind of steady, even-handed reporting that freed a writer from the knee-jerk reaction—right-wing or left— over the return-bout clause, Stepin Fetchit, Muslims, and the continued 1Y draft deferment as the Vietnam war stoked up. This balanced, somewhat, the strait-jacketed way *The Times* defined news as a series of recent occurrences or official pronouncements or logical, "responsible" speculations, often to the exclusion of moods, common knowledge, or "outsider" intelligence that was sometimes years ahead of the facts. A minor, but telling example: The editors decreed he be referred to as Cassius Clay, although he demanded to be addressed as Muhammad Ali (a name that stuck in the throats of many of my older colleagues who either quarreled with him about it or compromised by calling him "champ").

Ali's contention was that the Establishment was frightened by the power of his new name and the implication that Negroes would cast off their slave names and rise to freedom. *The Times'* official line, as far as I could determine through countless conferences and memos, was that until he changed his name legally he was Cassius Clay; I suspected that *The Times'* institutional adoration of words as ultimate definers of civilization was as much at stake in this case as in its refusal to allow certain slang and obscenities into the paper, even when they were essential to properly understand the character of an elected official or a public event.

I discussed this once with Ali, and was sorry I did. He patted my head and told me not to worry, "You just the white power structure's little brother." I brought that testimonial back to 43rd Street, too, and suggested it be put up on the trucks. Later, thinking about the smug arrogance with which editors had insisted that Ali was Clay, I remembered that Liston had stared at Ali a few weeks before their scheduled rematch and sneered, "Ahmed Mali, Mamud Wally, what's that? I met you as Cassius Clay, I'll leave you as Cassius Clay."

Poor dumb messed-over Sonny. He trained his ass off for that Boston fight, literally. He looked fast and sharp, lean and mean. A few days before the date I drove up to his training camp with Dick Gregory, who was collecting money to truck turkeys to Mississippi for the poor at Christmas. The camp was at a deserted summer resort overlooking Plymouth Bay, a dozen miles from Plymouth Rock, and that chill night there were only the mournful sounds of gulls and boats' horns and lonely dogs. When we went into Liston's cottage, Sonny was sitting in an overstuffed chair glaring at the television set; a movie called "Zulu" was on, and at that moment a handful of white men with repeating rifles was mowing down the cream of that proud black empire. Liston just glared; he did not twitch or move a muscle or say a word until a commercial called a cease-fire. Then he rose and walked into the kitchen with Gregory. Later, Gregory said there was no way in the world Liston could ever win the fight; his mind was blown.

Of course, we didn't find out right away. A few days later, Ali
suffered his famous hernia, which Liston sympathetically attributed to his opening his mouth too often to let in too much air,
and the fight was postponed. The dingy corridors of Boston City
Hospital swarmed with guards and rumors: Ali had been poisoned; Ali had inflicted the hernia upon himself because he was
scared; Ali was faking it on orders from—pick one—H. L. Hunt,
Bobby Kennedy, Elijah Muhammad. Nothing would ever be
simple and straightforward when Ali was involved.

On January 8, 1965, nearly two months later, I saw a wire-
service story that Leon 4X Ameer had publicly renounced the
Muslims. On Christmas Day, he had been beaten by Captain
Clarence X Gill and several other members of the Boston mosque
in the lobby of a Boston hotel. They had been caught running out
by an off-duty detective, and arrested. Christmas night, according to Ameer, several more Muslims came to finish the job. He
was found by a chambermaid the next morning in a bloody bath-
tub, and he spent three more days comatose in Boston City Hospital under twenty-four-hour police guard. He was released after
regaining consciousness. He tried to get justice within the
Muslims, he told his very own first press conference, but his wife,
who was the mother of his seven children, a blood brother, and
his Muslim brothers and sisters had all been turned against him.
Now, in fear for his life, he was ready to denounce the group as a
revolutionary conspiracy of black and white racists. Apparently
he still believed that notoriety afforded some insurance against
murder. I thought he'd have trouble getting much attention
when Malcolm's own predictions of assassination were generally
discounted by the white media as publicity stunts. I was only
vaguely interested myself. It sounded like a falling out of thugs,
and I'd be hard-pressed to pick a favorite between Leon and
Clarence.

Five days later Ali came to town to announce the signing of
radio rights for his as-yet unscheduled re-rematch with Liston. I
hadn't seen Ali since the operation. He began his press conference by saying, "Little old me, a country boy, raised in the sticks,
actually sitting here in this twenty-five-story skyscraper in New
York City. It's hard to believe."

It was also hard to take. I found myself uncharacteristically rising and asking questions about Ameer and his accusations.

"Ah-meer? Little fellow? I think I remember a little fellow who hung around camp, a little fellow who liked to go downstairs and get me papers." When Ali saw my pen poised for more, he added, "Now I hear he's telling lies, saying he was my press secretary," then shrugged and looked away.

Another reporter broke in to ask Ali about his weight. But I continued asking about Ameer, and Ali finally exploded.

"Any fool Negro got the nerve to buck us, you want to make him a star. Jim Brown said something about the Muslims and they made him a movie star. Ameer was caught with a young girl. He had a wife and nine children. That man stole $800, he was a karate man and he come down on three officials and he got what he deserved."

I asked about several other members of his entourage who had dropped out of sight at various times. Ali, controlled now but still angry, called them "weak believers out to get what they could" and said that "God burned their brain and made them go crazy." When I asked if Ameer was justified in being afraid for his life, Ali said, "They think everyone out to kill them because they know they deserve to be killed for what they did."

The sports editors were not interested in the Ameer material; it was not sports, they said. Sulking, I wrote a short dumb piece about the radio rights without mentioning Ameer. The next day, Ameer called me. He was in New York to appear on the Barry Gray radio show, and asked if we could meet. We made a date for dinner the following evening. That night, on radio, he called Ali "a victim of circumstances," and intimated that Elijah had Ku Klux Klan money and Swiss bank accounts. A carful of local Muslims was parked outside the studio building. New York plainclothes policemen escorted Ameer back to his hotel that night.

Ameer was no longer the hard little nut I remembered from Boston. Most Muslims have a healthful glow to their skins, a springy step, and righteously glittering eyes. But Leon's skin was now ashy, and he walked gingerly; he said there was a blood clot in his head he was afraid of displacing. We talked for several hours that night about how he had become a Muslim.

He had been 23 years old at the time, the same age Ali was now. He was loading dresses on a truck on Seventh Avenue when the black driver began cursing a passing white woman. When Leon questioned him, the driver suggested he attend a meeting of the Lost-Found Nation of Islam: "If you knew what I knew you'd be cursing that devil bitch, too." Leon thought about it for a few weeks, but characteristically did nothing. He had been drifting for years. He had joined the Marines at 18, in 1952, and found his first real home in the Corps: He loved the community, security, and discipline. But he was hurt in a training accident, and honorably discharged with a disability pension. At 5 feet 4 inches he was too short to be a policeman, the only other career that interested him. He rarely held a job for more than a few months, and occasionally took numbers arrests for runners who couldn't afford a bust that month.

A few weeks later, a friend who had lost an eye and part of a leg in Korea came back from a Muslim meeting thrilled and excited. Leon allowed himself to be dragged to the next meeting. He walked into a room of clean, disciplined black brothers and his life was changed.

He found what Cassius Clay would find a few years later—peace and order, a shield, a greater truth, a mythology, a language, a surrogate family. They got him straight, they put him under pressure to be healthy, respectable, responsible, and "a man." He quit liquor and policy, and married the woman he was living with. Ameer's experience offered an insight into Clay's.

As a boxer in training, Clay found it easy, even helpful, to observe the prohibitions against smoking, drinking, the eating of pork. He was also relieved of peer pressure "to hang out," to cruise, to chase women, particularly white women, which was expressly forbidden, since they were the "white devil's" ultimate weapon in the continued enslavement and corruption of black men.

The theme of black superiority—physical, cultural, religious—gave Leon his first positive psychic framework since the Marines. For Clay, it soothed many of the racial anxieties Cassius Sr. had whipped into him. For Leon, who had dropped out of high school, and for Clay, whose diploma was practically a gift for winning the Golden Gloves, the pseudo-intellectual mumbo jumbo provided a handy store of phrases and concepts upon which their bright but underexercised minds could feed and grow. Leon moved quickly up the ranks; he was encouraged to renew his interest in self-defense, he opened a health food store, became a karate teacher and goon squad leader, and eventually gave karate demonstrations at the national convention and at command performances for Elijah's family. Clay was offered special dispensation to continue an otherwise forbidden career in entertainment, and studied privately with Malcolm. Clay gained a platform from which he would become "the onliest boxer in history people asked questions like a Senator."

The Times was still not interested in Ameer's story, neither sports nor Outside, which was just as well. Ameer needed money badly for his family and for his medical expenses, and I was fascinated by the material and wanted to explore it with greater freedom. We arranged to write an article for *Look*. I called Malcolm, who was rising anew as an ideological leader with a broader, nonracist, international outlook. He laughed when I asked him about Ameer. He said: "If my life is worth 3 cents, then Leon's is worth 2 cents."

One weekend Leon stayed in my apartment while we worked. He complained of headaches and dizzy spells from the beatings. In the middle of a night that had suddenly turned colder, my wife Marjorie tip-toed into his room to cover him with an extra blanket. He was awake, coiled to counterattack, but feigned sleep. In the morning, when he told us about it, he was close to tears. In a sense, her gesture completed a circle begun nine years before when the truck driver cursed the white devil's bitch a few miles downtown.

In nine years, said Leon, he had seen the group "lose its spiritual eye" and become a hustle to milk blacks. Like Malcolm and like Ali, he found in the worship of Allah a religion better suited to the goals of black freedom than the missionary Christianity of the slave culture. Like Malcolm, he had seen the cult—which he carefully made distinct from the Moslem religion—become factionalized by local and national power struggles. And he had grown disenchanted with Elijah—his reported impregnations of teenage secretaries, his meetings with radical-right white leaders, his shifting of emphasis from religion and education to internal extortion and external pressure. Leon was convinced that the inevitable murders of Malcolm and himself would keep Ali in line as long as the group could use him.

Leon's bitterness was laced with frustration. The Muslims were able to exist, to prosper, because of white oppression. The Muslims gained their strength from the poor and the criminalized, from the forgotten and the flogged. So long as "colored killed colored," the police were not overly concerned about Muslim enforcers punishing "hypocrites" who dropped out and critics who charged criminal irregularities. So long as social agencies seemed to exist to perpetuate a black underclass, the Muslims could truthfully boast the highest cure rates from narcotic, alcohol, and gambling addiction. So long as the white man could be scared by black shadows instead of black substance, the Muslims would be hyped and harassed into headlines that made them community King Kongs.

Late in January, a Boston policeman told me that Leon's case against Captain Clarence was the kind of "sleeper" that could have "national repercussions" and "bust this Muslim thing wide open." While we waited for the trial, Floyd Patterson reestablished himself as a heavyweight contender by beating George Chuvalo, a relatively unknown Canadian, at Madison Square Garden. Biologically, George was white, but he had been cast in the traditional "black opponent" role for Floyd, a black playing the traditional "white hope" role in preparation for a future fight against Ali. The champion himself was at ringside that night "covering" the fight for *Life* magazine. He kicked off the advance promotion for his own fight with Floyd by writing that Floyd had been "tough and vicious" in his victory over Chuvalo.

The day after the fight Clarence and his men were found guilty of assaulting Leon, and were fined $100 each. No sleeper, no national repercussions. Leon was sure that Boston wanted to keep a lid on its racial pot, and the policeman agreed. Just colored killing colored again, after all.

Then *Look* turned down our article. Ultimately, I think, they decided the Muslims were too parochial a story unless we could prove that they either presented a real revolutionary threat to white America, or were actively stalking Malcolm and Leon for front-page hits.

Leon was not discouraged, only pressed for time; he said he could feel the clot swelling and moving inside his head. Specialists had told him there was nothing to do, but wait and rest. We talked a lot, mostly on the phone, and every time we talked he mentioned having eaten at my table and having been covered by Marjorie. He had never been in a white home before.

Five days after the *Look* rejection, on February 21, 1965, Malcolm was shot to death. Leon called, panic-stricken. He had talked to Malcolm several days before, and Malcolm had expressed concern because the annual Saviour's Day convention was coming up, and, he said, "the Muslims like to clean up loose ends and embarrassing people before they all get together." Leon went into hiding.

Saviour's Day came and went, and Leon was still alive. I went to Chicago to cover a match between Ernie Terrell and Eddie Machen for the newly created World Boxing Association heavyweight title. The WBA, the group that had denied its sanction to Ali's title, wanted its own champion ready to leap into the empty throne if anything should happen to Ali. Terrell won so ineptly he all but canceled his right to succession.

While I was in Chicago Leon called Marjorie several times. He said he rarely left his room; when he did he was sure Muslims followed him. He knew he was too weak to withstand a physical attack. His money was almost all gone.

A few days after I returned from Chicago, the call came from a friend. Leon was dead. It would eventually be ruled "natural causes" and the medical examiner would suggest an epileptic seizure or perhaps an overdose of medication. He downgraded earlier reports of the severity of Ameer's original beatings. Boston had fastened its lid.

In death, Leon had one small triumph, but few enough could enjoy it vicariously for him. The Associated Press report of his death appeared on the front page of *The New York Times*, and in the first paragraph he was described, incredibly, as having been mentioned as a "possible successor" to Malcolm X.

4

Unlike every other major professional sport in America, boxing has never had a strong, legal, central government. There is no logically scheduled sequence of bouts, no just system to assure a fighter he will succeed according to his ability. Good boxers have rotted waiting for their chances; mediocre boxers with crowd-appeal or cunning managers have become stars. There are no nationwide medical and safety criteria. A boxer brain-damaged in one state and medically banned in another will almost certainly find a third to fight in if he tries hard enough. There is not even a set of standard boxing rules—the weight of the gloves, the size of the ring, the roles of the officials, the rules for knockout, and the method of scoring are worked out for each bout; it would be like changing the size of the ball, the length of the field, and the number of points allowed for a touchdown for every football game. And, it goes without saying, there is no pension or welfare program for the old or ailing boxer.

Boxing was—and is—totally chaotic. There was no prestige or security for investors, so boxing traditionally was owned by "sportsmen," which is a euphemism in journalism for wealthy, socially connected gamblers with an itch for low-life, and by "alleged underworld figures," which is what we called their ethnic partners. Through the Joe Louis era and to the brink of the sixties, the sport was controlled by James Norris of the Midwest grain and real estate dynasty and Frankie Carbo of Murder, Inc. The Norris-Carbo alliance was known as Octopus, Inc.

It took a Supreme Court antitrust decision to break their hold on boxing, and the immediate beneficiaries were Floyd Patterson and his manager, Cus D'Amato, whose stubborn, often dangerous refusal to deal with the Octopus was eventually worth stringless millions. Patterson was, at best, a light-heavyweight or 175-pound class fighter, but he had been beefed up for good reason: Social progress had created an America in which the only prize with power in boxing was the heavyweight championship.

The strength of boxing had always been grass roots—neighborhood gyms feeding small fight clubs that depended on local fighters and regular customers. The postwar suburban migration changed the urban and rural neighborhood patterns, and minimum wage laws, social legislation, and higher standards of living made boxing a poor vocational choice for a ghetto or farm boy reaching for money and recognition.

The old ethnic rivalries were fragmented and dispersed, and the Jewish, Italian, and Irish fighters were replaced by the new urban disadvantaged—Negroes and Hispanics. But as more and more black fighters appeared, fan interest among whites dwindled except for so-called mixed matches, which were routinely promoted as little race wars, particularly when dark Puerto Ricans were involved.

Patterson, who was not committed to the old network of alliances, brought in his own promotional companies to subcontract the closed-circuit and other ancillary rights, companies that were really Chinese boxes of companies run by tweedy young financiers who regarded themselves as refreshing breezes in a stale-cigar business filled with what they called "the moustache boys." They all looked and talked Wall Street, and had an amusing habit of brushing their forefingers across their upper lips to signify that the person under discussion was a moustache, or old Mafioso, of the kind they were running out of the business. Their credibility was not enhanced by the presence of their own God-father, Roy Cohn, or their occasional board-room fist fights.

Liston was a legacy of the new promoters, and the boxing industry was vitally interested in the outcome of the second Liston-Ali fight. It was common knowledge that the Louisville Sponsoring Group's last option on Ali's original contract would be ending in a year or so, and it was not likely that either side wanted to renew. Ali would start his own promotional group, and it would be controlled by Muslims.

The machinery by which Ali was effectively stripped of his title went into gear in 1965. It was no monolith, and it did not have the appearance of a high-level conspiracy.

Closed-circuit television had returned boxing—at least the heavyweight championship fight—to the grass roots. The money was made in hundreds of local theaters, which were owned and operated by businessmen who had to respond to local social, political, and economic pressures.

The theater exhibitor could not afford to book an Ali fight if a local veteran's group threatened to picket. And if enough exhibitors around the country could not afford to book the show, there would be no show. The voice of the people would be heard.

Not surprisingly, the re-rematch was run out of Boston several weeks before it was to be held on May 25, 1965. It landed in Lewiston, Maine, a depressed mill town best known for the waters of nearby Poland Spring. Maine officials were delighted with publicity so close to their summer tourist season, the television promoters were grateful they could use most of the closed-circuit lines they had laid in for a Boston telecast, and the massed press corps was in high-spirited reunion; not only was press headquarters at a quaintly comfortable nineteenth-century spa, but a carload of black gunmen was driving up from New York at the speed of a story per day, to avenge Malcolm's assassination.

It seems a little gratuitous now to snicker over a 1965 non-murder. Contemporary history has long since canceled all such jokes. But even then the inky stench of the fresh press release hung over the story. At the beginning of buildup week, one of the promoters had said, "If I could assure the people an assassination in the ring I could sell a million tickets," and later took out a life insurance policy on Ali. Jose Torres, light-heavyweight champion and a rising journalist, had said, jokingly, that he didn't want a front-row press seat in the line of fire. · New York City plain-clothesmen, perhaps justifying their "special-duty assignments" in Maine, told Jimmy Cannon that some of Malcolm's hotbloods were "missing from their usual haunts," and he wrote it. Harold Conrad, the star publicist, took all the threads and began tying dry flies for the British. They bit. Once again, editors in New York began calling, and our stories could not ignore that Flying Dutchman of a killer car heading north to Lewiston with the only black men for hundreds of miles who were not accredited to the fight camps. Only the fighters seemed unconcerned. Ali said it was part of a plot to scare him, but would end up terrifying Sonny, who shrugged and said, "They're comin' to get him, not me, right?"

By fight time we had written ourselves into a high quiver. The reporters stalked Lewiston's ice hockey arena, searching every black face, which was usually a Muslim's behind a camera taking pictures of policemen searching women's handbags, suitcases, and technicians' equipment bags while dozens of local youths climbed in through unguarded windows and side doors. It was a fight to have been at, rather than to see, and the gate crashers did as well as the front-row press. Ali's one-punch knockout, which I did not see live, was rerun on a ringside television monitor at least a hundred times until those who thought it was The Perfect Punch no longer saw it, and those who thought it was The Phantom Punch, saw nothing else. Only the fighters seemed satisfied. "Will there ever be another like me?" screamed Muhammad Ali.

"All you newspapers, together now," yelled Stepin Fetchit. "NO."

And Liston, the next morning, overwhelmingly friendly in a snappy iridescent blue-green suit and a black straw hat with a gay colored band, obliged the only photographer who came to see him leave by kissing his wife on the steps of his training cottage. "I never kissed her like that when I married her."

"It's better to lose and not be hurt," she said, and Sonny grinned. I talked to him about the punch, which he said was a good one, and his career, which he said would continue. He turned to two hotel bellmen. "You been taken care of? Yeah? Good. Never can tell what happens, might have to come back here some time. Life a funny thing."

Laughing, he got into a station wagon with his luggage and his wife, and drove away with his last big payday.

I think he did take one on the button, but sometimes, when I wonder if all the people who yelled, "Fix!" could somehow be right, I think, Why not? We made Sonny the Beast; what made us think he'd always be a Good Sport?

On to Floyd Patterson, our last hope, the catcher in the rye, the free safety, the cavalry at the pass: He'll stop Ali and the Muslims before they take over boxing and maybe the free world as well. Because Floyd has God in his corner.

That summer, 1965, I went to Europe for three months, a combination of sports assignments and vacation. No one I interviewed had heard of the Mets or Yogi Berra or Mickey Mantle or Vince Lombardi or Joe Namath. Everyone wanted to talk about Vietnam and hear about Cassius Clay. Except in Sweden, where they wanted to hear about Floyd Patterson, whose photograph, unnamed, was featured on ads for a candy bar. Quite unexpectedly, I ran into Ali in the lobby of the hotel in Stockholm where we were staying. He was on a European exhibition tour, and he was tired but high.

"Ten days here, I'll have this country sewed up, too," he said. "Youth, I'm growing up with the youth of the world. When I'm 35, they'll be 35, running things, and I'll be something else again."

He couldn't believe I was actually on vacation, that I hadn't flown out from New York just to see him box a few exhibition rounds at a local amusement park. As we parted at the elevators, he said, "It's hard to get used to a new champ, like a new president. But people are getting used to me now."

The Swedish press, even the Communists, were most interested in his lack of interest in white women. They seemed concerned that he wouldn't be lining up local blondes like every other black fighter who had ever come through town. Angelo Dundee carefully explained to a press conference that it was nothing personal, merely religious, but the next day's newspapers all carried headlines about Ali not preferring Swedish blondes. The crowd at the amusement park, young and uniformed that night in clean army surplus field jackets with ROLLING STONES neatly lettered in English across the backs, shouted "We want Floyd" through several dull exhibition rounds, then jeered good-humoredly at doggerel they did not fully comprehend. They did not really cheer Ali until he accepted the traditional bouquet of roses from the management, and tossed them one by one into the crowd.

He invited me back to his hotel room after the exhibition. It might have been his hotel room anywhere, clothes and boxing equipment strewn around the room, the portable stereo record player with a stack of 45s on the changer. He kicked off his shoes and fell on the bed. Now he was tired and depressed. He was on this journey to suck up the energy of crowds and forget his problems—his marriage was over, for one—and now, disappointed by the lackluster response of the young Swedes, his psychic battery was briefly running low.

"Man, you just can't go strong all the time," he murmured into his pillow. "Can't be such a controversial figure, dodging all the traps . . . Just be myself . . . Go out among the little people, the children and the folks sitting in garbage alleys, and they say, 'That really you, champ? You know you couldn't pay Chubby Checkers and Joe Louis to come here and talk to us like you do.' That's what makes you powerful, the little people."

I flipped the stack of records on the spindle while he murmured on.

". . . Catch all this hell . . . don't drink or smoke or chase bad women, treat everybody nice, you know, nobody ever came to me and said, 'I'm going to become a Muslim because you are.' You have to live it and practice it and sacrifice and study. You don't love the cereal because Willie Mays eats it, but you might try it because of the man. But then you got to do the thing . . ."

When he finally fell asleep I let myself out and went back to my vacation.

The Floyd Patterson buildup and fight soured the liberals on Muhammad Ali just when he needed their understanding and support to counteract all the forces reacting to his "unpatriotic" posture. The liberals—I use the term loosely here for those who are not so much liberal as tolerant, bestowers of a kind of noblesse oblige made possible by their disengagement from day-to-day educational, housing, and employment problems—would eventually make Ali their champion, but not until their own antiwar passions had been activated and they were convinced that his constitutional rights had been flagrantly violated. Until then, his career would be at the mercy of television executives and boxing commissioners who saw in his unpopularity a way to squeeze out the last ounce of his promotional juice before responding to the will of the people and unloading him for a more cooperative champion.

The boxing industry wanted Patterson to win the title back, for a third time, in 1965. The Wall Street gang were financial rapists, but they were white and predictable in their greed. The peasants of boxing had long since learned that bandits always move on. But the Muslims were black and unpredictable; who knew what horrible, eternal surprises these mad-dog Allah freaks would wreak upon the land? Black ownership in boxing was rare, black promoters rarer, black control of a heavyweight title unheard of. Especially by what Eldridge Cleaver would call the "autonomous" black, in his own fanciful assessment of Ali.

SportsWorld was never quite sold on Patterson as were the liberals in general. While Patterson undoubtedly represented "the fulfillment of the American Dream," as one of Conrad's press releases pointed out, none of his actions could bear too close a second look. He might be living proof that there *was* a solution, but not that the solution was ultimately enough, or even worth the effort.

Floyd was materialistic, true, but not in that amenably gross way that SportsWorld encourages in its showcase superstuds—dynamite girls, "bad" cars, pie-in-the-sky franchises and investments. Floyd acquired and held and quietly invested and was so mean-spirited and skittish in negotiations that it was soon apparent that big money was not for fun, it was to certify he wasn't being taken advantage of.

He was subordinate, yes, but so much so that he depended upon white institutions for a constant therapeutic support they could not maintain. He was run out of Scarsdale, N.Y., by racial slurs and threats against his children; he took no direct action himself, but later complained bitterly about the local Roman Catholic priests (Floyd was a recent convert), who he felt made no concerted effort to stop the harassment. He proudly became a pet of the Kennedys, of top NAACP officials and Dr. Ralph Bunche, and later shifted some of the blame for his collapse against Liston to the burdens imposed by his new patrons. They had urged him not to allow such a criminal access to the title, and warned if he must fight Liston, he must also beat him. The Negro cause depended on it.

He was "hungry," of course, SportsWorld's code word for ambition so overriding that the athlete will do anything to win, and he proved it again and again with long periods of monastic training and inspiring moments of courage in the ring. But slowly it became apparent that Floyd trained so diligently to avoid his family and his responsibilities outside the arena, and he kept punching and getting punched through wrenching pain and blood and hopelessness not so much to win but to keep fighting, to stay in the life.

Psychoanalyzing Patterson nourished a thousand rainy-day columns. It was not the cheap pot-shotting it appeared. Floyd himself was an enthralled student of his head, often with his biographer, Milton Gross, a syndicated columnist and pioneer explorer of the athletic psyche. Floyd had never been so much a "juvenile delinquent" as a chronic truant hiding in sewers and abandoned subway tunnels, a behavior pattern he would repeat years later when he slipped away from ring defeats by prearranged escape routes in prearranged disguises. Floyd's early "rehabilitation" was credited to several schools for the emotionally disturbed, which were happy with the publicity, and to manager

Cus D'Amato, who took him on as a youngster and filled him with mystical theories of fear and violence that sound neurotic even when D'Amato explains them.

With all this baggage, Patterson was still the sentimental favorite to beat the best-looking, most exciting, biggest box-office champion of modern times.

In Las Vegas for the fight, scheduled for the second anniversary of Kennedy's assassination, November 22, 1965, there was no way to avoid the Holy War hype—the crusading Christian vs. Saracen metaphor planted by Ali, cultivated by Patterson, and left for the sportswriters to harvest or trample, but not ignore.

Leisurely rereading one's old, hastily written newspaper stories is always a squirmy business; the best-turned phrases, if they were really that good, are now clichés, and the precious fact that was exclusive the day it was reported is now an archeologist's shard beneath a ruined tower of misinformation. The eye tries to skip over all the clumsy phrases, incorrect details, pompous predictions, and off-the-wall insights. Reading old clips, you can only hope that the concept, the attitude really, of the piece holds up, that it is all still basically true.

When it is, when later events seem to confirm the "truth" of what you have written, you then begin to wonder if your piece contributed to those later events, if, in effect, the story helped give life to later events.

And if it did—God or Allah help us—could it be that there was more manipulation involved in your writing the story than there was the "right of a free press"? Could it be that journalism is so structured that the reporter and his reader are inevitable victims of that cynical setup called "news"?

Floyd's measured, articulated righteousness, sentences that often began "As I have often said . . ." and ended with his prayer that he would be able to "give the title back to America" cried out for satiric reportage. His theme—"The image of a Black Muslim as the world heavyweight champion disgraces the sport and the nation. Cassius Clay must be beaten and the Black Muslims' scourge removed from Boxing"—demanded review by an interdisciplinary panel of historians, psychologists, and theologians. At least.

Ali's reply, the latest refinement of our talks in the Hotel

Theresa nearly eighteen months earlier—"I'm certainly not going to attack his religion. How can I attack all these Catholic people, the Pope, and those wonderful people who run hospitals and help little children, why should I attack them for the sake of one fool?"—called for an ecumenical exegesis annotated by Lenny Bruce.

But we tigers of the typewriter were stuck with just spreading the story, like a flu, selling tickets to the closed-circuit telecast, disseminating yet more racist propaganda, scattering seed for better stories to come.

The fight itself was hideous. I filed a front-page story from ringside with no time to think, only to react, and so my instincts were microfilmed: "Like a little boy pulling off the wings of a butterfly piecemeal, Cassius Clay mocked and humiliated and punished Floyd Patterson for almost twelve rounds tonight, until the referee halted their heavyweight championship bout because the challenger was 'outclassed.'" Later, Patterson would say he couldn't fight back because a chronic back injury had flared up to cripple him, and Torres, Patterson's friend but as shrewd an observer as you will find, maintained that Ali tried and failed to knock out Patterson from the start. Yet there was no question in my mind that Ali was in total control, and his in-fight commentary, "No contest, get me a contender . . . Boop, boop, boop . . . watch it, Floyd . . ." was the fulfillment of his promise to "chastise" Patterson.

As crude as he was that night, he was subtle at the following day's press conference. He patronized Patterson and gently stuffed him down America's throat. "Floyd, you should get honors and medals the spot you was on, a good, clean American boy fighting for America. All those movie stars behind you, they should make sure you never have to work another day in your life. It would be a disgrace on the government if you had to end up scuffling somewhere."

"Last night I was beaten by a great fighter, Muhammad Ali," said Floyd, using the Muslim name for the first time. "I will not say I lost because of my back; the results might have been the same anyway. But the fight might have been more entertaining." Floyd kept his half-smile. Might have to come back here some time. Life a funny thing.

"I believe his back was hurt," said Ali, "because he don't want to publicize it. He's a man." And I might need this Nee-grow for a rematch some day.

The general reaction of the media was inevitable. *The New York Times* editorial page called for the outlawing of prize-fighting as "a tawdry exhibition of cruel and senseless savagery." *Time* magazine reported that its 1963 cover boy "spat carefully on the floor while Eddie Fisher was singing the *Star-Spangled Banner.*" Others pulled out "The Tale of the Tape," that chart of beefcake statistics to prove they knew it was a mismatch all along: Ali was 3 inches taller, more than 13 pounds heavier, and his reach was 8 inches longer. He was also 7 years younger. Ex post facto, Floyd's credentials as America's Instant Knight were withdrawn, his lance broken, milady's handkerchief plucked from his sleeve.

Next time, we'll send a lawyer to do the job.

5

The air is sweet and sluggish in the Miami afternoon, and Ali sits in a lawn chair under a palm tree watching the children straggle home from school. "Hey, little girl in the high school sweater, you not gonna pass me by today."

"Hi, Cassius, how you been?"

"Fine. Whatcha learn in school today?"

The children drift onto the lawn in front of the small, gray cement house, one of hundreds of such houses set in neat rows in this predominantly black neighborhood. The children surround him, they sit at his feet. Bold ones touch him, banter with him; shy ones circle and stare. He is very relaxed, drained of his physical energy; in the morning he ran, in the early afternoon he worked out in the Fifth Street Gym on the Beach. He has been here for several weeks now, in the early stages of training for a March fight in Chicago against Ernie Terrell, which will never happen. The date is February 17, 1966.

That morning, in my motel room, I watched a few minutes of the Senate Foreign Relations Committee hearings on the war in Vietnam. That was the day Gen. Maxwell Taylor said the administration intended to wage only a "limited" war, but he refused to be pinned down further. There was a very sharp exchange between General Taylor and Sen. Wayne Morse, who said he thought that before too long the American people "will repudiate our war in Southeast Asia."

Taylor snapped back, "That, of course, is good news to Hanoi, Senator."

The two men then set the lines on dissent as treachery or loyalty that would mark so many of the alliances, attitudes, public postures, and private actions of the following years.

Morse said, "I know that is the smear . . . you militarists give to those of us who have honest differences of opinion, but I don't intend to get down in the gutter with you and engage in that kind of debate.

"All I am asking is that if the people decided that this war should be stopped in Southeast Asia, are you going to take the position that is weakness on the home front in a democracy?"

Taylor, becoming angry, replied, "I would feel that our people were badly misguided and did not understand the consequence of such a disaster."

Morse said, "Well, we agree on one thing, that they can be badly misguided and you and the President in my judgment have been misguiding them for a long time in this war."

The committee chairman, Senator Fulbright, pounded his gavel to silence the applause and restore order.

I did not see much of the hearings. I had driven up from the Florida Keys the night before, and I had a reservation to fly back to New York that night. I wanted to spend as much of the day as possible with Ali. Things were cooking again. Jim Brown, the football star and head of the Negro Economic Union, was fronting a new promotional group called Main Bout, Inc. Other principals included several white closed-circuit promoters and two high-ranking Muslim officials.

Boxing had responded quickly to this potential junta. The New York Commission denied Terrell a license to fight in New York, effectively blocking a fight with Ali at Madison Square Garden. Terrell's association with his adviser, one Bernie Glickman, was adjudged "detrimental to the best interests of professional boxing." Years before, Glickman had been linked to Frankie Carbo.

Terrell had shown up at the Commission hearings with Elmer Gertz, the Chicago lawyer who got Nathan Leopold out of prison, and had defended Henry Miller and Jack Ruby. When the decision against Terrell was announced, the fighter turned to his attorney and said, "Now that you know me, you can't practice law anymore."

But hardly anyone believed the "exhaustive investigation" into Terrell's background was anything more than a delaying action against Main Bout, Inc. After a few other rejections, the fight was rebooked for Chicago, where it was thought that the combination of organized crime and Muslims would be strong enough to defeat even the *Chicago Tribune*'s crusade to run it out of town.

Ali, meanwhile, trained to get into shape and to shut out the world. Down in the Keys, I ran into Sonji Clay, as she billed herself, training for her own big time, singing next to the piano at Tony's Fish Market for roistering young officers from the Naval Station. She was very pretty and had some style, but her voice was thin even with the mike so close to her pursed lips she seemed to be kissing its head. At the bar between sets, she told anyone who would listen that the Muslims had stolen her man, "took his mind and spirit away," that she still loved him, and that he was far too smart to fail any old Army mental exam in the first place. Newspapers had been reporting that the Selective Service was reexamining Ali's draft status.

Ali had been originally classified 1Y during a period of higher Army standards and retested when public clamor over the draft touched such deferred athletic stars as Ali and Namath, who was 4F because of his bad knees. Ali apparently flunked the mental test the second time, too, which many people found hard to believe. Anyone who could remember all that doggerel could follow Army orders. I've always leaned toward a theory that the local draft board may have slipped Ali, then Clay, a 1Y as a gift to the Louisville Sponsoring Group, much as his high school diploma, and the disappearance of a juvenile arrest entry for a minor street misunderstanding, were hero's perks from the local Board of Education and the local Police Department.

It always seemed strange that he was reclassified 1A just when it was most convenient for the Sponsoring Group, for boxing, for the country. And for their purposes, his reaction could not have been better. As luck would have it, it came that day when General Taylor and Senator Morse were choosing up sides, and I was hanging around interviewing him and shooting pictures for a Sunday feature.

He got the news, I think, from a wire service reporter who called the house. He was playing with the children, then excused himself when one of the three Muslim women who cooked for him called him inside to the telephone. When he came out, he was angry and bewildered.

"Why me? I can't understand it. How did they do this to me— the heavyweight champion of the world?"

Soon, bright red television trucks pulled up at the house, confirmation of catastrophe. Interview followed interview on that patch of lawn in front of the gray cement house. "I've got a question," Ali might scream back. "For two years the government caused me international embarrassment, letting people think I was a nut. Sure it bothered me, and my mother and father suffered, and now they jump up and make me 1A without even an official notification or a test. Why did they let me be considered a nut, an illiterate, for two years?"

There was very little hard information beyond the announcement of the new classification itself, but some interviewers suggested Ali might be called up within weeks, and he became wilder.

"How can they do this without another test to see if I'm any wiser or worser than last time? Why are they so anxious, why are they gunning for me? All those thousands of young men who are 1A in Louisville, and I don't think they need but thirty, and they have to go into two-year-old files to seek me out."

Between interviews he sat on the lawn chair incongruously humming "Blowin' in the Wind," while Muslim bodyguards and friends chuckled at how the white devils were doin' Ali, proof of everything the Messenger ever said. They chipped in stories of their own about racial discrimination in the Army during World War II and Korea. Oh, brother, there are fat cracker sergeants just waiting to get you on the hand-grenade range, Muhammad Ali.

He'd be set off again.

"I'm fighting for the government every day. Why are they so

anxious to pay me $80 a month when the government is in trouble financially? I think it costs them $12 million a day to stay in Vietnam and I buy a lot of bullets, at least three jet bombers a year, and pay the salary of 50,000 fighting men with the money they take from me after my fights."

After awhile there were no more rest periods between rounds with the press, television, radio, neighbors, friends, promoters, and the lawn became a worldwide dump for questions, answers, advice, gossip, rumors, stories of death and dismemberment, accusations, anxieties, injustices, and always the interviewers— What do you think about. . . ? How do you think. . . ? Why did the. . . ?—and the Muslims, almost antic at this proof they were not paranoids but chosen people, and somewhere along the way a newsman asked for the fiftieth time what Ali thought about the war in Vietnam, and he shrugged, and the newsman asked, "Do you know where Vietnam is?"

"Sure," said Ali.

"Where?"

Ali shrugged.

"Well, what do you think about the Vietcong?"

And Ali, tired, exasperated, angry, betrayed, certainly without thought, carved his quote on the facade of history: "I ain't got nothing against them Vietcong."

6

"All great men have to suffer. Many people want Lyndon Johnson's position. He's worried, tense. You can't hold a high office or position and not have pressure. I'm living at a time when we have 22 million of our people struggling. I'm the top athlete in the world, my word means something, and I'm not wanting to follow the path of people beaten and killed. I'm taking a different path, a more difficult path; I'm giving 100 percent, not just donating some money, making one or two appearances for CORE, NAACP.

"A big Negro movie star called me up, 'You're showing us that we're not free either.' Another big Negro calls up, 'You're doing something we don't have the courage to do.'

"I'm run out of my own country, it makes me bigger. I always knew I was meant for something. It's taking shape, a divine destiny.

"Jesus was condemned, Moses, Noah, Elijah, Martin Luther King. To be great, you suffer, you have to pay the price. Why are so many powers on me? People just have to see this man the politicians are against. Who is this man they hold the meetings about?

" 'I want to see him,' the people cry.

"Nobody asks me how many miles I run this morning. Nobody asks me how's my left hook. You can't rank me with no fighter.

"You tell me, Lipsyte, what other athlete can you go to and always get something to sell papers with?

"I'm in a class of my own. I'm a jet compared to props. I'm cruising at 650 miles per hour, at 35,000 feet, and the prop is 450 miles per hour at 20,000 feet. You never be happy in a prop again, once you been in a jet.

"What you gonna say about a fighter? He smells a flower, it's his favorite pastime. He went to the hospital and visited some sick people. His double uppercut is sharp. What does a housewife know about that? But people talk to me like a congressman."

This time, the hotel room was in Toronto, the stereo on the bureau playing Carla Thomas' "Comfort Me." A sparring partner stood in front of a wall mirror mouthing the words of the song. Ali was stretched out on one bed. I sat writing on the other, surrounded by boxing gear, jock straps, sweat clothes, and underwear. Several foreign newsmen were brought into the room.

"The Americans are envious," said a Dutchman, "because you speak the truth."

"Let other people defend me," said Ali with a wave too grand for the small room, "because to defend myself would be cheapening." He turned to a Turk. "Am I well known in your country?"

"You are beloved," said the Turk. "On the streets of Istanbul, children wear pictures of you on their shirts, and cry 'I am the Greatest.' "

"They do, really?"

"Yes."

"Tell your people," said Ali, "that I will visit Turkey right after this fight with George Chuvalo."

"They will be happy," intoned the Turk.

The last year of Ali's first hitch as heavyweight champion turned into a road show that opened in Toronto's Maple Leaf Gardens and closed in Houston's U.S. Custom House, where he refused to be inducted into the Army. The travel was broadening for both of us. I had no idea at the time, but the year was my last as a reporter, the last time I would be able to stay with a continuing story on a long-range, day-to-day basis. I was leaving a phase of my career in high style.

Ali sensed he was a short-timer, too, and he seemed to take a greater interest in everything around him, absorbing information and attitude as well as energy from people who came to pay him court, to offer him fellowship, sympathy, a political hero-worship he had never experienced before. In Canada, England, Germany, where anti-American feelings became pro-Ali feelings, he began to develop the language of a world view. "Elijah is not teaching hate when he tells us about all the evil things the white man has done any more than you're teaching hate when you tell about what Hitler did to the Jews. That's not hate, that's history."

In America, when facing hostility, he might be moved to snap back, "I get booed and this makes me strong. If everybody said, 'Oh, champ, you is wonderful,' I'd just lay back. But if a guy says, 'Son of a bitch, I hope you get your ass whipped,' I got to beat him and everybody else."

But overseas he could softly explain to African and Indian students that those who were against him "don't like me because I'm free. The Negro has always sold himself out for money or women, but I give up everything for what I believe. I'm a free man, I don't belong to nobody."

He was a superb guest. In England he was constantly thanking "you Lords and you common market everyday people" for inviting him, and he praised British heavyweights so earnestly that people forgot that the term "British heavyweight" is generically derisive in boxing. There was even some grumbling in the press when the Prime Minister canceled a date with Ali and his first British opponent, Henry Cooper, apparently at the behest of the American Embassy, which had pointedly ignored Ali's presence because he had just applied for a conscientious-objector deferment. "It's somewhat disparaging when we are trying to present the image of a nation unified," an Embassy spokesman told me.

The foreign fights themselves were not so satisfying. George Chuvalo, a local last-minute substitute when Terrell dropped out of the Toronto fight, threw more than a hundred low blows, which Ali stoically absorbed to prove he could "take it" before jabbing George's face into raw meat and winning a decision. Ali split open Cooper's papery skin with snake-lick jabs, then tried to dodge the torrents of blood until the referee stopped the fight, Britain's first heavyweight title match in more than a half-century. Despite the outcome, the British invited him back less than three months later to knock out Brian London, in three rounds. He went on to Frankfurt where he knocked out Karl Mildenberger in twelve. I don't doubt the suggestion that Ali carried the German so that more commercials might be shoe-horned into the home telecast, assuring its financial success and sponsor receptivity to the next Ali match.

By leaving America Ali also enhanced his celebrity among Americans. His fights were usually replayed on the ABC television network, and he often discussed them voice-over with Howard Cosell before going on to a "controversial" or chatty interview that showed off both men at their bantering best. Long before Cosell clinched his national recognition with Monday Night Football, he was well on his way toward becoming the most important commentator on sports-related news in the country. A lawyer, Cosell became Ali's public advocate for civil rights, and for this alone Cosell's impact on the education and awareness of SportsWorld was incalculable.

By late 1966, the forces that had kept Ali from fighting in America allowed him back; perhaps they felt he was gaining too positive an image abroad, perhaps they didn't want to risk his running away from the imminent showdown with Selective Service. He fought three times in America, against competent, uninspired heavyweights, whom he played like remedial instruments: Cleveland Williams, Ernie Terrell, Zora Foley.

Against Williams, who still contained the Texas highway patrolman's .357 magnum slug that had ripped up his insides two years earlier, he unleashed the "Ali Shuffle," a little soft shoe that broke the monotony with as gaudy a bit of black jock style as the heavyweight division had ever seen. Against Terrell, a tall, awk-

ward fighter who insisted upon calling him Clay, he served up a
"Floyd Patterson humiliation," battering Terrell's eyes in a cruel
performance marked by such taunts as "What's my name, Uncle
Tom? . . . Give me another Clay, you white man's nigger . . ."

Ironically, it was Terrell, an intense, thoughtful man, who
offered the best perspective when SportsWorld's house organ for
boxing, *The Ring* magazine, refused to designate a Fighter of the
Year in 1967 because "most emphatically is Cassius Clay of
Louisville, Ky. not to be held up as an example to the youngsters
of the United States."

Terrell said: "It's illegitimate reasoning, and it's out of the
realm of *The Ring*. This will all be used as a stepping stone for
the Muslims to say they achieved something. If Clay did something illegal, put him in jail. But he didn't. I dislike what Clay
stands for, using boxing to further an extremist cause. But it's not
against the law to be a clown."

By now, Dr. Martin Luther King, Rep. Adam Clayton Powell,
who would soon be denied his seat in Congress, and Julian Bond,
barred from his seat in the Georgia legislature for his antiwar
stand until the Supreme Court ruled the action unconstitutional,
were citing Ali as symbolic of black manhood courageously re-
fusing to knuckle under to an illegal and immoral system.

As usual, however, the boxer had the last word—Applause!
"The whole world knows I'm not only the fighter of the year, but
fighter of the century."

Into the spring of 1967 now, and the question was simply this:
Would Ali go into the Army?

He said no, and it was known that his lawyers were proceed-
ing to secure him a deferment as a Minister of Islam. But the
boxing industry found it hard to believe that he would give up
the title when he could so easily take it into the service with him
for two years of exhibitions and public relations. The two Muslims who had taken over Ali's business affairs, Herbert Muhammad, Elijah's son, and John Ali, the national secretary, were
worldly, humorous men with a taste for high-life that was
thought by many whites to be an indication that a last-minute
deal could be whipped up. I didn't think so. I had spent a long
day in Chicago during the past summer with Herbert and John
and Elijah himself, talking in the Prophet's living room about

Ali's future, and I had come away impressed with their shrewdness and their conviction. Muslims did not go into the Army; Elijah himself had been jailed during World War II.

The day before the Terrell fight at the Astrodome, half-a-dozen white sportswriters and photographers were invited to hear Ali preach at the Houston mosque, probably to help substantiate his deferment claims. We were searched thoroughly, and our ballpoint pens were clicked in our faces as if they might be derringers. I remembered that Leon had gone through a similar procedure in 1956 when he attended his first Muslim meeting. The precautions must be taken, it is told, because Muslim teachings are so powerful first-time listeners often go berserk and attack the teacher.

None of the whites or curious black non-Muslims were so moved that afternoon, although Ali, comfortable and poised, ridiculed Negroes "so wrapped up in sport and play you'll fly across the country to see me box a few rounds, but you won't leave your boogaloo hangout to walk over and hear Elijah."

The regular mosque minister introduced Ali as "another of Elijah's ministers and the heavyweight champion of the world in that world." Ali told the audience that while heredity and talent had made him strong and a good fighter, "the teaching of Elijah made me a heavyweight champion."

He then launched into his famous pork-eating lecture, which included snuffling pig sounds and blackboard cartoons of "the nastiest animal in the world, the swine, a mouthful of maggots and pus. They bred the cat and the rat and the dog and came up with the hog."

After fifteen minutes, the whites were asked to leave and Ali continued speaking to the all-black audience for another hour, stepping up his attack, I was told, on the white man, that devil created by a mad scientist and doomed to destruction by floating space platforms manned by "men who never smile." It did not seem substantially different from what Leon had been taught.

The last fight before the deluge was held in Madison Square Garden, the one on Eighth Avenue between 49th and 50th Streets, since torn down, then known as "The Mecca of Boxing." Ali had never before fought there as champion. In fact, a few weeks after he won the title, Garden officials had refused to allow him to be routinely introduced from the ring with other guests one night if he insisted upon being introduced as Muhammad Ali. He insisted, and kept his seat.

Now, they could all pronounce Muhammad Ali like Arabs, and the name on the marquee was Muhammad Ali, and the bout was promoted as the last chance to see Muhammad Ali before he got one-to-three, a reference to the current sentence for refusal to be drafted. There was little else to recommend the match; Foley was a nice man with eight children, he called his opponent Mr. Ali, and he was rewarded with six rounds in which Ali danced around him, touched him with feathery jabs and powder-puff combinations, and allowed him to occasionally graze his beautiful face or brush his beautiful body with the tag end of long, spent punches. In the seventh, quite suddenly and with the quick mercy of a fine butcher, Ali knocked him out with one short, chopping righthand punch to the chin. It was a classic punch, and it would be the last one we would see for more than three years.

"When I'm gone boxing be nothing again. The fans with the cigars and the hats turned down'll be there, but no more housewives and little men in the street and foreign presidents. It's goin' to be back to the fighter who comes to town, smells a flower, visits a hospital, blows a horn and says he's in shape. Old hat. I was the onliest boxer in history people asked questions like a senator."

Another hotel, this one in Chicago. He had just closed up an apartment and stored a Cadillac. In the morning he would fly to Houston to face the draft. We were sitting in the coffee shop, eating lunch, watching a spring storm lash the waters of Lake Michigan.

"I don't want to go to jail, but I've got to live the life my conscience and my God tell me to. What does it profit me to be the wellest-liked man in America who sold out everybody?"

"Why don't you skip the country?"

"You serious? How long you been around me, Lipsyte? I got to stay here and lead my people to the right man, Elijah Muhammad."

"Well, you've talked about someone so poisoned with hate he'd kill you and think he was doing the country a favor. It wouldn't serve any point, your getting killed."

"Every day they die in Vietnam for nothing. I might as well die right here for something."

Another newsman at the table, Nicholas Von Hoffman, asked "What about just playing the game like other big-time athletes? You wouldn't be sent to the front lines. You could give exhibitions and teach physical fitness."

"What can you give me, America, for turning down my religion? You want me to do what the white man says and go fight a war against some people I don't know nothing about, get some freedom for some other people when my own can't get theirs here?"

Then his eyes softened and his voice deepened and dropped.

"Ah-lee will return. My ghost will haunt all arenas. The people will watch the fights and they will whisper, Hey, Ali could whip that guy. . . . You think so? . . . Sure. . . . No, he couldn't. . . . Wish he'd come out of retirement. . . .

"Twenty-five years old now. Make my comeback at 28. That's not old. Whip 'em all—if I get good food in jail.

"Allah okays the Adversary to try us. That's how he sees if you're a true believer.

"All a man has got to show for his time here on earth is what kind of a name he had. Jesus. Columbus. Daniel Boone. Now, Wyatt Earp . . . who would have told him when he was fighting crooks and standing up for his principles that there'd be a television show about him? That the kids on the street would say, 'I'm Wyatt Earp. *Reach.*'

> "Two thousand years from now,
> Muhammad Ali, Muhammad Ali,
> He roamed the Western Hemisphere,
> He was courageous and strong,
> He called the round when the clown hit the ground.
> Tell little children whatever they believe,
> Stand up like Muhammad Ali."

Two days later, on April 28, 1967, Ali refused to take one step forward, thus fulfilling legal technicalities that made his case eligible for a civil trial before a federal judge. In one sense, the non-step was a non-event; after all, nothing really happened, and

probably wouldn't for some time. There were many legal bridges
yet to cross. Two days earlier, one of the Beach Boys had finally
been arrested by the FBI, nearly four months after he refused to
step forward.

Yet, in another sense, the feeling on that cold, drizzly day in
Houston was that something quite extraordinary was happening,
that Ali was not only confirming himself, not only authenticating
his credo, "I don't have to be what you want me to be, I'm free to
be who I want," but giving strength to all who had passionate
conviction. Here was a man willing to give up the rewards of the
heavyweight championship of the world, the richest prize of
SportsWorld, for something as abstract as religious principle.
Who else had as much to lose?

Ali had little to say that day. He had been grimly laconic at
breakfast, silent after five hours in the Armed Forces processing
station. I spent the time roaming the building, the grounds, the
neighborhood, talking with other newsmen, reading government
fact sheets, calling *The Times* to exchange information, watching
my television colleagues stage a demonstration for the occasion:
They promised a dozen rubbernecking black secretaries and students time on the tube if they would whip up some black power
posters and march in front of the Custom House steps. By shooting close, the cameramen were able to create the illusion of a
sizable demonstration while the TV reporters provoked loud and
angry answers and shouts of "Burn, Baby, Burn" by asking deliberately insulting questions. It looked very exciting that night on
the news.

7

Boxing commissioners responded to Ali's refusal to be drafted by
either withdrawing their recognition of him as champion or re-
fusing to license him to fight in their states. Once indicted and
released on bail, Ali was not permitted to leave the country.
Thus, he was stripped of his livelihood long before he was ever
convicted of any crime, a gesture inconsistent with SportsWorld's
noble rhetoric about salvation and reformation through sports,
about fair play and due process, but consistent with its day-to-

day adjustments for control—boxing had been purged of its black economic threat, and the Muslims had had their sports platform kicked out from under them.

Although Ali made several appearances at civil rights meetings and peace demonstrations, most notably for CORE and Dr. King, he showed no inclination to become involved in the growing anti-war, anti-administration movements, actions that would have brought him into conflict not only with Elijah's philosophy of divorcement from white politics but with his lawyers' advice that he keep a lower profile while legal proceedings continued. Ali specifically declared he had no intention of becoming "a Negro leader," usually citing the hypocrisies and compromises necessary to such a station. It looked as though Ali had been boxed and shelved for the duration.

In the summer of 1967 he took a 17-year-old Muslim bride and slipped out of camera range.

But in the black ghettoes of SportsWorld, in all those dormitory rooms, airport lounges, superstars' pads, uptown bars, where the sprinters, defensive backs, outfielders, and forwards gather to escape their white "teammates," *Ali* v. *U.S.A.* became a case to pick at, study, turn upside down, and shake. Many black athletes disliked Ali for his aggressive anti-Christianity, for his stuffy moralizing against liquor and drugs and "race-mixing" sex, for his violating the taboo against degrading blacks in front of whites, for all the hard questions he forced them to consider. But there was no avoiding the implicit message for all of them in the government's handling of the case: No matter who you are, even if you are The Heavyweight Champion of the World, the Biggest, Baddest Stud on Earth, you are still a nigger.

Blacks have always had to answer to whites about other blacks, and it was no great problem to weasel with finesse about Ali to college recruiters and coaches and pro scouts and newspapermen who used the case as a psychic barometer to measure the "militancy" of any black under scrutiny. The slick athlete could easily take a stand that skirted basic issues of politics, economics, and race, and talk about religious freedom and due process—"Now, I'm not saying I believe in what he's doin', man, but until he's actually *convicted* of a crime . . ."—until the interviewers were satisfied or bored.

But when the black athlete finally came back to face himself and his black athlete brothers, to admit finally how tightly the drawstring had been pulled on this trick-bag, a cold and righteous anger swept the locker rooms. The turbulence in sports during the late sixties and into the seventies was not only a wan reflection of the death and destruction that tore through the streets beyond the arena. It was also a very real and separate movement of selfish, privileged young men—white and black—who, since childhood, had been told they were different, special, that God had granted them talents that they must protect and perfect for their advancement and for the betterment of mankind. Coaches had divided the world into athletes and non-athletes, doers and watchers, white hats and black hats, jocks and pukes. There had always been special rules for the athlete, perks and payoffs and deals. He paid wholesale if he paid at all, and he walked through side doors to beat the lines. Cops winked and toll keepers waved him through. He got money under the table, and passing grades he hadn't studied for but still thought he deserved. The better he was, the bigger a winner he was, the more good things came his way.

How *could* they do this to the heavyweight champ?

The implicit message of *Ali* v. *U.S.A.* hit black athletes first and hardest. Eventually all athletes came to terms with the government's warning to Know Thy Place, but not precisely in the way in which they were supposed to. The chilling effect was lost on most athletes who, after all, had been trained to respond obediently to authority. Instead they began to wonder what it was all about. How free *were* they to expand and develop to the limit of their ambitions and skills; how true *were* all those truisms about sacrifice and dedication and discipline leading to just reward? They began listening to voices beyond the arena, and the black college athlete was the most vulnerable.

The so-called Athletic Revolution was a mood more than a revolution. The gladiators never attacked the stands, and there were surprisingly few instances of either physical intimidation or extortion in which athletes threatened at the last minute not to play unless specific demands were met. In general, athletes did not know what they wanted beyond an end to "dehumanization" or "racism" or "exploitation," newly acquired abstracts with which most sports fans showed impatience since they thought athletes had it made in the shade.

While the world might be divided into athletes and non-athletes, the athletes were no more of a monolith than the non-athletes. There were amateurs and there were professionals, men and women, blacks and whites, stars and bench-warmers, jockeys and basketball players, all athletes yet all fragmented by peculiar needs and goals. Eventually, in their own time and in their own way, each group and subgroup would stage its own uprising, be it the long hair of the Harvard crew or the mass strike of pro football players. Ultimately, the most important reaction stimulated by the new militant mood of the late sixties would be the move toward unionism spearheaded by black basketball players.

But the first, and most dramatic, was the great racial upheaval in amateur sports, particularly track and field, inspired and articulated by Harry Edwards in late 1967. Actively supported by Floyd McKissick of CORE and Dr. King, Edwards called for a boycott of the 1968 Olympic Games unless certain demands were met, including the reinstatement of Muhammad Ali's title, the ouster of Avery Brundage (millionaire doyen of the American Olympic movement), the desegregation of the New York Athletic Club, the banning from Olympic competition of South Africa and Rhodesia, and the placement of black coaches and officials on the U.S. team.

Edwards had struck a nerve, and SportsWorld reacted with froth on its lips. College athletic directors, amateur officials, sportswriters, congressmen, the entire Big Boy network rose to defend the sanctuary by attacking Edwards as a Communist riot-monger and by pressuring athletes through their college scholarships, their club expense money, and their professional aspirations to reject him. Quite rightly, SportsWorld sensed the danger.

"If there is a religion in this country, it is athletics," Edwards had said. "On Saturdays from 1 to 6 you know where you can find a substantial portion of the country: in the stadium or in front of the television set. We want to get to those people, to affect them, to wake them up to what's happening in this country because otherwise they won't care."

Edwards was a SportsWorld renegade. Born in East St. Louis, Illinois, deserted by his mother early and raised by a father who

worked as a laborer, Edwards did poorly in school and ran the
streets. But he also grew to be 6 feet 8 inches tall, 240 pounds,
well coordinated, and brutally aggressive. A blue-chipper.

In high school he starred in track and field and football. On an
athletic scholarship at San Jose State he was captain of the basketball team and set a school record for the discus. He was big
and tough enough to attract several pro football offers, but by the
time he was ready to graduate he had discovered academic
scholarship. He went to Cornell on a Woodrow Wilson Fellowship, and came back to San Jose to teach sociology. When I first
met him, in 1967, he was 25 years old. We talked for several
hours, privately, the night of his press conference with McKissick
and Dr. King, and I was surprised by his relatively "moderate"
views.

"We're not just talking about the 1968 Olympics, we're talking
about the survival of society. What value is it to a black man to
win a medal if he returns to be relegated to the hell of Harlem?
And what does society gain by some Negro winning a medal
while other Negroes back home are burning down the country?

"We have to use whatever means are available to wake up the
country. We don't want a full-scale revolution—not even for one
day. It would be insane to pass up any means to avoid destruction and to gain human rights.

"It seems as though the only way we can reach a lot of the
people is by showing them that all is not well in the locker room.
No one attempts to change anything he's not in love with, and
the Negro loves his country, fights for it in war, and runs for it.
The tragedy here is that the country the Negro loves doesn't love
him back."

A few months later, now supported by H. Rap Brown, who casually suggested that athletes "blow Madison Square Garden up,"
Edwards returned to New York to his most resounding triumph,
the boycott of the New York Athletic Club's 100th anniversary
indoor track and field games, one of SportsWorld's glittering winter galas. There were fierce press conferences in Harlem, bomb
scares, and roaring mobs of demonstrators in black combat boots
and dark glasses surging around the Garden. Bullhorns, night-
sticks, Cause groupies screaming for murder in the February
night. SportsWorld had never seen anything like this before.

Inside the Garden, an eerie hush. There were relatively few athletes, mostly from white out-of-town schools. The audience was sparse, mostly club members and their families determined to show that they couldn't be intimidated. They seemed sullen and sad and a little bewildered; after all, for many years this meet had been a famous showcase for black athletes who went on to star on the U.S. Olympic team, itself a beneficiary of NYAC largesse.

A club member called me over, introduced me to his friends, and offered me a beer. We knew each other well; we had been childhood summer neighbors and he was personally hurt by my columns supporting the boycott. True, he admitted, the club was white Christian, but so had been the city when the club was first formed. As the club developed socially as well as athletically, club members took advantage of their right to choose with whom they would drink and their wives would dance. What's wrong with that? Negroes and Jews do the same thing. It's human nature to prefer your own.

The black athletes don't want to drink with you, they want to swim and run with you, I replied: Time, money, and interlocks with the major college and amateur organizations have given the NYAC the best facilities, the best coaches, the most travel of any team in the area; the systematic exclusion of blacks and Jews and Puerto Ricans from NYAC teams lessens their chances to develop their skills, to make Olympic teams, to compete on the highest levels. It's sports segregation of the same type that was practiced in Nazi Germany before the 1936 Olympics, and that is practiced now in South Africa and Rhodesia.

The club member listened politely, but his eyes had glazed over, and I realized that after less than four months as a columnist I was already sounding like one—I was quoting myself.

It was an exciting time to be writing a column, to be freed from the day-to-day responsibility for a single subject or the whims of the assignment desk. For me, after more than three years with Ali, the newly surfaced turmoil in sports seemed a natural climate, more so since I was sharing the internationally syndicated column—"Sports of the Times"—with Arthur Daley, whose approach was traditional, conservative, sentimentally nostalgic. We were perfect foils for each other, we appealed to different readers, we often took opposite views on an issue, and we got along very well, chiefly because he was a decent, honorable, kind, warm newspaperman secure enough in his own craft and niche to welcome and encourage a newcomer. Writing a *Times* column is like managing a store—you don't own the place but you work as if you do, and you can use all the help you can get.

My first six months on the column I did relatively little traveling—the Super Bowl, a fight in California, spring training in Florida, the Masters Golf tournament in Augusta, Georgia— while I concentrated on meeting people in New York and getting the feel of ideas and issues and games that had been outside my beat as a reporter. Late in April, a little more comfortable with the rhythm of producing three 800-word pieces a week, I flew to California for three days and my first real sense of the columnist's heady rip-and-run plunge through the cycle of the seasons, a style I had looked upon with contempt in those measured days when I donnishly observed Casey Stengel or Muhammad Ali.

I flew to San Francisco, rented a car at the airport, and drove down to San Jose to have lunch with Harry Edwards on campus. We had kept in touch by telephone since the NYAC boycott. I knew he had been receiving letters beginning "Shut up or you'll get Malcolm ex'd" and that his pet dogs had been killed and chopped up, but he was continuing his campaign for Olympic and sports reform. I had no intention of writing a column about him then; I just wanted to strengthen the contact for later. He was much more relaxed, and warmer than he had ever been in New York.

We ate in the college cafeteria. It was as messy and the food was as bad as in most college cafeterias, but he felt he had to comment on it, suggesting to the manager it be served in troughs, and each student pay 25¢ for five minutes at the trough and all the towels he needed. The manager looked as if he had heard it all before. At the time, I thought Edwards' comments gratuitous, later I realized that students eating starchy, processed slop was as central to any consideration of sports-health-fitness as the Olympic Games.

We talked for several hours. The success of the NYAC boycott had made him a celebrity—Dick Gregory and Marlon Brando called when they passed through town, he thought his phone was tapped, agents had registered for his classes, and he had been offered several subtle bribes to get off the Olympic case—but the early rush had subsided into a grind of meetings and details and appearances. He was also preparing to go back to Cornell after the Olympics and finish his Ph.D. requirements. He showed me an open matchbook he was wearing on a sweater under his jacket; it had no significance, he said, other than to "blow racist honkies' minds."

White girls kept coming to our table asking Edwards what they could do, how they could help. A little too brusquely he kept telling them to go back to their own communities and clean them up, that's where the garbage was coming from. He watched one girl twitch away. "Yeah, man, if things could be settled in bed they'd have been settled long ago, all the trips the slavemasters took to the barracks."

The next day I drove to Oakland to see Angelo Dundee, Ali's old trainer. He was preparing Jimmy Ellis, Ali's old sparring partner, to fight Jerry Quarry in the final match of a tournament cooked up by the World Boxing Association, the American Broadcasting Company, the Houston Astrodome, and the white survivors of Main Bout, Inc. Since the choosing of champions, like the making of presidents, is insiders' work, we must all be grateful for crumbs of ritual like primaries and elimination tournaments. The fights had been shown on home television, usually on Saturday afternoons, Cosell supplying the expertise and the credibility. The winner of the Ellis-Quarry fight was to be named the new heavyweight champion of the world.

Well, most of the world. The New York Athletic Commission, acting "in the best interests of boxing," had been the first to strip Ali's title after that famous non-step. Then it sanctioned its own heavyweight title fight between Joe Frazier and Buster Mathis, primarily so Madison Square Garden could cash in on the chaos. It was a routine example of a government regulatory agency acting in the best interests of the industry it was supervising—and acting illegally. Three years later a federal judge ruled the Commissions' decision unconstitutional. Frazier won the fight, in the Garden, of course, and reigned as heavyweight champion of the *world* in New York, Massachusetts, and Pennsylvania.

Dundee was too shrewd and nimble-tongued to be trapped

into a discussion of the politics of champion-making, or a comparison of Ali and Ellis. And I was too pressed for time to keep at him. The time difference between Oakland and New York was three hours, and my watch, always set to New York time wherever I was, read 4 P.M. The copy editors in New York were impatient for copy; in another hour they would be snarling. Angelo, as press conscious as any man in sports—he is deservedly famous for the wish-you-were-here postcards and telegrams he sends from exotic places to journalists who are stuck at home—began a charming monologue, anecdotal, quotable, in paragraph form, easily trimmed to 800 words, about all the clever ways in which he had built up the confidence of fighters who needed psychic additives, from flamboyant nicknames to punching-bag straps that conveniently broke to the long-term campaign to convince Ellis that he was not really Ali's moving target but his partner in training. It all worked out to a light, tidy, entertaining column, trivial but on time.

It was column number 84, of 544 written over a period of three years eleven months. Number 84 was written in perhaps a half hour, considerably less time than most. As with every column before or after it, the instant I made delivery, whether I handed it in to the slot man or telegraphed or telexed or read it over the telephone to a recording device in New York, my first thought was, What do I write next? My column appeared on Mondays, Thursdays, and Saturdays—Daley, when he was reduced from six columns a week to four picked the days on which he wanted to appear—and the character of what I wrote was as much formed by the peculiarities of my days in their seasons, and the 800-word length, as any prejudices, visions, talents, or ambitions I brought to the job.

For example, during the football season, the Saturday column, to be "right on the news," had to be an advance speculation on the college games being played that very afternoon, or the professional games scheduled for Sunday. Advance speculation can be as simple-minded and gambler-oriented as who is going to win, why, and by how many points, or as seemingly sophisticated to a *Times* reader as a deadpan report about quarterback Fran Tarkenton's use of prayer to clear his head in the huddle. In either case, the columnist being "right on the news" is providing free advance advertising for the staged entertainment.

The Monday column, to be right on the news, would be about the most important football game I had seen that weekend. If it had been Army-Navy or Harvard-Yale on Saturday, there would be plenty of time to disguise the dictates of the calendar with drollery, sociology, historical perspective, preachment. By the time I had delivered the column even I could briefly think that I had free-willed myself to Philadelphia or New Haven to give yet another American phenomenon that Lipsyte once-over.

If the most important game was a pro game on Sunday, I would write the column in the stadium after the game, frequently after a quick trip downstairs to the locker room to interview a player or coach. These columns usually concentrated on one incident or personality that figured prominently in the game; they were easy to write because they were more physical than mental exercises, more reporting than thinking, and they were fun. Often, however, an incident or personality became important merely because I wrote a column about it, not out of any intrinsic worth or real significance to the game, and this, of course, was what was wrong with being locked into writing a column whether or not you had something to write about. Turner Catledge, the former managing editor and executive editor of *The Times*, always resented what he called "the mortgaging of space" for columns, and for all but the three years eleven months I held a mortgage I've agreed with him.

The word count is another example of the control of form over content. Worse than having to condense a story worth 1000 words or pump hot air into a 450-word thought is the slow and subtle transformation of the columnist's perceptions into a rigid claw that scoops out an 800-words-worth chunk of the universe at a time, dumps it into his typewriter to be milled, then catches the newly ground words and empties them into the allotted hole. Whether the columnist writes in breezy bursts or chisels each word into stone, whether he writes clumsily or stylishly, foolishly or wisely, he is a slave to his space. Professionally, there is a challenge, for a while at least, to creating within formalized boundaries. Over an extended period of time, however, it's a poor way to transmit information. I first became aware of this after writing a column I was inordinately proud of, a neat package of Dave Meggyesy's thoughts. It was one of the first columns anywhere about the apostate pro football player, long before he wrote *Out of Their League*, in fact before he started his last season with the Cardinals. Several weeks after the column appeared, I received a friendly letter from Meggyesy, which ended with the hope we'd be meeting soon in New York for dinner. But it contained this paragraph, which rocked me:

"My main comment about the column is that you said too much but not enough. Understanding your space limitations and my intent, by giving the interview, to change the image of professional athletes in the public's eye, I thought the column was excellent. However I can honestly say the depth of my thinking is beyond the cliche-ish quotes contained in the copy."

Ungrateful jock. I just put that half-educated sumbitch on the map—the next time his phone rings it'll be the Dick Cavett Show or an editor from Random House. That was my first reaction. Then I got angry. How dare he patronize me! "Understanding your space limitations." And his "intent, by giving the interview," as if I hadn't tracked him down and talked him into opening up. When I finished getting angry, I realized he was absolutely right. After spending more than half his life in thrall to SportsWorld he was breaking out, reexamining everything he had ever believed about discipline and authority and loyalty and courage and manliness and beauty and goodness, undergoing emotional traumas, exultations, and depressions of which I had no inkling, which he would only begin to reveal in a full-length book, and I in my columnist's arrogance thought he should be glad I had given him an 800-word shot and fired it 'round the world. I answered Meggyesy's letter as best I could at the time, but never satisfactorily for myself until I quit the job.

The Meggyesy column, my apple of knowledge, was still more than a year in the future when I filed number 84 on Angelo Dundee and asked myself, What do I write next? For me, I had an easy answer. I had plotted my West Coast weekend carefully: Harry Edwards was in my notebook and Saturday's column on Dundee was delivered, and for Monday I would write about the Ellis-Quarry fight, scheduled for tomorrow afternoon, Saturday. Now it was Friday evening, and I was off to meet one Bozo Miller, a competitive eating champion, to gather information for a column I would write, probably when I got back to New York,

for Thursday's newspaper. All this advance planning would give
me a free day at home.

Bozo was terrific. He ate six club sandwiches before he suggested we go for dinner, and he confided that speed-eating was
the secret of his success, speed-eating psychs out all but the most
experienced opponents, and you can hold more if you down it
fast.

I was up all night with a stomach-ache. Early Saturday morning, walking up Van Ness Avenue in San Francisco searching for
a cup of hot tea, I heard a big car screech to the curb behind me
and someone yell, "Get him, don't let him get away." I turned in
time to see two big men jump out of a blue Oldsmobile. I started
to run but the car lurched forward and a third man, bigger than
the others, leaped out and grabbed me.

"You fast and you pretty, but if you thought you could get
away from me you'd apologize," said Muhammad Ali.

So much for careful plans. I got into the car, and we drove
down Van Ness. I never did write about the Ellis-Quarry fight,
and just did get to see it. Ali was in town to drum up business for
the Bay Area mosques, and he was on his way to speak at an
antiwar rally at Civic Center Plaza. With him were several unusually jolly Muslim officials and a Chicago booking agent who
seemed morose over a free appearance before a crowd of more
than 12,000.

At the plaza we sat in the car for a long time, sniffing the
marijuana smoke floating in. Ali pretended to get high. The booking agent was miffed. "I'll get you on right away so you don't
have to wait."

"No," said Ali, "I'll wait for my time."

One of the Muslims laughed harshly. "Muhammad Ali, you'll
wait for your time? The Man is going to see you get time, time in
jail."

Ali shrugged and watched several white balloons drift up into
a breathtakingly blue sky. "You think they stay up there forever,
just hanging up there in the sky till a plane hits them, or you
think they got to come down again?"

"What do you mean?" I asked, fishing for a profound metaphor, pencil poised like a rod.

"Air pressure," said one of the Muslims. "Gets thinner on the outside, the balloon pops out."

"Oh, yeah," said Ali, satisfied.

After the draft-card burners and the passionate radicals and several naked strollers and a rock band, the crowd was good-natured but not moved by Ali with his black leather briefcase and his black suit and his rude good health and his twenty-five-minute canned speech that seemed to boil down to several parables from the Koran as interpreted by Elijah Muhammad and retold by Ali to remind all that if black is to be beautiful it can't be diluted by white blood. At that, several interracial couples stood up, booed, and walked away. Ali ended his speech with a plug for the local mosque where he would be preaching over the weekend.

As we drove to his hotel, Ali played back the speech on a tape recorder, stopping now and then to make changes on large, hand-printed index cards. He was bringing the same methodical care and willingness to work hard to speech making that he had to boxing.

"You have to modify the speech for a radical audience," said the booking agent.

"I was too strong for them, they couldn't take it. People just can't stand the truth. They want to hear about violence or integration, but they can't stand the truth that can save them."

Later, back at the hotel, I wished Ali good luck and told him I'd have to hurry if I was to get out to Oakland for the fight. We chatted briefly, an actual conversation, which is very rare with him, and found that both our wives were in the eighth month of pregnancy. "Takes so long," he complained.

The booking agent, who was black, ambushed me at the door. "I just want to ask you one question. What's the difference between Gov. George Wallace and Elijah Muhammad?"

"I don't know," I said, expecting a punch-line.

"That's just what I say. I don't know. What is the difference between Wallace and Elijah Muhammad?" He was shaking his head when he left.

I enjoyed the Ellis-Quarry fight because I could watch it and make my notes without thinking at every turn, How am I going to describe this for Monday's column? Monday's column was already in my notebook. Someday I would write about the fight, just as someday I would write about visiting Harry Edwards in San Jose, but not right away, and for a columnist a spare column is more comforting than money in the bank.

When I started writing "Sports of the Times," the best advice I got was from Daley. He said, "Don't take the column to bed with you." When I knew him better, I realized he meant exactly what he said: Call a time-out to the workday so you'll at least get a decent night's sleep. But the phrase *taking the column to bed with you* seemed rich in implication. A column, if it is truly a column and not a glorified feature story or a collection of notes, is a columnist's appendage and wings, parasite and mistress, disease and plasma. The sense of power, though completely false, can be exhilarating, and the rhythm of rebirth, three times per week, of orgasm, of fulfillment, of imposing one's will upon the world, becomes the dominant rhythm of one's life. All for the column. Ultimately, one is in danger of rationalizing the rest of existence: Eat to be strong for the column, exercise to stay in shape for the column, read a novel see a film have sex go to a party visit Mom take a vacation play with your son to clear your head for the next column, even while knowing that the column doesn't love you back, that the column is merely a vacuum sucking out your life-force, and if you get sick or tired the people who own that empty space will get someone else to fill it because the column must go on.

Technically, the column worked best with sketches, profiles, sidebars to games, satires, and righteous socko editorials. For the reader who wanted a chuckle or a flush or one new lightweight idea with toast and eggs, it was perfect. For the editors who had given me the job, according to Gay Talese, to bring "a smooth literary touch" to the sports page, those columns were proof of their shrewd judgment. For the owners and operators in Sports-World those columns were a delightful series of free ads delivering their messages to a younger, better-educated, more sophisticated audience than they had ever reached before in *The Times*. I could con myself about a lot of things but I never thought my mailbox was stuffed with all those free tickets, books, hats, invitations to sporty resorts just because I was fast and pretty.

The column sometimes failed technically in my attempt to turn it away from staged happenings toward what I thought was really happening in SportsWorld, the beginnings of an intense internal reevaluation of nearly every traditional approach, concept, and role. But an 800-word column is, at best, a commentary on reported news, and if the current trends and events are not being adequately covered by the sports pages, then the columnist must either comment on trends and events unknown to his readers, running the risk of being obscure, or he must try to both report and comment in his space, which makes for dense, incomplete, hard-to-read columns, of which I wrote more than my share. There would have been even more except for the ground-breaking sportswriting of Leonard Shecter, Pete Axthelm, Sandy Padwe, Neil Amdur, Dave Wolf, Jack Olsen, and a few others who faced incredible inertia and hostility from editors, colleagues, and sources when they first began to cut through SportsWorld's candy and crackerjack curtain.

The 1968 Olympic Games shaped up as a bottomless well of controversy for the sports columnist, a fitting athletic entry in what Eugene McCarthy would call "the hard year." In the very beginning, there were objections raised to awarding the Games to Mexico City, because of its unusually high altitude. There were continued crises—the Soviet boycott of a dual track meet because of American "intervention" in Vietnam, Harry Edwards' black boycott, the alleged embezzlement of Olympic funds, the readmittance of South Africa, the student-led uprisings in Mexico, the Soviet "intervention" in Czechoslovakia—all brushed aside by Avery Brundage, then 80, who said, "If we stop the Games every time there is disorder in the world, there would never be Games. At least there is one place in this troubled world free from politics, from religion, from racial prejudice."

The Americans and the Soviets decided to ignore each other's interventions, and there was so much money that the allegedly embezzled funds were never really missed. The Mexican students were machine-gunned and hastily buried before the Games began. South Africa agreed to withdraw. The explanation for the decision was that Mexico was so racially mixed it could never assure adequate security for the all-white South African team. Olympic officials promised really tight security for the 1972 Games in Munich.

Which left us one last crisis, the black boycott. Harry Edwards never made it to Mexico City; he claims to have been turned away at the border; his critics claim he made only a token attempt to get to the Games. As a controversial figure, he was the subject of a great deal of speculation—was he threatened by imprisonment or death by the Mexicans, was he bought off by the CIA, did he opt to concentrate on his academic studies that October, did he stay away to avoid riot and bloodshed, did he realize his movement was dead?

One early plan had been for all black athletes to wear black athletic shoes to signify solidarity. That plan collapsed because many athletes were being secretly paid to wear Adidas or Puma shoes, distinguishable on television by their colors and designs. Other demonstrations were discussed, but the athletes were fragmented by their varying levels of radicalism, sophistication, intelligence. In some cases, athletes who thought they might be picked in the coming pro football draft were afraid of being labeled troublemakers, as were those athletes with government or college athletic jobs lined up. Under the circumstances, the simple raising of black-gloved fists by Tommie Smith and John Carlos was at once a courageous personal gesture and the mildest, most reasonable display of black power all that year.

CHAPTER
5

Sport of the Seventies:
Sly, Midnight Moves

1

NEW YORK's most salable human export traditionally has been its annual crop of college-bound basketball players, planted in the ghettoes, nurtured in the playgrounds and community centers, harvested in the high schools, and packaged for distribution throughout the country; rangy Irish gunners and scrappy Jewish playmakers and, by the sixties, game-busting black forwards and centers who could do everything with a basketball except read its label.

Products of the "city game," they reappear as college stars in South Carolina and Tennessee and West Texas and Wisconsin, often after a year of "prepping" at one of several small private academies in the South and West that seem to exist primarily to sand off the roughest of their streety ways and teach them to understand, if not speak, white English. The conventional Sports-World wisdom, that most of these young men would never have a chance to attend college without basketball, is absolutely true. And a condemnation of the educational system that barely needs comment.

One of the city game's finest products was a functional illiterate named Connie Hawkins who was shipped to the University of Iowa in 1960. He was 18 years old, almost at his full height of 6 feet 8 inches, and gifted with remarkable agility and body control. He had all the moves. He also had a general diploma, which was little more than a certificate of attendance, a kind of honorable discharge from high school for those the guidance counselors have pre-tracked for the city's pool of unskilled labor.

Hawkins has become in recent years a shining star in SportsWorld, another proof of locker-room homilies, You Can't Keep a Good Man Down, or, If You Come to the End of Your Rope, Tie a Knot and Hang On. But for almost the entire sixties Hawkins was a prototype of the SportsWorld sacrificial victim, the man left dangling when the going gets tough and the tough get going.

Hawkins attended Boys High in Brooklyn. When the neighborhood, Bedford-Stuyvesant, was white, the school was considered one of the best in the city. It drew future doctors and judges from all the boroughs. It was staffed by vigorous and idealistic young Irish and Jewish teachers eager to provide their younger counterparts with the tools to remake the world.

But by Connie's senior year, 1959–1960—which coincided with my own first year as a reporter, covering high school sports —the student population was more than three-quarters black, and the faculty was middle-aged and unprepared for the area's transition into a filthy, murderous reservation where crime and sports were prestige trades. The only respected badges of young manhood were the colors of a fighting gang and the varsity jacket of a Boys High team. For better or worse, the school's positive image was now based on its leadership in producing future college basketball stars.

Hawkins' coach, Mickey Fisher, was internationally recognized—he would abandon his high school team in the middle of Connie's last year to coach the Israeli Olympic team. Fisher was a classic inner-city coach, a white missionary who dedicated his life to saving black boys through sport. At the time, I did not question his role; I just nodded and smiled and took my notes and anticipated my by-lines as Fisher radiated energy and joy even as he complained of his personal sacrifices, his long hours, the occasional ingratitude of the community.

Fisher was relentless in pursuit of college scholarships for his boys, although he often placed them in colleges for which they were academically unsuited, colleges from which he must have known they could never be graduated.

Fisher bought his boys food and socks with his own money. He supervised their studies. He interceded for them with other teachers if their eligibility was in   jeopardy. He drilled them constantly in fundamental ball control and team basketball, but he was shrewd enough to allow them an occasional dash of ghetto playground style: Even Fisher's 5-foot 8-inch guards could spring above the rim to smash the ball down through the basket.

A self-styled psychologist, showman, platoon sergeant, Fisher assumed that his culture was superior to his players', that his love was more dependable than what they might find at home, that his way of integrating them into the white middle-class value system with a salable skill was the best way, and the only way.

The terrible presumption of this attitude, so typically SportsWorld, was not really challenged until the late 1960s, when it became a very hot issue involving black student groups and their liberal faculty allies on one side, and traditional athletic departments on the other. Of course, it rarely occurred on campuses where the team was playing well or where the team leaders had professional aspirations. For example, Coach John Wooden of UCLA, who coached some of the hippest black athletes in America, rarely had to take time from winning national championships to put down mutinies against his paternalism.

Had Mickey Fisher lived into the 1970s, when high school athletes were questioning their coaches, he, too, would have escaped rebellion as long as he was sincerely teaching them how to win, how to get into college, how to make out in the world. In his own time, as patient and kindly and perceptive as he was, Fisher would have been aggrieved and resentful if the assertion of black consciousness had disrupted his relationship with his players; after all, he hadn't made the rules, he was just trying to save souls—bullying, cajoling, yelling, even hitting the boys if he felt they needed that kind of physical proof that he really cared about them. It is easier, in retrospect, to criticize the Fishers for the colonial administrators they were than to praise them for the practical way in which they armed a few for battles beyond the ghetto. After all, the Fishers were also trying to survive in SportsWorld.

Fisher's players were hand-picked, scouted since grammar school through community centers, schoolyards, and junior high school tournaments. Connie Hawkins was auditioned for stardom.

A veteran starter from "The High" brought Connie around when he was a scrawny ninth-grader. Fisher looked him over with little interest, then asked him to try to touch the metal basket rim. Without a running start, Connie jumped straight up, grabbed, and swung from the rim with both hands. The coach's eyes lighted up. He had found a prime soul to save.

Connie's childhood contained all those neo-Dickensian touches the SportsWorld biographers love: He was the fifth of six children, his father left the family when Connie was 9, about the same time he started scavenging deposit bottles to redeem at the corner candy store where Mrs. Hawkins, who was losing her sight from glaucoma, got her telephone messages.

"Until I got good at basketball," said Connie many years later, "there was nothin' about me I liked, there wasn't a thing I could be proud of. I was kind of quiet and insecure. It didn't seem like I had anything going for me. I was ashamed of the way I looked. We all wore hand-me-downs. But my brothers were short and wide and I was long and skinny, so nothin' fit me right. I didn't feel sharp enough to talk to girls."

Boys High is an exotic outpost and Connie Hawkins an extraordinarily gifted and misused athlete, but the basic lessons of SportsWorld were here for me to learn in 1959. I failed the course. I went out to Boys High to attract attention within the paper, to practice technique, to test myself against the competition, to prepare for the Big Leagues. And so I saw Mickey Fisher as a kind of social worker in sneakers, a man with a mission to salvage what he could from society's slag heap; and I saw Connie Hawkins as a nice, but dumb, povert with a remarkable talent.

Only Mickey Fisher and the round brown ball would save him from a dull life, perhaps even jail. My own naked ambition could be served with positive stories about this worthy place and its worthy boys, and SportsWorld would applaud us all.

I never really knew Connie Hawkins or understood what happened to him until David Wolf described his rise and fall and rise again, first in *Life* magazine, and later in a rich and rewarding book called *Foul!* In grammar school, wrote Wolf, Connie was truant to avoid continual embarrassment; he was called Long Tall Sally, he looked weak, and was bullied. None of the fighting gangs wanted him. He had huge hands, mugger's hands, it was suggested, but he was too scared to try. His brother branded him a "chickenshit faggot."

Then he found basketball at the community center where his mother worked, and nothing else could ever be so important again. Perhaps because sports is play for most of us, and a relatively brief active career for professionals, the passion to participate is usually treated in a condescending or trivial way. But that moment when a poor, skinny, weak black suddenly realizes he has found the form in which to pour his energies and hopes is certainly as valid and dramatic as the pre-seminarian's epiphany or the future revolutionary's click. Then Connie found Fisher.

"Mr. Fisher was a father-type person," said Hawkins. "He treated me like a human being, never made fun of me. He took time to talk about my problems in school—and I had a lot."

Connie became Fisher's property; the inner-city coach has awesome clout—he is pope and police chief—and teachers might mock Connie or ignore him, but they didn't dare damage him.

The head of the English department told Wolf, "I suppose I was so fascinated by Connie's playing that I looked the other way when he didn't come to school or missed some classes. At Boys High, it took a hell of a lot of courage for any teacher to flunk Connie Hawkins. And few did."

Summers were orgies of basketball for Connie. The New York ghetto playgrounds in summer are justly celebrated for basketball as a macho performing art. Collegians and pros drop back to show off, work out, test the young bloods, and serve the SportsWorld Gods of cool, style, and put-down. The individual is supreme: One-on-one, and the winner must do it with moves that can rouse a crowd that has seen the best. Connie perfected fabulous sleights of body, dips, turns, twists, fakes, leaps, that eventually made his name synonymous with the balletic school-yard style.

There is a mystique about the quality of New York schoolyard basketball that implies that if dope and malnutrition and emotional depression were somehow eradicated, every National Basketball Association team would be starting two blacks from Harlem, two from Bed-Stuy, and one white from Indiana as mix. The "world's greatest player" has always just overdosed. Basketball almost saved him, but . . .

But basketball is a hard drug, too. On the coldest winter's night in any slum playground you will invariably see a boy alone, swimming in an outdoor lamp's eerie yellow pool: He is driving toward a netless basket, he fakes an imaginary defender, dribbles hard so the ball bounces into his hands as he rises toward a backboard so cold his skin would stick if he touched it, pauses . . . in mid-air . . . turns away from a grove of blocking arms . . . hangs suspended as he pumps the ball twice to his stomach before slamming it two-handed down the throat of the world. He is not practicing to gain the recognition of his peers or to impress girls or to get a college scholarship; at that moment he is on a trip, and for as long as he is on it, he is everything he wants to be. It should not be surprising that so many playground aces are junkies with dope, too.

Hawkins smoked grass and sniffed coke once or twice, but cheap wine was the main high of his day. Watching him play then I sometimes wondered if he was lazy or loafing along as a gesture of style or so incredibly efficient in movement that he made everything look easy. It did not occur to me that he might be high, which he wasn't. He was carefully pacing himself because years of inadequate diet and recent spurts of growth had left him with less stamina than he needed for an entire game at full tilt.

More than 200 colleges were actively recruiting Connie, including several fronting for pro teams who wanted to get him into their draft territories. The Boston Celtics, according to Wolf, were willing to pay Hawkins an under-the-table salary to attend Providence, so they could claim him in four years. Colleges offered him the standard car-apartment-sinecure. Colorado reportedly promised Connie a job clearing seaweed from the football stadium, which Wolf pointed out was more than a thousand miles from the nearest ocean. Connie took it, and went out to Boulder for summer remedial courses in reading and math. Connie took a brother along and his brother took a gun. All three were back in Brooklyn shortly.

Eventually, he decided to attend the University of Iowa. The Iowa recruiters were low-key, and they offered the next-best deal; among other perks, a weekly paycheck without a job and round-trip transportation for a neighborhood girl whenever the stud needed one. Later, when the deal was made public, Iowa received a year's probation. By then, Connie was long gone, in ruins.

The counselors at Boys and the admissions officers at Iowa were aware that Hawkins could never make it through college. One Boys teacher, working daily with Connie, raised his IQ score from 65 to 113 in a few months, and his reading level from seventh grade to eleventh. But there was no way to overcome all the years of malignant neglect during which he had drifted through school without learning how to study or organize information or take a test; all the years in which he began to think he was indeed a moron. Wolf speculates that a year in a prep school or junior college might have brought him up to a level at which he could have coped academically with Iowa. Had Iowa wanted to give him time to grow another inch, or fill out, or perfect a different style of play, he doubtless would have been farmed out for a year. But Iowa was in a hurry. Unlike any other major sport, basketball requires only one superstar to carry a whole team, to pack the fieldhouse, to plug a college into the national Good News Network.

"Connie's classes—which the recruiters had told him he could handle—were more overwhelming and humiliating than his worst experiences at Boys High," wrote Wolf in *Foul!* "Unfamiliar words buzzed about his ears like angry mosquitoes, and reading assignments for a month totaled more pages than he had read in his life. People were not unfriendly; they smiled and said how happy they were he had come to Iowa. But Hawkins soon found life on the college campus dull, lonely, and sexually frustrating."

In a few years, colleges would become very sophisticated at this sort of thing, recruiting their athletes under special admission programs for minorities. There would be federally funded tutoring and relaxed grade standards for varsity eligibility. They would enlist the nearest black community to make the athletes feel at ease; they would institute black studies programs and scholarships for black girl cheerleaders to create an instant ghetto on campus. But in 1960, the problems of the high-priced black athlete in an otherwise white northern school were a private matter between the boy and his coach.

By the time Connie got to Iowa, however, he was probably

past help. While his freshman basketball season was a sensation, his freshman academic year was a total wipe-out.

He was also carrying a time-bomb that would blow him off campus long before he would ever be flunked out.

The summer before he went west he had met Jack Molinas, a former Columbia all-American who had been thrown out of the NBA in the middle of a fine rookie season for betting on games. It has always been maintained that Molinas only bet on his own team to win, but by the time he met Hawkins he was mastermind of a nationwide gambling ring paying dozens of players to fix games. Connie, who had been 12 when Molinas was banned, thought the 28-year-old lawyer was just a basketball freak who bought him some meals, drove him to games, and offered him walking around money. Hawkins borrowed $200 from Molinas, which was returned by one of his brothers. There was never any evidence that Connie shaved points, gambled on games in which he played, or tried to recruit fixers. Apparently, Molinas was just softening up Connie for the future. Molinas was jailed in 1963, for five years. He was murdered in 1975.

When the 1961 college basketball scandals broke, Hawkins was one of many players hauled off campuses, locked up in New York hotel rooms with detectives, and brought before a grand jury. He was never prosecuted. But when he returned to Iowa a few weeks later, he was dismissed from school.

There was a cynical logic to this: While Iowa was perfectly willing to make an unethical arrangement with a potential all-America, it could hardly be expected to break rules for a freshman with failing grades and a tainted name. Financially, it was minimizing its losses. Had Hawkins not become involved in the investigation, Iowa probably would have found a way to keep him eligible; and had Hawkins been passing his courses, Iowa probably would have welcomed him back to school, as did other colleges whose players were mentioned in the same investigation. Iowa's action seems to have been critical to the National Basketball Association's later decision to blacklist Hawkins; other players who returned to college after a grand jury appearance were allowed to play in the NBA.

It took eight years, a painstaking investigation by lawyers and by Wolf, and the threat of a $6 million treble damage suit against the NBA for conspiring to keep Hawkins out of the league before he finally moved into the company of Wilt Chamberlain and Oscar Robertson, where he clearly belonged. By the time he got to the Phoenix Sons in 1969, Hawkins was 27, married, a father, an articulate and confident man. He was also a recent millionaire thanks to the league's sudden desire to settle the case out of court. And he had clearly been cheated, a SportsWorld victim lucky enough to find champions before his skills were gone.

The same year Hawkins finally made the NBA, Bob Cousy returned to the pros after six seasons coaching Boston College; he quit the amateur game, he said, because of the "rat race" of recruiting players. The NBA approved his coaching job with the Cincinnati Royals without a thorough investigation of a two-year-old *Life* report linking him socially with known gamblers. A teary denial of wrongdoing at the time had been good enough. After all, if Cousy, one of the game's most celebrated figures, its premier white for many years, had indeed been feeding information to gamblers during all those glorious years with the Boston Celtics, the NBA would be retroactively smeared. It would lose public confidence. It might never fully realize the predicted boom of the seventies.

SportsWorld has always put a greater premium on the appearance of innocence than on innocence itself. For example, almost all pro sports have rules against players "fraternizing" with opposing players, especially while in uniform, lest fans get the idea they are "electing a winner," or that they are friends and might try to avoid hurting or embarrassing each other. Yet no sport I know of has rules against coaches and owners lying to the public, directly or through the press. When a commissioner suspends a player for "alleged association with undesirable characters" he invariably declares that the player was doing nothing really wrong, but in the interests of public confidence and for the good of the game . . .

Like most fans, I immediately assume either a cover-up of deep scandal or the periodic sacrifice to the shade of Caesar's Wife, the most frequently invoked woman in SportsWorld.

Hawkins was sacrificed by the pros, he was sacrificed by the college sport, and he was sacrificed by the high school game. He was sacrificed by his country. Fisher's abandonment of his team for a State Department-sponsored Israeli tour is not defensible; it smacks of all those CARE packages handed down from tailgates in other countries' ghettoes. Where was all that guidance, that character building, that protection of innocents that physical education lobbyists unfurl at every hint of a budget cut? Fisher's replacement, a black assistant coach who had once played for Fisher at Boys, came late and lame with his overview: "I don't feel that what a lot of the college recruiters did was much less dishonest than what the gamblers did."

Not good enough, but then high school coaches cannot afford to be too righteous about college recruiters. Not when they're busy recruiting players from junior high school. It is a common practice nationwide, and in coaches' jargon it is called "proselytizing." In cities where open enrollment gives students a free choice of high schools, the competition is intense, and coaches promise boys starting positions and summer jobs. Players who go from coach to coach looking for the best offer are known as "shoppers." They are sometimes helped by "spooks," free-lance scouts who tag hot prospects at 12, and hang with them for a few years hoping for a payoff from college recruiters looking for information or an inside track.

In cities without open enrollment, the proselytizer sometimes arranges for a player to move into the neighborhood his high school services, or at least register with a local address. The only coaches who are ever caught are those who proselytize so blatantly that they endanger the system for everyone else. When this happens, there is a great deal of ethics committee rhetoric, and the player is declared ineligible, which in many cases is a sentence back to the street. Sometimes a death sentence.

Eligibility disputes—overage players, transfer students, so-called super seniors in their fifth or sixth year of high school attendance, as well as simple "address cases"—are the common virus of high school athletics, and invariably the player and his team are punished rather than the coach.

At worst, the coach may be censured, which will be remembered when he goes looking for a college job. He'll be marked as a man who will do anything to win. It's the best recommendation you can get.

2

On May 4, 1965, Ferdinand Lewis Alcindor, Jr. held a press conference, his first, on the floor of his high school gym. Off to his
right, some women, including his mother, were hanging decora-
tions for a parents' association dance. In front of him were several hundred reporters, columnists, photographers, broadcasters,
and television crewmen, self-conscious and cranky at having
been summoned at the whim of a teenage goon whose claim to
fame was that almost all of his contemporaries were shorter.

Alcindor, barely 18 years old, slightly taller than 7 feet, was
quite obviously on his way to becoming the first athlete to destroy his own sport, or so they said. A mere seventy-four years
after Dr. Naismith nailed up peach baskets in a Massachusetts Y
to drain off the energies of college boys in wintertime, this sim-
plest, least contrived, most economical of major American sports
was to be wiped out by a freak with a pinhead and tennis racquet
hands.

Alcindor had dominated his high school game and would
surely dominate his college game.

The pro game had a scant four years to figure out defenses
against him.

Very little was known about Alcindor that day. His high school
coach had never allowed him to be interviewed, and his recruitment had been the subject of a great deal of sportsblab rumor
and speculation. At least sixty colleges had seriously bid for his
services, and some of the deals must have been hefty packages:
Landing Alcindor virtually assured a college four years of positive national publicity, winning teams, and a financially profitable basketball program. As far as most of us were concerned,
Alcindor might be the biggest and the best, but he was still just
another ghetto black redeemed in the shadow of the Hoop. So it
was widely assumed that he would either fall into St. John's, a
local basektball power, or leave the area with his young and
ambitious white coach for a college that would hire them both.

That day was the first time I had ever seen Alcindor. Aside
from his height, which was accentuated by the unformed slim-
ness of his body and the marionette jerkiness of his limbs, his

most striking features were his sweetness and his seriousness. Gulliver, not goon, I began to think. We swarmed about him, Lilliputians in mind as well as body. One of my colleagues asked, "Are there any liabilities in being tall in basketball?" and Alcindor kindly replied, "None that I can think of."

Over the years, always from a distance, I've watched Alcindor bake in the kiln of publicity, that seriousness turning hard-edged and protective, that sweetness becoming a dreamy remoteness. I've thought about that first day and how we never knew Alcindor, and we will probably never know Kareem Abdul-Jabbar, not as long as the sports press is as white as it has been, so middle-class, so steeped in the fakelore of SportsWorld.

Our reference point for Alcindor, at first, was Connie Hawkins, then clowning for the Harlem Globetrotters. Alcindor was obviously more intelligent and socially aware than Hawkins had been in 1960, and better prepared for life beyond the high school gym. We could report that while Hawkins had been poor and father-less in the black ghetto of Bed-Stuy, Alcindor grew up a carefully supervised only child in a predominantly white Manhattan neighborhood with trees, a river view, and a semisuburban atmo-sphere. While Hawkins went to black public schools, Alcindor went to white Catholic schools. But we reported these details as facts, as prospected nuggets of truth, rather than using them as the raw material for insight and interpretation. We did not—could not—differentiate between their experiences. We lumped them together, first as blacks, then as jocks.

But what different men they always were. Hawkins' parents were from rural North Carolina, products of the southern slave culture that came north in the great wave of World War II im-migration. Connie was a street boy, barely educated, unguided.

Alcindor's father's father came from Trinidad, where Alcindor Trace was a place name. Alcindor's father was a Transit Author-ity policeman who was not grateful for a civil service job. He had trained as an orchestra conductor, and was a graduate of the Juilliard School of Music; at the least he would define himself as an out-of-work jazz trombonist. His son would pitch in the Little League, take music lessons, join a HARYOU-ACT training pro-gram, attend UCLA at the urging of such alumni as Jackie Rob-inson and Dr. Ralph Bunche.

The press did not understand Alcindor, but then we only had
racist assumptions to go on. Until that day in May when Alcindor
announced the college of his choice, Jack Donohue, his coach,
had allowed him no formal contact with the press. No postgame
interviews, no telephone calls, no casual conversations that might
slip into a question and answer session. But Donohue, who saw
Lewie every day, knew his parents, had access to all his test
scores and records, traveled with him, showered with him, spent
summers with him at a camp he operated, would seem to have no
excuse at all. In a revealing memoir in *Sports Illustrated*, Alcindor describes an incident in which Donohue, during a half-time
critique of his Power Memorial team, suddenly turned on his star
and said, "And you! You go out there and you don't hustle. You
don't move. You don't do any of the things you're supposed to do.
You're acting just like a nigger."

Alcindor was stunned. The two other blacks on the squad
urged him to go home, but he finished the game in a daze. Power
Memorial won, and Donohue said, "See? It worked! My strategy
worked. I knew that if I used that word it'd shock you into a
good second half. And it did."

That word. "The instant you do something wrong in front of
the white race you're not only a misdoer, but you're a nigger,
too," wrote Alcindor with Jack Olsen in *SI*. "They hold that word
back until you slip up, and then lay it on you like a crowbar."

Alcindor went home that night and told his mother. His father
was working. She calmed him down. "I'm afraid we'll just have to
wait till you're through with that man." There was little choice,
of course, now that Alcindor was locked into SportsWorld. If he
quit the team or transferred to another school, he would lose his
senior year of varsity basketball, weakening his bargaining position for a "free" education at a quality college. He would have to
string along with Donohue until he was graduated from high
school.

When the *SI* series was published, Donohue, by then coaching
at Holy Cross College, said he was surprised and hurt. Alcindor
had misunderstood; in long talks he had appealed to the boy's
pride, said Donohue, he had "tried to impress upon him that if he
didn't play up to his ability, if he took the easy way out, if he
didn't work hard, people would call him that."

We knew none of this at the time. There was some grumbling, and a few half-hearted attempts to get at Alcindor, but for the most part the Establishment white press respected Donohue's protectorate: Of course a black family had to be shielded from bad, tricky whites, spook scouts, Jack Molinases, hit-and-run journalists, college recruiters, jock chasers, who could overwhelm and ruin their simple lives. As usual, we blew the story and looked like fools, as we always do when we play ball with news sources, from Power Memorial to the Bay of Pigs.

After his formal announcement, Alcindor excused himself to return to class. All the TV cameras and most of the press left soon afterward, but a few of us stayed on the chance he might come back, which he did, perhaps an hour later. Alcindor seemed slightly more relaxed now as we crowded into Donohue's small office off the gym. The sweetness, the seriousness, were even more pronounced. He had a gentle llamalike quality to his face and a warm smile. He told us he was sports editor of a neighborhood newspaper and that he was seriously considering a career in journalism. We urged him to take as many television courses as he could at UCLA because the future of sports journalism was electronic. He thanked us for our advice and we felt magnanimous. It was a very warm, human moment. Then he excused himself again. He had a Russian history class.

The next Alcindor press conference I attended was in a banquet room of the Americana Hotel in New York on January 25, 1968, nearly three years later. Alcindor was a college junior. He was at least as great as the gaudiest predictions. After his first two years, during which his team never lost, intercollegiate rules were changed to forbid dunking or stuffing the ball down into the basket. It was unofficially known as the Alcindor Rule. In this third year of his era, the rule was proving to have far less effect on Alcindor than upon a generation of less talented schoolyard-trained blacks who had to revamp their techniques. UCLA had lost only one game in which he played, on a night he was still suffering double vision from an eye injury.

Now, recovered, on the night before his first game in New York as a college player, he rocked silently on a straight-backed chair and regarded some fifty newsmen arranged in rows before him. We stared back at him. His modified Afro intimidated or angered a few, but he did not seem hostile so much as defensive, on guard. Milton Gross, naturally in the front row, whispered, "Lew, you find all this," he gestured at the assembled press, the ornate room, "ridiculous?"

Alcindor smiled and shook his head. "It's kind of expected," he said.

Speaking evenly, in complete sentences, he answered questions about his eyes, the recent defeat, being ranked No. 1 in the country. *Newsweek* had recently reported that Alcindor's arm-span was 7½ feet, his intelligence quotient 131, his grade average B—. We had all the stats, but we tried, in clumsy conference fashion, to get closer. Did he think he was moody and reserved, as profilers seemed to indicate? "My peculiar personality comes off that way," he said. Were they true, the reports that he wasn't happy at UCLA? "I enjoy it sometimes. I don't like Los Angeles that much." In effect, we were asking him to comment on our reportage.

Someone who had been in Donohue's little office that day asked him if he was still interested in journalism. Did the sudden flicker of coldness in his eyes reflect my anticipation or was it truly there? He looked us over carefully before answering.

"I'm majoring in history now. I'm no longer interested in journalism."

He grew more confident, his answers became longer, more voluntary, as the conference continued. He said he had not yet decided whether or not he would respect the Olympic boycott; he thought Harry Edwards had some good ideas and some mistaken ideas, but was on the right path. He said he had yet to become accustomed to strangers asking about his height. "I don't appreciate it. People make you a fall guy because you're different."

Suddenly, Gordon White of *The Times*, whose neck had been reddening throughout the conference, turned to Coach Wooden, who was sitting near Alcindor. "Where is the rest of your team? Do you consider this in the best interests of amateur sport, one athlete and the coach being interviewed? Isn't this a team sport?"

Wooden considered him coldly. "If this is a bad thing, it's bad because of the way the press handles it. I've gotten 300 requests for personal interviews for Lewis. I don't like to have my entire team sitting here while you direct all your questions at just one or two players." The conference was over.

The University of California at Lew Alcindor, as we called
UCLA then, played twice that visit, first romping over Holy
Cross ("Lewie was as great as I remember him," said Donohue
cheerlessly), the following night beating Boston College ("Alcindor could be better than Chamberlain and Russell," said Cousy).
In postgame interviews Alcindor was unfailingly courteous in a
businesslike way and very precise in his language, as if he expected to be misinterpreted. When we remarked on how cool he
remained while other players punched and shoved him under the
backboards, he said, "I'm going to learn how to cope with it but
not how to get used to it." He kept his parents and Dr. Bunche
waiting one night while he obliged photographers, and I tried to
eavesdrop on their conversation. Alcindor Sr. was answering Dr.
Bunche's questions about his height and his wife's height, and
Dr. Bunche was saying, "Well, we're trying to reach a peaceful
solution."

Alcindor was booed during the two games, and it was easy to
see why. It often seemed unfair that he should be on the same
court with those little white boys who were trying to shoot over
his head or drag him down by his underarm hair. He was so tall,
so mobile. He sometimes looked goofy on court, mouth open,
ropy arms dangling as he loped along or just stood loafing in a
corner, but in the moment of scoring or rebounding everything
worked so efficiently; there was no scramble or tussle or herky-
jerk about Alcindor. He seemed to know exactly where he was
going and how to get there without knocking anyone down or
using force of any kind. For me, his finest moments came when
he gracefully rose like a genie from a bottle, the ball resting on
his outstretched right palm as if it were on a silver tray, and,
suspended aloft, almost casually it seemed, tipped the tray and
let the ball slide off and into the basket. It was an artistic instant,
at once a finished performance and a coming attraction. There
was such a sense of deep resources about Alcindor—he was playing only as hard as he needed to play to win—that one could
hardly wait to see what would happen when he was truly tested,
extended to his limits by the pros.

That sense of deep resources was apparent off the court as
well. Always veiled, always in control, he answered questions
only as far as they needed to be answered; he had no need to
chatter, preen, pontificate, joke to keep reporters smiling and

nodding, their pens scratching away. Wooden had kept the press away during Alcindor's freshman year; after that it was probably Alcindor's choice, too. The last thing he needed during those college years, 1965–1969, were sportswriters tugging his sleeve and asking the equivalent of "How's the weather up there?" just when he himself was trying to find out.

It was the worst of times for a freak-sized jock with an even bigger advance reputation and the best of times for a proud son of black princes who understood he was far from completion as a human being. He seemed to have navigated his four years as well as any top athlete ever has: He was graduated with his class, which is not typical at his superstar level, he avoided serious confrontation with the law or conventional morality, he played to everyone's expectations, and he established a persona that was clearly special. Alcindor could boycott the Olympics, travel for the U.S. State Department, spend summers teaching New York ghetto children.

He became a Sunni Moslem, legally changing his name to Kareem Abdul-Jabbar, Generous Strong-Servant of Allah. The Sunnis are not connected with Ali's separatist American splinter group; in fact the 1973 murder of seven Sunnis, including five children, in a Washington, D.C. house Abdul-Jabbar bought as a U.S. center for his orthodox Hanafi sect, was blamed on Black Muslims.

Through ballgames, through murder, through the bidding for his services, Abdul-Jabbar moved with a curious detached dignity, a man who seemed in constant communion with himself. He was, of course, an immediate pro success. The Milwaukee Bucks, who won him in a coin toss, made a $300,000 profit his first year after losing $370,000 the season before. His salary—at least the figure leaked to the press—was $1.4 million over five years.

He was merely sensational his rookie season, carrying the Bucks from last place into the championship playoffs, but sheer talent was not quite enough. Old pros knew too many ways to thrash and elbow him, and the team he played with could not help him enough. It was also the year of the Knicks. The last game of his rookie year was in Madison Square Garden, back home in New York, and late in the third period, the contest long lost, his coach benched him. As he walked off the floor, a high, hard, nasty song rolled out of the balcony, was echoed and multiplied until it flooded the cockpit of the arena. "Good-bye, Lewie, Good-bye, Lewie, Good-bye, Lewie, We hate to see you go." Some of the Knicks seemed embarrassed by the fans, *their* fans, the ones they had praised all year, and later, Walt Frazier would excuse it as a "sigh of relief." After all, everyone had heard the rumor and the prediction, which turned out to be true, that the Bucks were buying Oscar Robertson and couldn't miss winning the title next year. But at this moment the singing seemed malevolent, unnecessary; even the price of these tickets didn't include such a breach of sportsmanship. Abdul-Jabbar's face held no expression. He flashed the peace sign before he sat down. Later, in the locker room, he had little to say about the incident. "I don't feel anything at all about it. It's their problem, if they want to act like that."

Someone pressed him. "Why do you think they did it?"

Very softly, he said, "Maybe because they're scared."

3

Basketball and hockey are complementary sports for the arenas that house them; cover the ice with portable flooring for a basketball game, pick it up and you're ready to skate again. The foundations of the present National Basketball Association were laid after World War II by hockey owners who needed more events for the arenas they operated. Professional basketball was a rough game, like hockey, and it was encouraged to stay that way. The referees called fouls "selectively" so as not to slow the brawling action. Veterans in the league "put the question" to rookies with their elbows and fists. With only slightly more finesse, they still do.

For most of its existence, pro basketball had been regarded by the casual sports fan as a kind of competitive carnival: Rubber-hoofed goons storming back and forth on a polished hardwood raft, building suspense for the last two minutes of the game, the *real* game, and for the dash to the airport for the next one-night stand. But the game hung on, and it prospered. It was relatively cheap to produce. It had a hard-core following. The owners, being businessmen rather than fans, were willing to experiment with such radical changes as a twenty-four-second deadline to shoot and a limit to team fouls, which improved the quality of play. And pro basketball was very lucky. The 1951 college scandals reversed the conventional wisdom that the pros were shady and the amateurs pure. In 1961, the college game was again revealed as infested with dumpers and shavers, and the NBA, above suspicion, stepped forward into its contemporary era of stabilization and expansion and black superstars.

But pro basketball did not truly burst upon the national consciousness—or at least upon the consciousness of the trend hustlers, advertising executives, television programmers, pop culture promoters who hype and sell fashions in clothes, entertainment, and ideas—until the New York Knickerbockers were on their way to their first league championship, the 1969–1970 season when "the city game" was proclaimed the Sport of the Seventies.

The New York-based national hype machine was already geared up and humming for the Namath-Jets and the Everyman-Mets, and it was simple to cast a few new dies for the Knicks. Wow! What a groovy team! Charismatic, classy, smooth, lithe, sexy, dynamic, yin and yang, Gestalt, Hegel, the greatest ever! Suddenly, in New York, everyone was talking about (writing about, broadcasting about) the pick-and-roll, the backdoor-play, the high-and-low-posts, as if they had just been invented and would slow the decline of the West. And why not? If a Louisiana farmboy and a banker's son and a beer-guzzling Detroit ethnic and a black Atlanta dude and a 33-year-old workhorse guard could submerge their egos in a quest for group success, if the basic concern for looking good and getting your buckets could be disregarded for helping each other and hitting the open man, then maybe we could all come together and stop the slide and get back on our feet and turn the country around. There was a droll little coach named Red (his hair was sandy-gray and sparse) who said "I'm just an ordinary man" so many times that we knew he was a genius. Dustin Hoffman and Robert Redford and Elliott Gould were photographed at Knicks games, pop stars certifying pop stars, and there were so many chic women at Madison Square Garden that pop sociologists argued whether they came to see the scantily clad beefcake stretch and strain or to be seen at the latest hot-ticket event. No one considered the possibility that the women might be basketball fans.

George Lois, the advertising superstar whose demonstrative passion at games won him the Knickname Superfan, has written that Bill Bradley's "presence at the Garden helped make the game acceptable to the white New York woman." A WASP from Princeton, a Rhodes Scholar, a man whose business agent declared before his rookie season, "I believe he will be President of the United States. He's further along toward that goal than any other 24-year-old in the country," Bradley actually made the game acceptable to many white New York men, including writers, editors, television producers, network executives, publishers, and advertising men. The fact that Bradley spurned the pro game for two years while he studied at Oxford was interesting, even a little unsettling for some who might daydream of being old Satin Pants on the Garden floor; but it was eventually understandable. Bradley was already so rich, intelligent, handsome, well connected, and famous that what could he gain by playing a game for spades? But after two years of communing with the spirits of Bentham and Locke, and five months in the Air Force Reserve, Bradley appeared in New York and coolly said, "I'm available to play basketball." We asked him why, knowing that $500,000 over four years could not be enough of an enticement, not for this Perfect Boy, and he answered, "I want to test myself against the best."

SportsWorld never entirely trusted Bradley. He was not dependent upon the kindness of owners, coaches, and sportswriters. He obviously wasn't "hungry" in the way that promoters understand. His angle was not clear. And he was so close to the model son that SportsWorld promised to produce, he seemed so often a hero of postgame sermonettes, that SportsWorld sometimes wondered if he might not be an absolute fraud, an imposter, some kind of infiltrator. One thought of spy movies in which the foreign agent was unmasked because he spoke English too well to be native-born. SportsWorld knew that Bradley could not be real. Did Bradley know?

His father was the bank president in a small town thirty miles south of St. Louis, Crystal City, Missouri. His mother, a former junior high school teacher, was an energetic clubwoman and golfer who had played basketball in high school. The Bradleys carefully created a renaissance boy of their only child—music lessons, sports instructions, Scouts, religious training, political discussions at the table, attention to his studies. When Bill's interest in basketball became intense, the Bradleys black-topped their backyard and installed a hoop at exactly the regulation ten feet.

Black Knicks, who seemed bemused by the less than Greek configuration of Bradley's body (Walt Frazier called it "funny"), recognized how hard Bradley had worked to become so accomplished. "I make it that he knew he didn't have the body for this league," Willis Reed told Roger Kahn in *Esquire*, "so he did special things." And in recognizing the extent of his effort, they of course wondered why. What was he trying to prove or find out or escape from? They knew he had worked as hard as any of them, although he wintered in Palm Beach until he was 13 and practiced his dribble down the corridors of the Queen Elizabeth at sea and went to Princeton without a scholarship.

He was considered a potential pro in high school and his mother made scores of chicken-in-wine-sauce dinners for the coaches, vice-chancellors, and Latin teachers who swarmed into town after the country's hottest prospect. Princeton had been Bradley's first choice since he was 8 years old and pretended to be Dick Kazmaier in touch football games. But in May of his senior year, 1961, the temporary victim of what he would later call "a carefully orchestrated recruiting job," he decided to attend Duke. His father, disappointed, sent him on a summer European tour to think it over.

Duke had come on strong with the Bradleys, a tailor-made rush that would not have fitted the Alcindors or Connie Hawkins. Legions of Duke alumni in the St. Louis area called to offer postgraduate business connections, assistant coaches arrived with dorm blueprints and dietary charts, and important administrators sent informal notes to Mrs. Bradley once they learned she favored handwriting. Using Bill's own description of his college requirements—a well-balanced school offering an intellectual, athletic, and spiritual experience—they picked apart the opposition: The athletic competition would be good and tough at St. Louis University, they would say, but he would learn nothing, and at Princeton and Yale he would atrophy as a ballplayer and lose his religion in the atheistic atmosphere.

"We were kind of taken in. My mother made a big chart of the pros and cons of the different schools, but it was like playing cards with a rigged deck. It came out Duke."

We were sitting in a motel coffee shop in Salt Lake City, in the midst of a Knicks road trip that championship season, and I remember how Bradley's narrow face, usually thoughtful and humorous, darkened at the recollection of his recruitment.

"I'm very much against this whole thing now—recruitment, scholarships, letters of intent. It's organized for adult men to manipulate 18-year-olds to come to a university and provide it with a winning team, some money, and fame. Now that doesn't often lead to a situation where an athlete can develop his talent against good competition and still be a serious student. There has to be another way, because the extremes are to either break down all sports to intramurals, or admit that there is a professional class of athletes in college whose role includes providing vicarious excitement for the rest of the student body."

That summer after high school, the only male on a guided tour with twelve girls, Bradley found Oxford and began to enjoy the intellectual fantasies that would bring him back four years later. When he returned to Crystal City in August, he broke his ankle playing baseball and spent the rest of the summer reading about Oxford, its tradition, the scholarships available. The day before he was to report to Durham, North Carolina, he showed up in Princeton, New Jersey. It was several years before he completely justified in his mind an early feeling that he had compromised his integrity by reneging on his letter of intent to Duke.

His integrity. When he used that word in the coffee shop, I noted it without reaction. Speaking slowly, carefully, often in complete sentences after seeming to examine my questions for catches or flaws in the fine, cool chambers of his mind, Bradley appeared as formidably moral, even arrogantly so, as any athlete I had ever met. During that interview, which lasted more than four hours, I brought up the topic of penal reform; I had heard he was interested in it, I said.

"Yes, I'm interested in penal reform," he said, biting off the words.

"Why is that?"

"It's a pressing need." The lips clamped shut.

"What do you do about penal reform?"

"Well, I don't run around looking for a television camera and when the red light goes on deliver my three-minute package on penal reform." He seemed slightly angry.

"You don't talk about it?"

"Until I know what I'm talking about, I won't talk about it."

"Do you know why you're interested?"

The lips relaxed, the voice softened. "It's one area of American life that's easy for people to forget about and still feel good. People can forget about the ghettoes because they don't live there, but when they face the reality of the ghettoes they agree that conditions have to be changed. But when they face the realities of the prisons, most people just say, that's what they deserve. This concept of punishment is eighteenth-century. We have to give people a chance to be productive members of society." By the time he was finished, his voice was high and the words were tumbling out.

I wrote them all down and they appeared in my column. In 1970, before Attica and before Jimmy Hoffa and Clifford Irving and former members of the Committee to Re-Elect the President made penal reform a talk-show staple, Bradley's concern, like his unselfconscious use of the word integrity, was remarkable. Much later, thinking about it, I wondered how many SportsWorld superstars had been able to afford so many material, intellectual, and emotional luxuries as Bradley. No scholarship in college, no pro contract before graduation, no commercial endorsements as a pro. No obvious compromises. Integrity.

One thinks of Spencer Haywood, 19-year-old hero of the 1968 Olympic basketball team, who got his chance when Alcindor, variously excusing himself because of the pressures of college study, the atmosphere of racism in America, and other interests, refused to play. Haywood came home to a hero's job—a fat scholarship to a four-year college—which he soon quit to turn pro. Then he jumped leagues. Haywood's credo: "If you're from the ghetto, it doesn't matter what you do or how you get it, only if you got it. What loyalties you got? To your family. To your [black] brothers and sisters. But to basketball? To some team? Forget it."

The classic debate formed around Haywood. Liberals blamed his attitude on a society that had exploited his race, his family, and him. Conservatives argued that to deny Haywood individual responsibility for his actions not only patronized, even castrated Haywood, but endangered society. Haywood, above (below?) the debate, drove for his cash and his buckets.

The Olympic boycott came up during Bradley's first press conference as a Knick, in December 1967. An obvious opponent of the boycott challenged Bradley for a statement. It was my first good look at Bradley, and I studied him while he carefully chewed on the question. At a quick glance, he seemed like a SportsWorld natural; at 6 feet 5 inches he was quite tall without being abnormally so, and there was a looseness about his body that suggested Gary Cooper and Jimmy Stewart film characters, those decent, uncomplicated Americans, self-protective and inner-directed, who were stubbornly (if secretly) devoted to Good. Bradley had dark hair clipped neatly in the fifties mode, and he wore sober Ivy League clothes. Later, it would turn out that his lack of flashy fashion was as much an affectation as the outrageous taste of teammates Dick Barnett and Walt "Clyde" Frazier. Bradley smiled at odd moments, as if he enjoyed a private, humorous relationship with himself, and his eyes, beneath permanently vaulted brows, were very alert. Over the years, I have never shaken the feeling that Bradley is snapping mental photographs which he later studies.

When he finally answered the boycott question, he surprised most of his interviewers and displeased quite a few. He said that as a former Olympian he understood the thrill of testing oneself "at the highest amateur level," and he understood that the Olympic ideal was "one of individual excellence" rather than the "nationalism it has become." Therefore, he respected the Negroes' "right to do what they think is right."

It was not exactly a popular answer. Most newsmen wanted Bradley to blast the unpatriotic black goons, or at least chide them for being ungrateful. But Bradley was too reasonable, too politic, and paradoxically, too much his own man. Curry favor with newspaper reporters? Impossible.

It was not hard to imagine the 19-year-old Bradley bracing himself for Princeton home games by listening to "Climb Every

Mountain" from *The Sound of Music,* and, according to his biographer, John McPhee, improving Princeton's moral climate by his unselfishness, religiosity, and spiny values. Bradley's coach at Princeton, Butch Van Breda Kolff, told McPhee that "I think Bradley's happiest whenever he can deny himself pleasure," and McPhee reported that the words "concentration" and "discipline" seemed the two most frequently repeated when Bradley discussed basketball as an undergraduate.

For those who marveled at Bradley's dedication and his willingness to sacrifice, McPhee suggested an early clue: Growing up, Bradley had been somewhat isolated—as an only child, as a rich man's son, by his family's winter hotel vacations—and he used basketball to make friends. Watching Bradley in the Knicks' locker room in the late sixties, it seemed like a useful clue indeed. His infrequent grab-assing and his banter with teammates always seemed forced. He had spent as much time in locker rooms as any of them, he had played on as many teams, yet he was not one of the boys. He seemed to enjoy the joking about his baggy pants and absent-minded air and haphazard grooming; it was not for the hilariously vain dudes to know that Bradley was signifying his caste as surely as they were signifying theirs. If he seemed to lack an easy jock chic in the Knicks' locker room, it was more than compensated by his appearance at social gatherings, especially dinner parties he himself had organized. Here, where strokes were subtler, where a raised eyebrow was as effective as a snapped wet towel, Bradley was a wit, a graceful host, and the mugging storyteller he must have been as the only child at the family dinner table.

While an undergraduate, Bradley was the subject of a *New Yorker* profile by McPhee, which was later expanded into a book, *A Sense of Where You Are.* McPhee is a highly respected journalist —his magazine has a mystique of its own—and never before had a college athlete been treated so seriously at length. Bradley's basketball technique, his peripheral vision, his most interesting games, were examined in tech-manual detail and with poetical style. Coaches and players thought he was one of the finest college basketball players of all time; but it was as an attractive, intelligent white jock at Princeton that he became a national celebrity. There is no way of judging if Bradley was "worth" a

New Yorker profile at 21, but there is no doubt that the profile established his public image. Every journalist who followed Mc-Phee had to deal with a character defined by McPhee as a self-made athlete who envisioned a public service future in which he would "set a Christian example by implementing my feelings within the structure of my society." But five years later, Bradley was revising his emotional history. By his junior year, he now said, he had become aware of the price he was paying, emotionally and intellectually, to play basketball at Princeton. "Those last two years," he told me, "were a matter of playing out my hand and proving to myself I could play high-level athletics and still do good work. So when the chance came to study abroad, to read and take my time about it, two years of experimentation and introspection, there was no way to make me sign a professional contract.

"I thought I was finished being an athlete, channelized by society, perhaps considered a smart athlete, or an athlete with character, but still a particular kind of object instead of a particular human being. The Knicks were very nice and understanding; they never pressured me the way the colleges did. I guess that's why I was able to come back later and sign a contract."

He remembered a gray, rainy mid-winter day at Oxford, spent reading. Deep in a reflective mood, he went to tea and began a personal conversation with an English friend. He talked about basketball and celebrity, what he calls "the publicity syndrome," and his friend looked at him blankly.

"For a moment I was a bit disappointed that he was unable to respond to a personal need I had, but then I found it refreshing. It was friendship on a whole different level. He had no idea who I was."

Athletic princes are always fantasizing moving through the masses in disguise (the new champ Cassius Clay was going to dress in rags and walk down country lanes until he found a pretty little girl who didn't know who he was and would love him for himself) and are always returning to the castle, refreshed or relieved or rueful. Bradley never quite threw away the basketball while abroad (he played for an Italian pro team and earned a half-blue at Oxford), and just before returning home for his military duty he had "a fine and true experience," almost religious in nature as he described it, shooting baskets in an Oxford gym. SportsWorld seemed surprised when Bradley offered himself up again, but it shouldn't have been. If Nixon the benchwarmer could never shake free of SportsWorld, what chance had St. William of Hoops?

Bradley has always seemed very sensitive to what people expect of him. On one level he can publicly say, "Thousands of people who don't know me use my participation [in sports] as an excuse for non-action, as a fix to help them escape from their everyday problems and our society's problems. The toll of providing that experience is beginning to register on me."

Yet, on another level, his dogged determination to be witty, concerned, cultivated, in a nonjock way for all his artistic-professorial-political friends who, like his own father, are "waiting for me to do something with my life," sometimes calls up images of a lanky teenage Bill making the honor roll, perfecting his hook shot, teaching Sunday School to become the son his mother envisioned.

Bradley keenly felt the pressure of expectations when he turned pro. Knick fans wanted him to lift that mediocre team into championship contention. Sportswriters wanted a clear-cut story, either an Ivy League intellectual unable to answer "the question" in the NBA or the white Oscar Robertson tearing the league apart. Only the Garden management, which wanted an instant box-office boost, got satisfaction that season. Bradley averaged about twenty minutes and 8 points for the forty-five games in which he appeared.

"I was disappointed with the way I played," he said, "but I wasn't surprised since I had no preconceptions. I had control over myself, but there are many more variables than oneself in the game."

Through the next season, the team was broken down and reconstituted through trades and shifted positions. Red Holzman, the chief scout, became the new coach, and a basketball collective was created: Willis Reed, a majestic man who forced himself through injury and pain to stand as anchor for the speedy four around him; Frazier, gifted and quick, whose moody performance sometimes disturbed teammates who realized how dependent they were on his ability to set up plays and lead the defense;

Barnett, steady, shrewd, pacing himself until a sudden, almost unexpected move was needed in some ignored corner of the court; Dave DeBusschere, fierce, relentless, wildly juiced by competitive instinct, driving, scrambling, leaping, all sharp bones and hard edges; and Bradley, moving constantly to a stream of self-directed profanity he rarely used off-court, getting himself into position for long, uncanny shots and fighting his own razor wars against the sharpest knees and elbows in the league. Bradley was not the star of the team as he had been the star of every other team on which he had ever played, but he was integral to the Knicks, an essential ingredient of what came to be called "team basketball as it should be played." That championship season, 1969–1970, was exciting even without the magazine covers and television specials and ballooning press coverage that was trumpeting the emergence of a new national sport.

The season ended with a near-mythic denouement. Reed, his badly injured right leg leaden with Carbocaine, dragged himself out on the Garden floor minutes before the start of the last playoff game against Wilt Chamberlain and the Los Angeles Lakers. Murray Kempton thought of El Cid strapped to his horse, dead as he led his troops to victory against the Moors. The crowd rose in a thunderous ovation for Reed and did not stop roaring until the Knicks were the new champions, and then the crowd chanted, "We're No. 1, we're No. 1," the same words in the same cadences that construction workers had used that morning after beating up young antiwar pickets in a well-organized attack on a Wall Street demonstration.

One is the most perishable of numbers. After a heady spring and summer of banquets, awards, endorsement contracts, and taped memoirs (Bradley, characteristically, was off on an extended Asian tour), the Knicks reassembled to find Alcindor, now in his second year, joined with the slick Oscar Robertson, middle-aged as a player but hungry for his first pro championship after nine seasons in Cincinnati. As expected, the Milwaukee Bucks won. The Knicks' "dynasty" was over before it reproduced, and so was the Sport of the Seventies: The national media had given basketball a boost that would keep it running at high speed for a few years, but they didn't stay on for the ride. Basketball was too black.

First of all, it was too black for the sportswriters. White males who had never understood Russell or Chamberlain or Hawkins or Abdul-Jabbar as individuals were suddenly faced with the first major sport in which they felt racially outnumbered and culturally alienated. There were black coaches, black general managers, rumors of a black commissioner. Two-thirds of the players were black. Sportswriters began floating the self-fulfilling prophesy that basketball had peaked because most fans were basically too racist to accept black heroes for their children. When sportswriters could, they covered white players; Dave Cowens, Pete Maravich, and Bill Walton, whether revered or ripped, got more attention than they deserved.

Those fans who did grow away from basketball for the sake of their children were probably less motivated by considerations of race than of class. Basketball was cheap—it reeked of settlement houses, schoolyards, rusty hoops on telephone poles. It had been their game because there was little else, and now it was "the city game" of junkies, purse snatchers, welfare cases. If the fans wanted something better, more expensive, exotic, difficult, suburban for their children, there was hockey, a perennial prep school favorite (remember *Love Story*?). Peewee leagues were being formed by the energetic ice rink owners who needed that 6 A.M. business to pay the interest on their building loans.

For sports investors, a pro hockey club offered the same tax shelter as a basketball franchise, the same local celebrity, and an even warmer feeling in the groin at meat-inspection time—the hockey players were mostly normal-sized, white, toothless, uneducated Canadian farmboys grateful to come south on nonresident alien visas while those black giants were not only pulling down enormous salaries and benefits but openly articulating their liberation from plantation sports. Robertson once told me that he had refused a plea to "cool" a ghetto uprising by informing the Cincinnati mayor's office that since their kind of white people had caused the underlying social problems, they could solve them, too; and, furthermore, until they started dealing old Oscar into their land grabs and stock swindles they had no call on him during their troubles.

A 1975 survey by *Newsday* showed that in fourteen of the twenty American cities that had both pro hockey and pro basketball franchises, the hockey team outdrew the basketball team. A losing hockey team often outdrew a winning basketball team. Violence, novelty, and racism were all suggested as factors in what appeared to be a hockey boom at the expense of a basketball decline. Actually, I'm more inclined to think that the rise and fall of basketball was announced by the same media chartists who declared baseball and God dead, and who announced the appearance and disappearance of the counterculture. The Sport of the Seventies, sold in 1969, was recalled in 1974; five-year decades may be the price of progress.

It would make little difference to SportsWorld, basketball or hockey or volleyball or j'ai lai. The arenas that house indoor sports are operated by businessmen, not fans. But the athletes, often victimized, frequently misunderstood, were no longer such amenable objects in the overall game. Bill Bradley, discussing his opposition to a pro basketball leagues merger in 1970, might have been speaking at any time for any athlete when he said, "The athlete is imbued with certain tenets held by society at large—work hard, be a millionaire, anyone can be president, if you make the most of what you have everything will be all right.

"Now he's a professional athlete, and he realizes that because he's an athlete he's not going to be a millionaire or the president or a really engaging intellectual mind, and the only thing left is to fly as high as his ability allows, and because he's a professional athlete this means, also, make as large a living as his ability allows.

"But, no, this is denied him, too. This leads to disillusion. And this isn't just an economic argument, it has to do with faith in one's society and in its collective achievement, its laws, its constitution."

CHAPTER
6
The Back Page

1

THE SO-CALLED Golden Age of Sports, the twenties and early thirties, was really the Golden Age of Sportswriting. The glories of the Babe, the Manassa Mauler, the Four Horsemen, were tunes composed on portable typewriters by gifted, ambitious, often cynical men who set customs and standards of sports journalism that are being dealt with to this day.

Without the aid and abetment of sportswriters, Judge Kenesaw Mountain Landis would never have been able to revirginize baseball after the 1919 Black Sox scandal, Tex Rickard would never have been able to introduce the million-dollar boxing gate, and college football would never have been able to grow into America's grandest monument to national hypocrisy. The Golden Age sportswriters hyped the country's post-World War I sports boom, rode the gravy train and then, for the good of the game, maintained the myths and legends as the country slid into a bust. Most of them must have agreed with the historian John A. Krout, who in 1929 wrote, "During depressions, with thousands out of work, sports help refocus our attention on the Great American values and ideals, and also help us to remember that life does not begin and end with the dollar."

The prototype superstar sportswriter of the Golden Age was Grantland Rice, columnist, broadcaster, sports newsreel commentator, who is best remembered for the opening paragraphs of his description of an Army–Notre Dame football game. It is the most famous lead in sports journalism history because it was both the most liberating and the most destructive. The following ap-

peared on the front page of the New York *Herald Tribune* on
October 19, 1924, under the headline, "Notre Dame's Cyclone
Beats Army":

"Outlined against a blue-gray October sky, the Four Horsemen
rode again. In dramatic lore they are known as Famine, Pesti-
lence, Destruction and Death. These are only aliases. Their real
names are Stuhldreher, Miller, Crowley and Layden. They
formed the crest of the South Bend cyclone before which another
fighting Army football team was swept over the precipice at the
Polo Grounds yesterday afternoon as 55,000 spectators peered
down on the bewildering panorama spread on the green plain
below.

"A cyclone can't be snared. It may be surrounded, but somewhere it breaks through to keep on going. When the cyclone
starts from South Bend, where the candle lights still gleam
through the Indiana sycamores, those in the way must take to
storm cellars at top speed. Yesterday the cyclone struck again as
Notre Dame beat the Army, 13–7, with a set of backfield stars
that ripped and crashed through a strong Army defense with
more speed and power than the warring cadets could meet."

Half-a-century later critics dismiss Grantland Rice with Red
Smith's gentle question: At what angle had Rice watched the
game to see the Notre Dame backfield outlined against the sky?
(I tend to concede Rice's point of view, having once described
the sun rising out of the Gulf of Mexico in a story filed from the
west coast of Florida. A friend on the desk, Tom Rogers, telegraphed: "Forget about Mets, please cover irregularity of sun.")

But the metaphors and hyperbole of Rice's opening paragraphs
liberated sportswriters from the traditional humdrum recitation
of points scored. They were free to exercise their imaginations
and flash their often prodigious stores of book-learning. There
had been lively sportswriters before Rice, but none so important
within the SportsWorld establishment. He was famous, he was
highly paid, he had a large following, and he was not using sports
journalism as a stepping-stone to political writing or fiction, as
did many of his betters, such as Damon Runyon, Ring Lardner,
Westbrook Pegler, Heywood Broun, Paul Gallico, and John R.
Tunis. Rice was a True Believer, even though (for the good of
the game) he wrote:

"When the One Great Scorer comes to write
against your name—
He marks—not that you won or lost—
but how you played the game."

Thanks to Rice, sportswriters embellished the games they
covered with Biblical allusion (David vs. Goliath was a favorite), with odd bits of Greek mythology and endless similes from
warfare, the assembly line, and natural phenomena. Clever
writers produced some amusing even self-mocking, metaphorical
stories in the twenties and thirties, but by my time it was pretty
much of a hack's technique, although we all used it when
jammed for time. It was a way of sugar-coating what might
otherwise be a dry pill of statistics. Of course, it got out of hand:
Stanford could never merely win a game, it was the Stanford
Indians, with stealth and a lightning attack, massacring the foe as
tacklers counted coup and ball carriers bit the dust. The practice
reached its logical conclusion, I hope, in a 1972 *New York Times*
story that began: "No longer called the Indians, Dartmouth's
football team went on the warpath anyway today..."

For all the excesses he is charged with fostering, Rice did help
open up sportswriting as surely as Knute Rockne made football a
more entertaining spectacle by popularizing the forward pass.
Like Rockne, Rice was a showman and he was successful. Even
jealous or disdainful colleagues had to be grateful for the positive
image of the sportswriter he was projecting to the public.

Whether his creative writing was good or bad, there was a
perverse honesty in Rice's approach: He was reporting a staged
spectacle in a mock-heroic manner, extending the entertainment
from the field to the page. The current debate over whether ballgames should be covered as hard news, like a fire, or as sociological indices, is absurd. If a game should be covered at all, beyond
a box of statistics in a paper of record or a consumer-oriented
evaluation, it might as well be in the spirit of the show, with
crunching adjectives and smashing verbs.

So much for Grantland Rice the Liberator. He was far more
potent as a SportsWorld propagandist. Painting a lily is not only
presumptuous, but ultimately destructive. The flower dies. By
layering sports with pseudo-myth and fakelore, by assigning

brutish or supernatural identities to athletes, the Rice-ites dehumanized the contests and made objects of the athletes.

The writer who criticizes a ballplayer for muffing a grounder, no matter how nasty he gets about it, is still dealing with the ballplayer within his context. He is judging the athlete as a working professional. But the writer who likens a ballplayer to Hercules or Grendel's mother is displaying the ultimate contempt—the ballplayer no longer exists as a person or a performer, but as an object, a piece of matter to be used, in this case, for the furtherance of the sportswriter's career by pandering to the emotional titillation of the reader/fan. Rice populated the press boxes with lesser talents who insisted, like the old master, that they were just sunny fellows who loved kids' games and the jolly apes who played them.

Rice's name often came up in the reminiscences of other sportswriters. He was one of the heroes of Jerome Holtzman's *No Cheering in the Press Box,* a rich collection of taped memoirs in which George Strickler, the retired sports editor of the *Chicago Tribune,* recalled the genesis of Rice's famous lead. It is a particularly instructive anecdote.

In 1924, Strickler was a sophomore at Notre Dame and was Knute Rockne's publicity man. Between halves of the Army game that year, he was standing in the aisle of the press box chatting with several sportswriters, including Rice. The score was tied, 7–7, he recalled, but the Notre Dame backfield was outstanding —"just like the Four Horsemen," said young Strickler. He does not admit to purposely sowing the seed. His mind was filled, he claims, with a movie he had seen earlier that week back in South Bend, Rudolph Valentino's first big hit, *The Four Horsemen of the Apocalypse.*

Strickler awoke the next morning to a press agent's dream, a winning team tagged with a Higher Symbolism. He quickly capitalized on it. He hired four horses on which he posed the Notre Dame backs. That famous photograph fixed Rice's lead in the nation's mind, made Stuhldreyer, Miller, Crowley, and Layden SportsWorld immortals, added another layer of gilt to the Golden Dome, and netted Strickler nearly $10,000 that year in picture royalties.

Rice's own recollection of the Four Horsemen episode is somewhat different. In his 1954 autobiography, *The Tumult and the Shouting*, Rice traced the seed of his lead to the 1923 Army–Notre Dame game, which he covered from the sidelines. On one end run, the four backs swept off the field and leaped over Rice, who was down on his knees. "It's worse than a cavalry charge," he told a companion. "They're like a wild horse stampede." A year later, he remembered his own quote, and refined it.

In 1928, four years after the Four Horsemen, on an autumn night before another Army–Notre Dame game, Rockne came up to Rice's Fifth Avenue apartment to drink by the fire and lay in the legend of George Gipp, the vagabond athlete who died of pneumonia after the 1920 season, his best. According to Rice, Rockne told him that Gipp's last words were these: "Rock, I know I'm going . . . but I'd like one last request. . . . Someday, Rock, sometime—when the going isn't so easy, when the odds are against us—ask a Notre Dame team to win a game for me, for the Gipper. I don't know where I'll be then, Rock, but I'll know about it and I'll be happy."

One imagines Rockne and Rice swirling their drinks and staring into the fire until the coach softly says, "Grant, I've never asked the boys to pull one out for Gipp. Tomorrow I might have to."

Tomorrow, of course, Jack Chevigny smashed into the end zone crying, "Here's one of them, Gipper," and Johnny (One-Play) O'Brien caught a pass for the other touchdown as the Fighting Irish beat the Cadets, 12–6. Rice wrote that he "knew they were playing with a 12th man—George Gipp," who "must have been very happy."

Rockne died in 1931, under somewhat less romantic circumstances. He had just signed as sales promotion manager of Studebaker, which was contemplating building a car called the Rockne, and he had been offered $50,000 to play the coach in RKO's version of *Good News*. He was en route to Hollywood to discuss both the RKO deal and a football movie for which he would serve as technical director and for which Rice would write the script, when his plane crashed in Kansas. He was just 43. As they say in SportsWorld, he went out a winner.

When Rockne died Grantland Rice was 50 years old, the so-called dean of American sportswriters and founder of what

Stanley Walker, the *Herald Tribune* city editor, called the "Gee Whiz" school of sports journalism. The founder of the "Aw Nuts" school was W. O. McGeehan, whose name invariably appears near the top of lists of all-time best sportswriters. McGeehan was celebrated for puncturing windbags, according to the listmakers, but there was a drop of poison at the tip of his needle. After years of traveling with Gene Tunney as a friend, McGeehan turned sour on the former heavyweight champion and his intellectual posturings. He began a story, which is often quoted, "Gene Tunney, who has written one book and read several others . . ."

But even the toughest "Aw Nuts" have a "Gee Whiz" somewhere under their shells. While McGeehan could snicker at those who "compare a fat young man swinging a club at a little ball to Thor of the Hammer," he unleashed his own metaphors for Lindbergh, "the perfect sportsman."

In his *Herald Tribune* column, "Down the Line," McGeehan wrote, "Hermes, of the winged foot, alighting on a 'heaven kissed hill,' never carried a more important message, even from Olympus, than did his successor, young Lindbergh. And not the least significant part of the message is that it took the clear eyes of youth to see the way and the indomitable spirit of youth to keep on it to the end."

One man's god is another man's jock. Reviewed through hindsight and history, McGeehan looks a little foolish, not so much for pulling out all his stops for Captain Prometheus, but for not realizing that Lindbergh and the Babe were SportsWorld brothers under the skin.

By the late thirties, Rice and McGeehan were both old school. Young men were climbing into the press box who had grown up reading the Golden Agers and knew that the ballpark was a motherlode of story material and that the sports department was a wide-open town for wordslingers with talent, no matter how idiosyncratic. The three most important writers of this new generation were Jimmy Cannon, Red Smith, and Arthur Daley, all nationally syndicated and New York-based, but each totally different from the others in style and sensibility.

They did not form new schools of sportswriting so much as they inspired the next generation by extending the possibilities of the craft. And they broadened SportsWorld's spheres of influence. Cannon's passion and Smith's wit and Daley's prestige helped make America's second major postwar sports boom seem not only significant and interesting, but somehow psychohistorically inevitable, like manifest destiny.

Cannon was a high school dropout who educated himself by voracious reading and relentless conversation. He was born in what he called the "unfreaky" part of Greenwich Village in 1909, the son of a minor Tammany Hall politician, and he began his career as a 14-year-old office boy on the *Daily News*. At 16 he was a rewrite man. His heroes in journalism were Ben Hecht, Westbrook Pegler, and Damon Runyon, whom he met while covering the Lindbergh kidnapping trial. Runyon thought he had a "natural style," and talked him into leaving Hearst's *Journal* for a job as sportswriter on Hearst's *American*.

Cannon became Runyon's protege and, eventually, a self-consciously Runyonesque character himself, a "night guy" who lived in a hotel off Times Square, ate breakfast in Lindy's at noon, dated Broadway actresses, hung out at Toots Shor's, the Stork Club, The Friars, cultivated cops and crooks, closed down the city from a rear table in the Stage Delicatessen, if he wasn't in Las Vegas or Miami Beach. He never married and had no children, but among his spiritual descendants were such worthy and grateful sons as Pete Hamill and Jimmy Breslin, with whom he characteristically quarreled—Cannon was a competitor and he saw them as challengers.

In his heyday, the late forties and fifties, Cannon posed as a romantic tough guy—Humphrey Bogart with a typewriter. He wrote, "I think of a girl standing on a bridge in Prague and beyond were the onion-shaped churches. She asked a question history answered for her. 'What is to become of us?' she wanted to know. Who stands on that bridge now?"

He overwrote. "The fog of time conceals the filth of the vanished years. Distance donates a bogus tranquility."

Once, in the fifties, he chilled me with a description of the J.C. Penney clothes fitted to mannequins set up on a desert A-bomb target to test reaction to heat and blast. Of all his contemporaries, Cannon was the most socially conscious. He saw and wrote about racism in sports long before it was fashionable to do so, and his assessment of psychoanalysis—"Freud gave a whole

generation a way to cop out"—seems less outrageous now than
when he said it.

He had his own spiny integrity—he turned down Sinatra's request to collaborate on an autobiography because the singer
wouldn't tell everything—yet he looked upon sportswriters as
"the vaudevillians of journalism" and was quick to take his own
turns. "It was always the policy in my old neighborhood that a
guy was a fool if he fell in love with a girl he couldn't knock
down with the first punch."

His column devices were frequently parodied, but no one since
has come up with the likes of

"GUARANTEED TO HAPPEN AT ANY RACETRACK—An
absolute stranger will claim a jockey winked at him in the pad-
dock as a sign the horse can't lose."

"YOU'RE WILLIE MAYS—Kids forget the squalor of their
childhood as they emulate the shambling urgency of your gait."

"NOBODY ASKED ME BUT—I'm depressed when I see a
homely young girl drinking a midnight soda alone at a fountain
on a Saturday night."

By the time I met Cannon in the early sixties he was a crabby,
opinionated, lonely, middle-aged "sportwriter" railing incessantly at most younger writers, all liberals, and black militants.
His time had passed, the Broadway scene was dead, but he had
neither the capacity for change nor the willingness to step back
into an elder statesman's role. After his brilliant postwar years at
the *New York Post*, a relatively liberal independent paper, he had
gone back home to Hearst's reactionary *Journal-American* for a
rumored $1000 a week, which made him the country's highest-
paid sports columnist. He was not popular among other writers.
He had a wicked tongue. After putting someone down, especially
another sportswriter, he would crow, "I zinged 'im pretty good,
huh?" repeating the "huhs?" until you agreed. When he was on
target the zinger stuck forever. Among his most famous lines was
the question he asked Leonard Koppett as that statistically ori-
ented sportswriter climbed into a press box carrying a heavy
briefcase—"Whatcha got in there, Lennie, decimal points?"

By the late sixties, when New York was down to three daily
newspapers, none of which carried his column, he was a carica-
ture of Jimmy Cannon. He became an Ancient Mariner button-

holing new boys to repeat the best lines of the column he had just filed. He was on the phone incessantly, for hours, reminding the Big Apple he was still around. For years, his column had reached out and grabbed New York by the lapels for him, he could walk into Toots' or the Garden or the Stadium pressroom and there would be people discussing what he had just written. Now, in New York, he couldn't even stroll down to a newsstand and buy himself.

Even his technique was obsolete. The old sporting scene was now fragmented. The traditional midtown "watering holes" were usually deserted of athletes, sportswriters and publicists. The new moguls—lawyers and agents—all returned each evening to their suburbs. There was no place to hang out where he could be sure of "picking up stuff for the column."

Along with other newspapermen, Cannon became more dependent on making postgame locker-room hits, but the locker rooms were more crowded now and the younger athletes were more responsive to the demands of television interviewers. Cannon asked good, sharp questions in a crowd, but pack journalism was not his style, and he began to write more and more out of his head. And as he got older and his column appeared in fewer papers and his favorite subjects, Joe Louis and Joe DiMaggio, became less important to sports page readers, Cannon turned sour. He wrote columns that seemed to rage at a dawn he was trying to hold back. His prose became wilder and more purple, parodies of Jimmy Cannon columns without the inside dope and the pinpoint reporting that had made the originals click. I think he sometimes attacked people in his columns for the human contact of a counterattack: I thought of slum kids who cursed cops to get a response that confirmed their existence.

His relationship with younger sportswriters was complicated. On one hand, he had a generously fraternal attitude toward all newspapermen. On the other, he had a jealously competitive spirit. It was Cannon who labeled as "Chipmunks" (because, he said, they reminded him of furry little animals scampering and chattering and clustering in the press box) a lively and talented group of young afternoon paper writers who would, collectively, make as important an impact on their times as he had, alone, made on his. Cannon found fault with the Chipmunks' clothing, hairstyles, their frontal interview techniques, their choice of subjects (Jim Bouton, for example, was an early Chip hero, as was Bo Belinsky), and their demeanor in public places. Yet Cannon realized that if he was not the Chipmunks' spiritual father, he was at least their uncle, and he genuinely liked and respected some of them. They, in turn, were pleased by his attention, and they institutionalized Chipmunkhood although they were no mob: Phil Pepe, Larry Merchant, Stan Isaacs, and Maury Allen, among others, approached games and life and writing with distinctly separate styles.

Cannon suffered a crippling stroke in 1971 and died on December 5, 1973. Red Smith waved goodbye in a column that shared its final tribute with a recently deceased race horse, Count Fleet. "No disrespect to Jim," claimed Smith.

Stanley Woodward brought Red to New York in 1945, at the age of 40. Born in Green Bay, Wisconsin, graduated from Notre Dame, Smith covered general news and sports in Milwaukee, St. Louis, and Philadelphia before joining the *Herald Tribune* and plugging into national syndication. By a process he describes as opening a vein and squeezing out one drop of blood at a time, Red easily outdistanced all previous records for consistently producing the purest, most crystalline, most delightful fresh running prose in sports.

In university English departments he was regarded as a "minor American stylist," no small praise. Whether Red was "rocking from cheek to cheek" in a Helsinki sauna in 1952 or covering baseball in 1963—"The Yankees are slobs/Who are good at their jobs./Us losers, we worship the Mets"—he was that rarest of newspapermen, the perceptive and complete reporter who could enlighten and entertain in elegant style, on deadline.

Red's impact on the technique of sportswriting was inspirational, but not direct. His talent was too large and special for his style to be successfully imitated. However, the mere presence of that talent on sports pages throughout America lifted the level of sportswriting: Readers raised their expectations, editors demanded better writing, and more young writers could now consider the sports department worthy of their talents.

Red plinked major league greed and amateur hypocrisy and official pomposity, the traditional targets of the better sportswriters, but his aim was to tickle, not disable. When he did set his lance at men or issues, they were usually too small to matter or too big to care. Through most of his career Red's talent was spent polishing the SportsWorld silver, and the generation who read him believed that everything was basically all right in sports because Red, who lent the weight of his own repute to the values of the game, never said anything was basically wrong.

Unlike most writers, however, Smith's scope has broadened and his thinking has become more flexible as he has grown older. By the time he reached *The Times* in 1971, as my replacement, he was displaying a remarkably fresh new approach to sports and a raised consciousness. Red himself has commented on the change, and attributed it to his second wife, "who is younger and more of today than I was," and "five stepchildren who are very much of the current generation."

"I won't deny that the heavy majority of sportswriters, myself included, have been and still are guilty of puffing up the people they write about," Red told Holtzman for *No Cheering in the Press Box*. "If we've made heroes out of them, and we have, then we must also lay a whole set of false values at the doorsteps of historians and biographers. Not only has the athlete been blown up larger than life, but so have the politicians and celebrities in all fields, including rock singers and movie stars.

"When you go through Westminster Abbey you'll find that excepting for the little poets' corner almost all of the statues and memorials are to killers. To generals and admirals who won battles, whose specialty was human slaughter. I don't think they're such glorious heroes."

The sportswriter is certainly no more guilty of "Godding up those ballplayers," as Woodward phrased it, than are political reporters or foreign correspondents or cultural reporters of enhancing their subjects' wisdom or grandeur or appeal. But just because the sportswriter is in "the toy department" dealing with "fun and games" in which no one is purposely killed, starved, or made homeless, that is no alibi for acting any less professional. In fact, the sportswriter should feel a greater responsibility for complete and honest reporting because his job is basically so easy— what other newsmen have their subjects and their events so visible and so accessible?

If Red Smith was the son of McGeehan and Pegler, and if Jimmy Cannon was whelped by Runyon, then Arthur Daley sprang full-blown from the brow of Grantland Rice. In the manner of Rice, Arthur was determinedly sunny, rarely wrote about people he didn't like, and performed uncountable acts of violence upon the fair bodies of Metaphor and Classical Allusion.

Smith and Cannon were essentially writers who happened onto sports. Daley, tall and athletic like Rice, became a writer to extend his sporting life. In his junior year at Fordham, Arthur broke his left arm in a football pile-up. It would not be fully healed until the varsity baseball season. So, to occupy his convalescence during the basketball season, Arthur joined the weekly Fordham *Ram* as assistant sports editor. As a senior, he was sports editor and columnist.

Three months after graduation in 1926 he joined *The Times* as a sports reporter. He was 22. Ten years later he covered the 1936 Olympics in Berlin, the first *Times* sportswriter to go abroad on assignment. On Christmas Eve, 1942, he replaced the original "Sports of the Times" columnist, John Kieran, who apparently was made to choose between *The Times* and the radio show *Information Please*. Kieran's column was ostentatiously erudite and "literate"; Kieran was a penner of rhyme, an aggressive "nature lover," an academic commando whose Greek and Latin obscured a nineteenth-century sensibility. Arthur was given the column "until further notice," and by the time he was no longer intimidated by Kieran's shadow and felt secure enough to put his own imprint on the column he was on a merry-go-round that must have felt like a treadmill. He produced nearly 1000 words each day, for seven, later six, days each week.

He cranked out more than the equivalent of three novels a year, and to assemble the wordage he traveled, interviewed, attended events, made telephone calls, answered mail, filled out expense accounts, conferred with editors, read sports books, magazine articles, and competing sports pages. He amassed an enormous sports file. There was little time to think, to take his wife to the movies, or play ball with his sons. The price was professional as well as personal—there was no time to keep up with the world.

When I began reading Daley regularly in 1957 he was the best-known writer on *The Times*, and ex officio the country's most influential sports journalist. He had just won the Pulitzer Prize for local reporting without pressure of deadline, the first sportswriter so honored, although two others had received Pulitzer awards. His column was nationally syndicated, and in many other papers it was titled, simply, "Arthur Daley," with a postage-stamp picture of him on top. He was very popular among his colleagues because he was unfailingly friendly and helpful, dignified without being stuffy, and generally noncompetitive. He was willing to use his *Times*-based prestige for the common good, such as improved working conditions at an event or access to a reluctant subject.

Sportswriters of my generation ridiculed his stilted, bowdlerized quotes and charged him with relaying a false image of sports —the Daley version certainly did not prepare me for that first run-in with Mantle. In exciting times, Arthur extolled the past and rewrote himself. Bill Klem and the Babe, Jesse Owens and Bronko Nagurski, the Flying Dutchman and the Fordham Flash and the Whizzer, the Gipper, the Clipper, and the Happy Hidalgo were still young in his columns. Arthur exuded a boy's delight at meeting athletes, although more and more often he was better known than the man he was interviewing, whose words he copied down on unlined paper on his omnipresent clipboard. Arthur could never quite cope with the self-promoting, draft-avoiding, Allah-worshipping Muhammad Ali, so he recalled the 1960 Cassius Clay, who had charmed him in Rome, and called Ali "misguided." Magnanimously, he wished Ali happiness.

If his column often seemed untouched by the convulsions in the locker room and beyond, so did he seem untouched by time and experience. In Tokyo or Paris or Mexico City he demanded his breakfast eggs and 6 P.M. meat and potatoes, and his God-fearing, right and wrong, decent, honorable, true-blue, all-American, clean "civilization." *Herald Tribune* baseball writer Harold Rosenthal's epitaph for such transient workers as sportswriters—"The road will make a bum of the best of them"—did not apply to Arthur.

He was not a graceful writer, and his simple-minded columns

maintained outworn myths. Yet I think that his readership, educated and sophisticated, accepted him as a gentle trivialist offering them morning mind-breaks. Arthur sensed this and performed accordingly. He was an old-timey anecdotalist, a sports folk-singer with few pretentions. He gave pleasure.

But young sportswriters on other papers who felt they were up against King Arthur of *The Times* saw him as the enemy, the champion of all that was repressive and reactionary in sports. Arthur would have been bewildered and anxious to think that such bright sports columnists as Stan Isaacs, Len Shecter, Larry Merchant, Jerry Izenberg, Sandy Padwe, Ira Berkow, and Pete Axthelm took him so seriously and in trying to counteract his influence advanced the progress of sports journalism.

Professionally, I could not have created a more convenient person with whom to share a column. We were usually diametrically opposed on major issues. We saw all events so differently that it was sometimes incredible that we often had been sitting together. We could perform a joint interview and select entirely different quotes. We were thus perfect foils for each other and we provided *Times* readers with a polarized view of sports (a few actually complained there was no middle-of-the-road). We could plan our schedules independently without fear of duplicating each other.

My age-group counterparts on other papers seemed pleased when I started covering Arthur's sins of omission—the growing discontent of athletes, racism, sexism, distorted nationalism, the sports-politics interface. By appearing in *The Times*, these stories got instant credibility. It became easier for other writers to get such stories past their own editors. Such is the power-by-default of *The Times*. Parenthetically, I was not waging any lonely, courageous avant-garde action at *The Times*—I was generally given my head, and my copy was rarely questioned. The same lax policy toward sports that had allowed Daley to write his way for twenty-five years now applied to me.

Personally, my relations with Arthur were warm and mutually respectful. He was helpful and encouraging. He taught me creative expense accounting and he introduced me to his friends and news sources. He shared what he knew of *Times* intrigue. We

were infrequent social companions out of town, but I have a
number of warm memories of him. We shared a room at the
Ali–Liston fight in Lewiston, Maine, and I remember one night
we both tucked in early and Arthur sat at the foot of my bed and
told me old boxing stories. I was 27 years old at the time and
generally brimming with myself, but that night I was folded into
a dream of cozy childhood.

Arthur died on January 3, 1974, on the way to the office, six
months from a forced retirement. He died, wrote his son Robert,
the novelist, with "the next column moving about in his head,
where it stayed."

Once, when writing about Arthur for *The Times'* house organ,
I called Joe DiMaggio, who said of him, "I've watched the way
he works. He'd be there, at a mass interview, hanging at the
edges, taking it all down. Then he'd get his man in a corner,
alone. He'd never come on strong. Shy and quiet and serious and
friendly, he'd look you straight in the eye. With a little smile. I
knew I could trust him from the first day I met him."

2

The first time I saw Dick Tiger he was waiting for me in front of
the old Madison Square Garden, a homburg perched on top of
his head. The homburg was much too small, and I thought he
looked comical. It was years before I learned that he always
bought his hats a size too small so he could share them with his
brothers back home in Nigeria.

I introduced myself to Tiger and he shook my hand gravely.
Then he turned and began moving down Eighth Avenue on the
balls of his feet, like a big black cat. His manager and I followed.

"Nigerian fighters are very good, very tough," said his manager. "They're closer to the jungle."

Over his shoulder, Tiger said, "There is no jungle in Nigeria."

"It's just an expression, Dick, just a figure of speech," said the
manager. "I mean they're hungry fighters."

Tiger stopped. "Hungry fighters." He winked at me. "We eat
hoo-mon bee-inks. Medium rare."

We walked a mile and a half to the gym where he was training because Tiger would not consider a cab, even if I paid. It was said around town that Tiger had the terminal cheaps. I followed him into a dressing room and watched him shed the comedy of his clothes. As the homburg, the brown sports jacket, the blue tie and white shirt disappeared into a rusty metal locker, Tiger seemed to grow larger. The blue tribal tattoos across his chest and back rippled over knotty muscle. He seemed suddenly savage, dangerous.

But there was only gentleness in his eyes, and humor twitched at the corners of his wide mouth. I watched him tape his hands with great care, slowly, first winding the dirty gray bandages around and around, then placing the sponge across the knuckles, then wrapping on the adhesive. I asked him why he didn't have his manager or trainer take care of this daily chore now that he was middleweight champion of the world.

"I am a travelin' man, and I got to do things myself, a fighter should know these things," he said. "This is my business. I don't want to spoil myself for someday when there is no one around to help me."

He was 34 years old at the time, and had been champion for less than a year. He was training in New York, where facilities and sparring partners were the best, for the second defense of that championship, to be held in Ibadan, Nigeria. Tiger was taking this fight very seriously. It would be Nigeria's first world title fight, and his own real homecoming. "It is very important I win," he said. "For pride. They receive me different, people, when I am champion."

This was June 1963, and I had interviewed few fighters. I watched Tiger work out for two hours, methodically, intensely, oblivious to sound and movement around him. Great silver globules of sweat formed, swelled, exploded on his forehead, and he never wiped them away. He weighed about 160 pounds then, and his 5-foot 8-inch body was unusually hard and fit. His calisthenics were so violent that they seemed beyond human tolerance; I was sure his eyes would pop out of his head as he twisted his neck, that his muscles and veins would burst through his skin.

We talked again after he was finished. His voice was softer now, his body more relaxed. He had been born in Amaigbo, a

remote Eastern Nigerian town in the rain forests of the Binin
River delta, a town that appeared on few maps. He was raised on
a farm and educated in English and Ibo at an Anglican mission
school. At 19, he went to the city of Aba to work in his brother's
grocery store. At a local boys' club he learned to box.

He had been christened Richard Ihetu, Ibo for "what I want,"
but assumed the ring name Dick Tiger for his early pro fights
against the likes of Easy Dynamite and Super Human Power. He
kept the name when a British promoter brought him to England
to fight on the Blackpool-Liverpool circuit. He was lonely and
chilled in the dank foreign gyms, and he lost his first four fights.
Letters from his family in Nigeria were beseeching him to give
up the foolishness and return to his father's farm or his brother's
grocery store. Tiger gave himself one more chance. In his fifth
fight, Tiger knocked out a Liverpool boy in ninety seconds, and
Richard Ihetu, farmer and clerk, disappeared forever.

He first came to America in 1959 and lived in third-rate Manhattan hotels with his pregnant wife, cooking meals on a hot
plate and running in Central Park. He slowly gained a reputation
among boxing promoters as an honest workman. He was always
in top condition, he always gave his best. He would never be
spectacular, he did not have a great deal of boxing finesse or
personal "color," but he was dependable and tough. His wife
gave birth to twins, then a third child in 1960. Tiger sent her
back to Nigeria and began commuting between New York and
Aba. Now he lived in fourth-rate hotels, walked whenever possible, window-shopped for entertainment, sent every penny
home. After he won the title in 1962 he was able to send more
money home, but he did not improve the quality of his living
conditions or his clothing. I asked him if he was saving his money
for something special.

"This will not always be my business. I want money," he said,
rubbing his fingers together, "$600,000 to start a big business.
Now all I have is a house and a Peugeot, that is all."

We left the gym together and took a subway uptown. We
made small talk on the ride, and he told me the only tiger he had
ever seen was in a cage in the Liverpool zoo. My stop came first.
I got off the train, and looked back at him through the window.
In his clothes again he was just a chunky man in a too-small

homburg, hanging from an overhead strap, jostled by a rush-hour crowd.

I went back to the office and wrote a tidy Sunday feature story, my specialty. A month later, I read that he had won his bout in Ibadan. I was glad of that, which surprised me: The results of sporting events almost never moved me. Something about Tiger had touched me.

In December of that year, 1963, he defended his title against Joey Giardello in Atlantic City. It was my first championship fight, and my notes were unusually voluminous and included the first stanza of the Nigerian anthem, which was played before the fight began. "Nigeria, we hail thee,/Our own dear native land./Though tribe and tongue may differ/In brotherhood we stand."

Tiger lost the fifteen-round fight by a decision. I knew he would be very upset. He had become a national hero in Nigeria: He had been awarded a medal, Member of the British Empire, in Lagos, and he was amassing property in Aba. In a few days he would be returning home a loser.

But the next morning he smiled at me and said amiably, "Look at my face. I don't look like I was in a fight last night. I did a bit of dancing last night with Giardello and I am a fighter not a dancer. I thought I did enough to win, as he kept running away."

He shrugged and sighed. "These days you get a title by running away."

We shook hands gravely and said goodbye. I would have liked to tell him that I was sorry he had lost, but the words stuck in my throat. It seemed somehow unprofessional, and Tiger was a professional.

Giardello promised Tiger a rematch within six months, but it was two years before the fighters met again. Giardello enjoyed his championship hugely and did nothing to endanger it, like fighting someone who might take it away. Tiger, meanwhile, waited patiently and rarely fought: His reputation as a head-down, hands-up, straight-ahead slugger who plodded into his opponent and beat away scared off anyone who didn't need to fight him for a payday or a shot at the title.

By the time they met again I was a regular boxing writer, veteran of the Clay–Liston spectacles, a seasoned observer who knew A. J. Liebling's *The Sweet Science* almost by heart. I even kept my own scorecard, which usually conflicted with the judges'. I was also a great deal more appreciative of Dick Tiger now that I had interviewed many other boxers and watched them train and fight. Of all athletes, boxers are generally the friendliest, the funkiest, and the most dedicated, and Tiger had the most heart and soul of them all.

I liked Joey Giardello but I was secretly rooting for Tiger to win back his title the night of the rematch in Madison Square Garden. Tiger was shorter and lighter and older than Giardello, but from the opening bell, when a Nigerian *etulago* set a thumping drumbeat, Tiger doggedly followed Giardello around the ring, pressing and battering and slugging. Giardello stayed on his feet as a point of pride. At the start of the fifteenth and last round, with the decision certain for Tiger, Giardello leaned forward and whispered, "Nice fight."

Tiger did not hold the title very long this time either. He was over 36 years old now, and the strain of keeping his weight below the 160-pound middleweight limit sapped his strength. Emile Griffith, the welterweight champion, who could no longer keep his weight below 147 pounds, moved up in class and beat him. So, logically, Tiger decided to move up in class, too. In the winter of 1966 he beat the brilliant but erratic José Torres and became light-heavyweight champion. The morning after that fight I visited his shabby hotel room. He greeted me with the same amiable win-or-lose smile.

"The people all said that Tiger is finished, that he looks a hundred years old, and now they come around to pat my head and tell me I'm a good boy." He shrugged. "That's life."

His investments in Nigeria were doing well, he told me, although he was concerned by the mounting violence and political instability. Many thousands of his fellow Ibo tribesmen had been slaughtered in pogroms in northern Nigeria. The Ibo, who were Christians, were civil servants and small businessmen in the Moslem north. Ibo were fleeing back to their eastern native lands. Tiger's holdings were in Aba, in the eastern region, where he lived in a large air-conditioned home, owned several buildings, operated several businesses and shops, and had a chauffeur for his Mercedes Benz limousine. He was still optimistic about the future of his six children and the many nieces and nephews he took pride and joy in supporting.

Tiger fought Torres again the following spring, as usual giving away height and weight and age, and he beat him again. This time, when the decision was announced fights broke out in the balcony and bottles of wine and rum smashed on the Garden floor and sprayed the crowd with shards of glass. There was blood and a number of injuries. I wrote most of my story crouched under the Garden ring with my typewriter on my knees. The incident was discussed and written about for several days, and then dismissed as one of those cultural-ethnic-economic-sporting inevitabilities. Garden officials blamed "a few nuts or hoodlums" who wanted to read about themselves in the papers. Torres said he was proud of his fellow Puerto Ricans for showing their "support" of him, and Lipsyte analyzed the random violence as an expression of the class struggle. The Boxing Commissioner declared, "A hundred years ago Charles Dickens went to a fight with William Makepeace Thackery and wrote about a riot in London."

It was an ironic send-off for Tiger, who flew back home into the Nigerian civil war.

The next time I saw him, in March of 1968, the smile was gone. His mouth was twisted, his voice high and tense. His square hands plucked at his baggy gray suit pants.

"I used to be a happy man, but now I have seen something I have never seen before. I read about killing and war, but I had never seen such things. Now, I have seen massacres."

He bounded from the straight-backed hotel chair and began fishing in his bureau drawers, through pamphlets and books and newspaper clippings. "Ah, here," he said, almost reverentially opening tissue paper. "This is Aba." He spread the photographs on the bed.

"The hospital. There were eight patients and a doctor when the planes came and threw bombs around. Hired pilots. The Nigerians can't fly planes. They are a thousand years behind civilization; that is why they are doing everything wrong.

"The open market, look at that. In that corner, that is a hand. A little girl's hand. What does she know of war? This woman burned. These men dead, not even soldiers. This is a woman, too. No, it is not rags, it was a woman."

He carefully repacked the photographs, and sat down again. "The Nigerian radio says Dick Tiger of Nigeria will defend his light-heavyweight championship against Bob Foster in Madison Square Garden on May 24. Dick Tiger of Nigeria. They still claim me and they would kill me, they want to kill us all. I am a Biafran. And we just want to live."

I asked him about his family, which now included seven children. He said he had moved them back to Amaigbo while he tended his businesses in Aba. "I do not worry so much anymore. The children have learned to take cover quickly when they hear the planes. It is the fighter planes we worry about. The bombs fall slowly. If you see them you can run away. But, you never see the bullets."

Foster knocked him cold in the fourth round of their fight. Tiger went straight down, his head smacked the canvas sickeningly. He twitched on his back like a turtle on its shell. He had to be helped up. Back in his dressing room he managed a smile at the crowd, which included various countrymen, boxing buffs, and Giardello. "Since I been winning I never had my fans stay in my dressing room so long. Now, I'm a loser and everybody's here. I guess I am a good man."

He left the United States without his light-heavyweight title, but with enough currency to buy a plane load of tinned meat and powdered milk in Lisbon and fly it into Biafra.

In the summer of 1968 there were reports of 6000 Ibos a day dying of malnutrition and disease and wounds. Occasionally we would hear that Tiger was dead, too. And sometimes we would hear that he was hiding out in Brooklyn.

He reappeared in September to fight an upcoming young light-heavyweight, Frankie DePaula.

I visited him in training. I was completing my first year as a columnist, and I had tried to stay away from boxing, to break the identification and establish my credentials in other sports. But Tiger had become a touchstone for me; I think I derived some symbolic nourishment watching him tape his own hands. The honest, independent workman, a man of dignity and courage.

"If I had been a flashy fellow," he told me, "with fancy clothes and many women and big cars and nightclubs every night, I would have trouble. But I have never been a flashy fellow, I eat what there is to eat, I just dress, you know ..."

"And still you have nothing now."

"This is true. I saved all my money and brought it home. I had apartment buildings in Lagos and Port Harcourt and Aba, and a movie and factories and shops and now, with the shelling, I guess it is all gone. Everything I have saved. But I am not sorry. If I had been a flashy fellow when I had lots of money, what would I do with myself now?"

He was training in the evenings now because he could no longer afford professional sparring partners; he sparred against dockers coming off work. He spent his days at the Biafra Mission, reading cables and dispatches. He disputed reports in American newspapers that the Nigerians were in complete control of almost all the cities.

"In every city they are still fighting," he said. "The Biafran fights to the end, the Nigerian will kill him anyway. The plan is to kill every Biafran over 2 years old. Then all the children will pray to the sun and moon instead of God, and never know who their fathers were. That is why we fight to survive."

We walked out of the dressing room to the training ring. In the hallway, a schoolboy caught his own reflection in the mirror of a vending machine, and jabbed at it.

Tiger smiled. "When I was young, if I ever saw my shadow I had to fight it, I always boxed at mirrors. No more. I am just one old man."

He was 39, and he seemed even older in his fight with De-Paula. Tiger won, but in the late rounds I thought he seemed to be melting like a used black candle.

He took his money and disappeared again.

I didn't see him for more than a year, my second year as a columnist and probably the most interesting. The Mexico City Olympics. The Jets Super Bowl. The Aqueduct Boycott. The Mets World Series. The start of the Knicks' first championship season.

The rehabilitation of Muhammad Ali began: Liberals discovered that his antiwar stand was compatible with theirs, even if his racial views were not, and sprang to defend his constitutional rights. Together they would prove that the American legal system worked perfectly for anyone with the money and the power to go all the way.

I began to wish I had more time to think and read and talk to people, to stop writing so much and with such assurance. Columnists have to write with assurance because they are paid to raise the Truth. As that second year slipped into a third year, as the column became progressively easier to write, as my work brought me greater access to people I wanted to talk with, I found I was less and less sure of what I absolutely knew. Was I growing wiser, losing my nerve, taking myself too seriously, getting bored? Was I over the hill, choking in the clutch, hearing footsteps, getting fat? Describe your malady, SportsWorld has a metaphor for it.

In November of 1969 Tiger sluggishly won a dreary decision over a light-heavyweight no one had heard of before or would hear of again, a victory that had meaning only when translated into milk and salt and meat. On December 5 we sat down at a table in a publicity office of the Garden to discuss a matter that had suddenly become very urgent to Tiger. The medal he had received in Lagos in 1963 had grown too heavy in his mind to keep. When he read that John Lennon had returned his Member of the British Empire award for reasons that included Britain's involvement in the Nigerian civil war, Tiger decided to mail back his medal, too. But he needed help with the accompanying letter. Garden officials had not wanted to become involved in his protest, and had called Dave Anderson, then covering boxing for *The Times.* Dave called me.

I had misgivings. I felt I was stepping over some invisible boundary—an unsurveyed one, but a boundary nevertheless. I had always been contemptuous of those sportswriters who acted as go-betweens for professional clubs and city governments, for high school athletes and college recruiters, for out-of-work coaches and potential employers. They were no longer honest journalists, I thought; they could no longer be trusted by their readers. They were supposed to cover stories, not make them happen.

I rationalized it, of course: I had known and written about Tiger for more than six years, he had always been cooperative and friendly, it was the least I could do to help him out; I would be his amanuensis, no more, not a single idea or even word of mine would slip into the letter; it would make a good column for my readers, my kind of column, a famous athlete taking a princi-

pled stand on a headline issue that transcended sports. I didn't
think This is a very important cause, life, freedom, justice, I
should be involved and make a worthwhile contribution as a
human being. In those days I thought being an honest journalist
was enough.

We wrote the letter and addressed it to the British Ambassador, Washington, D.C.

"I am hereby returning the M.B.E. because every time I look
at it I think of millions of men, women and children who died
and are still dying in Biafra because of the arms and ammunition
the British Government is sending to Nigeria and its continued
moral support of this genocidal war against the people of Biafra."

He signed it, Dick Tiger Ihetu.

We walked across Eighth Avenue in the brilliant, chilly afternoon and up the post office steps. Tiger said, "If they ask me how
much it's worth, what should I say?"

I shrugged. "We should try to pawn it and find out."

"I'll say a million dollars." Tiger laughed for the first time. "I'll
say fifty or a hundred, just so it gets there."

The clerk behind the registry wicket hefted the package and
shook his head. "No good, you got Scotch Tape on it. Go around
the corner, they'll give you some brown paper."

Another line. He stood very quietly, a small black hat perched
on his head, his body muffled in a fur-lined coat. I would always
remember him for being overdressed and patient. He was always
cold, and he was always willing to wait, for a bout, for a return
bout, for a shot at a title. He was 40 then, picking up fights
wherever he could, waiting for one more big payday. If there had
been no war, he would be retired now, in Aba, a rich man. He
had been financially wiped out, but he said he could not complain, many others had lost all their property, and many, many
others had lost their families and their lives.

A clerk finally handed Tiger a long strip of gummed brown
paper and a wet sponge in a glass dish. Tiger took it to a writing
desk and began to tear the brown paper into small strips, his
thick fingers careful and precise, the fingers of a man who had
taped his own hands.

When he finished the package he proudly held it up for me.
"Now I know there is something else I can do."

We waited for the registry clerk silently. "Okay," he said, nodding at the package, then flipping it. "What's in it?"

"A medal," said Tiger softly.

"What?"

"A medal."

"What's it worth?"

"I don't know. Fifty, hundred dollars?"

"No value," said the clerk, to himself. He weighed it, registered it, asked Tiger if he wanted it to go airmail. Tiger said, "Yes."

"One sixty."

Tiger gave him two dollar bills, and counted his change. He readjusted his scarf as he walked out into the bright street, and smiled, and shook my hand gravely and could only say, "Well . . ." and shrug, and start down the steps. I never saw him again.

It was a good column. It drew much favorable comment and mail, and it won a prize as best sports news-feature of the year. But I did not mention in the column that I had helped Tiger write his letter, and I have never resolved my feelings about that, or about the involvement of journalists and the use of journalists. After awhile I wondered if I just wasn't being a bit too fine, and beating my breast like a drum.

That summer, on vacation, I read that Tiger had lost a ten-round decision to Emile Griffith. I figured that should end any chance he had for major bouts. Would he now take short pay-nights as an opponent, a trial horse for new contenders? I made a note to call him when I got back to work, but never did.

Ali came back that fall. The afternoon of his fight against Quarry, Shecter and Plimpton and I sat in his training cottage outside Atlanta and met his "Jew brains," the lawyers and accountants he had collected to take care of "my corporations, my businesses, my financial dealings." We all took a walk around the neighborhood. Ali found a seven-foot pole in the wet grass along the road and brandished it like a prophet's staff.

"History is being made, a walk with the champion." He looked slyly down at me. "Most writers wonder where the champ is, what he's thinkin'. 'Oh, if I could just talk to him on the telephone.' And here you're walkin' with him. Something to tell your grandchildren."

LBJ at the ranch, JFK at Hyannisport, it must always be the

same thing, I thought, invite a few friendly journalists into the vestibule of the great one's existence while reminding them how lucky they are to be here, and at what narrow sufferance. As if it really mattered in this case. No matter what I wrote about Ali now, I was selling tickets to his next fight.

The Quarry fight did not last long enough to determine how much Ali had lost in the three and a half years of his exile from the ring. Athletically, that is. As a celebrity he had jumped into a new league. Diana Ross and Coretta King were waiting for him outside the ropes, and Jesse Jackson and Sidney Poitier and Andrew Young and Bill Cosby and Julian Bond and Hank Aaron. The Reverend Ralph Abernathy used the postfight press conference to present Ali the annual Dr. Martin Luther King Jr. medal and call him "a living example of soul power, the March on Washington all in two fists."

Every time I wrote about Ali in those days I would get a flood of letters praising me for being courageous or liberal or irreverent, attacking me for being un-American or a nigger-lover or a fool. The letters more or less neutralized each other. But sometimes I would get a sad, thoughtful letter reminding me of all the young Americans coming home in rubber bags while Ali and I were free to prattle. Once, I might have replied that young Americans were fighting and dying so Ali could be free to practice his faith and I could be free to write about it. After all, that was what I learned in school. But it seemed a hollow answer now, especially since I no longer believed it was true, that the dead bodies had any connection whatsoever with Ali's rights or mine or the public's vaunted right to know. To know what?

As I write this I glance at two photographs to prime the pump of my memory, but I glance at them warily, afraid I will see in them shadows and nuances that were never there. The first one, a wrinkled black-and-white UPI telephoto is dated February 26, 1964. Its caption reads, "MIAMI BEACH: Cassius Clay gestures as he's interviewed at Convention Hall. The new heavyweight champion was on his best behavior at the press conference."

Clay fills the left side of the photograph. He is seated, in profile. His face looks smooth, untroubled. He is pointing his right forefinger, pedantically. He is probably saying that in the jungle redbirds stay with redbirds and bluebirds with bluebirds. In the crowd of newsmen immediately below him I easily spot the late Milton Gross, half-glasses perched at the end of his nose, characteristically the closest of all to the subject. There is Plimpton, near the center of the photograph, arms folded, chewing on his lower lip and staring off toward the right where Sonny Liston has begun his press conference. Nearby, Arthur Daley watches Liston, as does a friend of mine, Will Bradbury of *Life*, a former *Times* sportswriter who has promised to share his Liston notes with me so I can stay with Clay.

And there I am, bottom right, pale face no larger than Clay's dark fist, eyes huge, lips compressed. What am I thinking? Am I shocked, sorrowful, intense with study? Am I wondering how I will begin my story, where shall I go for lunch, will I be able to fly home tonight? I look very young to me, the face unformed, without much character. If eleven years later I could reach into the picture and grab my own ear, what would I say? "Way to go, boy, just hang in there."

The other photograph is famous. It was taken the night of March 8, 1971, at Madison Square Garden, and it appeared on the front page of the *Daily News*. Variations of it appeared on the front pages of most newspapers around the world, color versions in most magazines. Ali is on his back, eyes shut, mouth open, and Joe Frazier stands over him, fists cocked. Arthur Daley is in many of the pictures; so is Phil Pepe of the *News* and Dave Anderson, chewing on a pencil. I am in most of them, shouting into a telephone, my face contorted. Am I shocked, sorrowful, intense with study? There is a little more character in the face now, more lines, less hair, a scar beneath the right eye. What did I learn for sure those seven years? If I could reach in and grab my own ear in this picture, I'd say, "Remember, you always used to say no matter what happened to Ali you'd never feel sorry for him? He was into a cosmic game, and the rest of us didn't even know the rules? Well, don't start feeling sorry for him tonight."

I was not writing that night. My only immediate responsibility was to hold open a direct phone line from ringside to the sports desk and keep the editors current on the fight's progress so they could plan headlines and extra editions. After a few rounds of perfunctory description I had responded to very little urging and turned broadcaster. Everyone who heard my version of the fight was surprised when Frazier was awarded the unanimous decision.

Although I thought Ali had won by a close margin, I thought the decision could have gone either way. I had my bias: I wanted Ali to win and I had predicted in a column not only that he would win, but how and in what round—a knockout in twelve. It was the first time I had ever gone on record with a sports prediction of any kind.

The ring officials had a bias, too, as crucial to their judgments as my bias was to mine. The Madison Square Garden press kit had declared of Frazier, "Not since the days of Joe Louis has a black man done so much for his race. Not since the days of Joe Louis and Ray Robinson and Floyd Patterson has a black man brought so much dignity to boxing."

It was a clear mandate.

For Ali, of course, just beating Frazier could never be enough. He would have to do it with a special style, as part of a fantasy-vision. The theme of this fight, this so-called The Fight, was the proving of Ali's manhood to SportsWorld. He had decided to prove he could take Smokin' Joe's best punches. He was going to stand and slug, swallow the smoke and blow it back as dragon-fire. And he did, and he lost. On a night of flash and fame, with Burt Lancaster broadcasting for closed-circuit television and Frank Sinatra shooting pictures for *Life*, and Mailer, Schulberg, and Saroyan covering for magazines, and Bernadette Devlin, Ethel Kennedy, Hugh Hefner, Abbie Hoffman, and Marcello Mastroianni in shouting distance, Ali won the only medal left, the bum's accolade—He Can Take It.

I went home that night saddened. But for whom? Ali? He had made $2.5 million, and he had completed his rehabilitation. He'd win the title back some day, perhaps when the war cooled down. It would be so much easier now for the Supreme Court to reverse his conviction for draft evasion, so much easier for all the forces against him to back off without losing face. He was no longer champion, no longer the baddest stud in the land, Mr. Man. And you could see by the way he stood up to Smokin' Joe that boy was no coward, no siree, he must of really been against the war. Religious boy. Sincere.

I stayed up that night and loosed my mind. . . . Could it have been the most artful fix of the century, The Dump? . . . Had Ali let SportsWorld mess up his mind? . . . Should I be sad for myself, was I off the track, had I missed a signal on some curve or switchback down the line?

The next morning I went back to the city and sat in Ali's hotel room for a few hours while he entertained the press. I was keeping voluminous notes again.

"Just lost a fight, that's all. . . . More important things to worry about in life. . . . Probably be a better man for it."

One radio newsman, obviously upset by Ali's apparent insouciance, gestured at the crowd around the lounging fighter, the television correspondents crouched at his boots, the hunched newspaper reporters, the sweating cameramen. "This is very important. Look at all the people here."

Ali shook his head. "News don't last too long. Plane crash, ninety people die, it's not news no more a day after. My losing not so important as ninety people dying. Presidents get assassinated, civil rights leaders assassinated, you don't hear so much about that no more. World go on, you got children to feed and bills to pay, got other things to worry about. You all be writing about something else soon. I had my day. You lose, you lose. You don't shoot yourself."

He stirred in the parlor chair to sign autographs for some of the newsmen. "A great leader has his followers. When the leader falls, his followers cry. I don't cry, so maybe they won't cry. I have to rejoice in defeat like I rejoiced in victory so my followers can conquer their defeats, the tragedies every day, someone in the family dies, you lose your property . . ."

The newsmen came and went in shifts all day. Once, between shifts, I thought of that very first day I ever met Cassius Clay, the day of the Beatles, the day he lay on a rubbing table and said that if he should lose to Liston he would be on the sidewalk the very next day hollering, "No man ever beat me twice." The scarred old 1971 Lipsyte remembered how the smooth young 1964 Lipsyte had written that down, almost sure it was the key.

I reminded Ali of that day and what he had said. He nodded and closed his eyes and leaned back and as the new shift filed in he began to chant, "Fight him again. . . . I'll get by Joe this time. . . . I'll straighten this out. . . . I'm ready this time. . . . You hear

me, Joe? . . . YOU HEAR ME? . . . Joe, if you beat me this time
you'll really be the greatest."

I wrote it down and stood up and left them, sensing that, one
way or another, I was not long for this job.

That summer, 1971, after working briefly as a guard in the
Metropolitan Museum of Art, Dick Tiger returned to his native
land. He was penniless, and took home nothing except the cancer
in his liver. He died that December, in Aba, at 42.

By that time I had quit.

CHAPTER
7
The Body Biz

1

By the summer of 1971, when I finally got around to learning how to play tennis, the game had turned middle-class. The proliferation of indoor courts was making tennis a suburban woman's sport. The traditional kept amateur was practically extinct, replaced by hard-working prole pros. And cigarette money, shut off from television, was aggressively promoting tournaments into big-league spectator events. Philip Morris, roller of Marlboros and Virginia Slims, spread sickness and health simultaneously.

I wrote about the tennis boom for several years without completely understanding the attraction of the game. From outside the fence it looked like a pleasant, social sport, classier and better exercise than golf or bowling, although not as good a workout as jogging or handball or swimming, my own occasional recreations. And certainly more expensive. At parties, tennis talk had replaced money talk and sexchat as social lubricants. Among men, the tennis elbow had replaced the old football trick knee as jockdom's million-dollar wound. I once heard a woman discuss her husband, disparagingly, as a "reactive baseline player who just won't go to the net." People talked about their pros as they had once talked about their psychoanalysts. I listened politely, but without interest. If you don't play seriously, nothing is as dull as an analysis of someone else's game. And I certainly was not playing seriously. In fact, a friend of mine from *The Times*, Steve Cady, and I would sometimes hit a tennis ball back and forth on the quiet street in front of his house: We had the anarchistic notion that tennis without a net or boundaries of any kind was a truer "disport" or joyful diversion than a regulated contest.

Playful innocence. By the summer of 1971 I had regressed to regulated contests in a resort town gripped by tennis frenzy, and I decided to learn how to play properly.

My first tennis pro, call him Claude, had a beach boy's smile and a personal greeting for all comers—"Hi, champ." He remembered the names only of people who drove big cars or treated him like a servant or promised to invite him over to their summer places for dinner soon. He claimed to have been ranked in Europe for a season, but now, at 26, he managed three all-weather courts off the highway and gave lessons with soft, dead balls.

He was not a gifted teacher; his patience was limited and he could not explain and describe in the clear, simple language a beginner needed. I had already heard "Keep your eye on the ball" and "Get your racket back" from most everyone I had ever played with, and Claude had little more to offer besides good nature and enthusiasm. Sometimes, while rallying, his eyes would become very bright, as catlike as the sudden turn of his body and the graceful arc of his arm. The ball would streak past me, and Claude would sigh loudly, then ostentatiously remember where he was and what he was doing, and stick out his tongue in a small boy's gesture. Poor Claude, playing pitty-pat with a lame when he should have been tuning up for Forest Hills.

I deserved Claude. I was looking for a bargain, and I had seen a sign offering early-bird cut rates. I took my lessons at 7 A.M., in the morning ocean fog.

I always arrived a few minutes before 7 since I had to wake up Claude. He slept in the lounge-pro shop on a bare mattress behind the counter with a sweet and pretty girl who helped him keep the reservation book and clean the place. The assistant pro who was a few years younger than Claude, slept on a bare mattress in front of the counter. When I knocked on the glass outer door, the assistant pro would turn in his blanket and kick the counter. The girl would pop up, windmill into a bra and sweatshirt, then disappear. A minute or two later Claude would stagger to the door in flannel long johns. There was no heat in the building. Claude would cheerfully say, "Hi, champ," as he un-

locked the door, then lead me over the assistant pro and down to
the courts. I would practice my serve while he dressed, did a few
stretching exercises, and drank coffee.

Claude was so cheerful and open that customers did not question his living arrangements. And Claude, in return, gladly accepted his customers' postures. There was, for example, a couple
who arrived each morning in a chocolate Cadillac and strolled
grandly oncourt in finely tailored and pressed tennis costumes
with gut-strung super-rackets underarm. They opened a new can
of balls each half-hour. Their games were terrible; she scraped
the court on all low shots, he hit the ball like a bear swiping at a
beehive. They did not look as though they were having much
fun. Occasionally, Claude would shag over, flash his wonderful
smile, and say something that would set them both nodding seriously. I never noticed much improvement. After they finished
playing, they would sit in the lounge and consider Claude's urging that they take more lessons and fulfill their obvious destinies
as mixed-doubles champions. He would often perform long, gos-
sipy monologues about tournament and circuit life. Like so many
golf, ski, and tennis teachers, Claude had that courtesan's sense
of when a customer wanted to stroke or be stroked.

My own relationship with Claude was friendly, but businesslike. I was not entirely convinced that I should be spending all
this money, and so I was determined to pack sixty minutes of
blisters and sweat into every hour. When Claude took his time
picking up loose balls, or left in the midst of a lesson to answer
the telephone, a meter clicked away in my head, mocking my
extravagance and my athletic pretensions. I would say to myself,
You should be home with your family. I'd answer, But they're all
asleep. Then why aren't you researching your next column? Because I'm on vacation. Don't you have anything better to do with
your time and money than fritter it away on an elitist sport you'll
never master? Look here, tennis is a lifetime activity, and you're
always preaching that people should be out participating, not
spectating, right?

"Ready, champ?," Claude would cry, and before I could answer he would cheerfully blast one into my stomach.

In the middle of the summer Claude took off a Saturday morning and entered a local tennis club tournament. I went over to

watch. He was knocked out in the first round by a college player. There were flashes of what he once might have been—that season in Europe—but his serve was erratic and fatigue weakened his groundstroking. After the match he was grumpy and full of alibis. It wasn't fair, he said. The college boy had a rich father and had spent his summer practicing on clay while poor old Claude had a tennis elbow and a jammed back and poor timing from swatting beginner's high balls for ten hours a day on hard courts. He looked at me as if I should apologize. And furthermore, he said, he had had too much sex lately.

One morning I arrived just in time to see Claude and his girl and the assistant pro dumping their suitcases into the back of a red convertible. They all seemed rather cheerful, especially the assistant pro, who held up recently worn tennis socks and asked if anyone wanted a souvenir. Claude said the management had demanded too much of him—he was a tennis player, not a bookkeeper. This might be the best thing that ever happened to him, he said; his elbow would heal, his back would straighten out, he would get his head and his game together and start playing all these new pro tournaments with all that big money. Later in the day I called up the management and a very tough voice said, "These college boys get a little money and quit. No sense of responsibility."

Claude stayed in town a few more weeks, spinning out the season with occasional lessons on borrowed courts. I don't know where he was sleeping. He called me several times for lessons, but I begged off with one excuse or another. Actually, I had found a new pro, a powerfully built drill sergeant named Paul who taught tennis by the numbers. Backhand, one, two, three, stroke; forehand, one, two, three, stroke; and although I improved it was not fun at all. It was like counting while dancing.

My third and last teacher that summer was a warm little man named Yale who filled me with dreads. He taught me to rush the net with my racket in front of my face like a catcher's mask so the ball wouldn't drill me between the eyes. He taught me to make every backhand a long, soft fly to the opposite corner, presupposing correctly that I would never develop a whippy attacking backhand. But Yale was humanistic, the only teacher to tell me I was doing all this for fun, that victory and even form were secondary to pleasure.

I learned enough tennis that summer to talk about my weaknesses at parties, to spot the phonies who said volley when they meant rally, and to realize that I could never be truly serious about the game. I had no killer instinct. I didn't care enough whether I won or lost. The game was obviously not hooked into my image of myself, my ambition, my competitive spirit, my manhood. Or was it so basic to my psyche that I had to *pretend* not to care so defeat would not destroy me?

I discussed this once with a friend, a Westport psychiatrist, who listened sympathetically. I unveiled my latest theory: Only men with nothing else going for them, dead-end jobs, loutish children, dry sex lives, no cultural interests, have to symbolically murder other men on the tennis court. After that we played. His serve came in like a grapefruit and his groundstrokes were ordinary. He routed me on nothing but sheer animal ferocity.

For a year after my three-pro summer I played irregularly, and when I did play I was beaten by an economics professor who laughed insanely when he blew one past me. It didn't help to learn that he had a brother-in-law who laughed insanely when he blew one past the professor.

Tennis, I decided, was a despicable game; like golf, it was both elitist and vulgar. With half the world starving, how did America justify setting aside fertilizer for the upkeep of golf courses? The American housing industry was grinding to a manipulated halt, yet huge sheds were being financed and built for indoor tennis courts.

Corporate America's television sponsorship had made golf an enormously rich spectator sport—our latest livingroom heroes were men in picnic clothes who charted their comparative standings not by victories or even great performances but by the amounts of money they earned.

The most popular of them all, Arnold Palmer, had not won a tournament in years. He was applauded for the size of his weekly payroll, and for the tanks of fuel his private airplane burned getting him from engagement to appearance to board meeting to match to the opening of a trade show.

The best golfer, Jack Nicklaus, was unattractively overweight.

He didn't slim down until it was obvious he'd never get those pants and shirt endorsements with that belly.

And tennis was struggling to grow up to be just like golf. The top player at the time was a faceless God squadder named Stan Smith who earned so much prize money as a U.S. Army private that his income had to be tucked away into various team funds to avoid the embarrassing bulges. It was considered bad form to ask Smith about money or Vietnam; when I did, for one of my last columns, his long body tensed and he grinned like a dummy and kept repeating, "The Army's been very good to me." In return, apparently, he had been asked only to wear his ARMY TENNIS warm-up jacket to sudden-death battles in Philadelphia, Washington, Cincinnati, London, and New York.

The game was stoking up in the early seventies. Agnew and Mayor Lindsay posed in their whites; so did Gilbert Roland and Jim Brown, Dinah Shore, and Elke Sommer. My dentist flew off to Caribbean hotel tournaments after every extensive cap job. The local A&P was jammed with ladies in white tennis dresses and autographed leather shoes, cunning little pink pom-poms peeking over their heel-tops. Aging executives carried racket bags instead of attache cases to work. Ethel Kennedy announced the first annual Robert F. Kennedy Pro Celebrity Tennis Tournament at Forest Hills. At parties now women talked about their elbows and their gut tension as promiscuously as men.

In the summer of 1972, before the game passed me by entirely, as had the Acid Age and the Sexual Revolution, I decided to try again. The county's latest tennis barn had been thrown up only three miles from my house, and the resident teaching pro was . . . *Althea Gibson!*

I decided to take a lesson from her. Two at the most. For show. When people started name-dropping their pros, I'd ice the conversation. Althea Gibson. I had interviewed her eight years earlier when she was starting out as a tournament golfer, but I was sure she wouldn't remember my name or face. I would be just another anonymous student, as I had been with Claude and Paul and Yale. I made an appointment over the phone for a lesson and met her a week later on a court.

"Hello there, Bob," she sang out, referring to her schedule. "If it's 11 o'clock you must be Bob." She looked up. "You forget to shave this morning, Bob?"

"I'm letting my beard grow."

She looked faintly displeased. I wondered if she was a Lombardi-style teacher, We don't have time to grow beards, Bob. But all she said was, "Take four laps to loosen up, then we'll see what you've got."

Nothing, as it turned out. Althea broke her impassive silence only once, when I rushed to net behind my racket mask.

"What's that?" she yelled. "Now don't tell me you're afraid of getting hit in the face."

I was going to tell her it was one of my ex-pros who was afraid for me, but I was out of breath, a condition which lasted through the next eight months of weekly lessons in which I tried to do what she told me to do, rarely succeeded, but occasionally saw glimmers of the game.

That was a fine season. For the first time in my life there was a self-composed rhythm to my time. Six days a week I worked on a novel called *Liberty Two*, an artistic and political statement that was important to me. And three times a week I played tennis.

At least one of those times I played with an old friend who had sat next to me in kindergarten and roomed with me in college and now lived in the next town. We played a very friendly, relaxed game; we each tried to give the other a strenuous physical workout rather than playing merely to win. I could rush the net without my mask, secure that Mark would never drill me between the eyes just to shake me up.

And once a week, the anchor of my week, I spent an hour with Althea. By winter we were playing mock games, Lipsyte flat out, a foaming retriever who collapsed at the bell, and Gibson just hard enough to make her returns appear effortless. She was loose and graceful, and I had to consciously remember to watch the ball, not her. Every so often I scored a nice point. It would be on a day she had lingered too long over too large a business lunch and her mind was drifty with schemes and she was taking me lightly and preening for the gallery of women and children. I would angle one past her and laugh insanely, then watch in awe as the juices kicked in and turned her briefly back into the monster she had been in the fifties. The monster had to punish me, reclaim the gallery, reassert its omnipotence. If it was my serve, I would lay it in and get my racket up to my face as quickly as possible. If it was her serve there was nothing to do but turn sideways, as in a pistol duel, and wish myself as small as possible. WHOP. A little memo from the champ: Don't get too perky, fool.

Of course, I was never absolutely sure that I had really won the point, that Althea wasn't letting me drop one in now and then to tickle my fantasy and keep me coming.

Althea was more serious about my game than I was. She was very fussy about rules, dress, and deportment, and she inspired me to run more, concentrate harder, think creatively about what I was doing on the court. It sometimes seemed absurd, this all-timer concerned with my game, a jet pilot tuning a Volkswagen motor, and it was an incredible luxury, elitist and common at the same time.

The season ended too soon. The novel was finished, and I reluctantly let it go. Althea was off for a summer of appearances and clinics. Before she left, she urged me to enter the club's intermediate singles tournament. She was a great believer in the crucible of competition. I asked her for a preview of my chances. We were fairly relaxed with each other by then. I had even shown her the 1964 feature story and revealed my secret identity to a mild "Well, how about that." She looked me over like a used car, ran her finger down a list of entrants and guessed I might win half my matches, a pipe dream as it turned out.

Her parting words were, "Got to get out there and see what you're made of, Bob. Only way to learn."

I told her I was going to wear a T-shirt with the message, "I just completed thirty lessons with Althea Gibson." She looked so alarmed I said I was only kidding.

My first opponent was a short, chunky, bow-legged man at least ten years older than I. He was very friendly in the locker room, which made me even more nervous. He told me he hadn't played singles in five years. He wore a red shirt and canvas sneakers. During warm-ups he came to the net with his racket in front of his face and made every backhand shot a long, soft fly to the opposite corner. When the game started, he took a position in the center of the court near the service line, the so-called no-man's land where Althea had warned me never to be caught, and hit back every shot softly and to my forehand. He never missed. I might as well have been playing a wall. And walls always win.

But I was elated. My first tournament match. True, I was now 0–1, and up ahead was an ambuscade of big servers and fake limpers and cheaters and dink artists and "A" players dropping down to hustle the hardware, but I had been blooded, I had lost one without losing my spirit, when the going gets tough the tough get going, look out for the Comeback Kid.

Two days later Ethel Kennedy called. We had never spoken before. Her voice was high, light, merry, insistent. She began by telling me what a success the first Robert F. Kennedy Pro Celebrity tennis tournament had been. The Comeback Kid was cool although he could not classify himself as either a pro or a celebrity. Mrs. Kennedy trilled on, the second annual Robert F. Kennedy Pro Celebrity tennis tournament would be even a greater smash thanks to Mr. Lipsyte. I thought, restring the racket, get a spare, time for more lessons? Mrs. Kennedy said she knew it was a terrible imposition, but so many people had told her how fabulous I was. The Kid felt panicky, would it be him and Althea versus Ethel and Pancho?

Just a few dozen short biographies, she said, one for each of the pros in the tournament, in your own terrific style, you're such a dear, Mr. Lipsyte, it will make the program book a veritable collector's item.

2

June 15, 1968. It is a very hot day in New York City, and I am standing, in my regulation jacket and tie, on a rutted asphalt parking lot behind the Joseph Bulova School of Watchmaking, in Astoria, Queens. I have been interviewing a buxom, red-haired young woman from Chicago, Linda Laury, who tells me she is 26 years old and works for the government in social security administration. She is nervous because in a few minutes she will compete in her very first athletic contest, a 60-yard dash.

She tries to be flip. "I didn't come to set records, I came to have fun."

"Sure," says a friend of hers, a blonde named Ella Cox, who won this event two years ago, setting a record, and lost it last year. "You going to race with your pocketbook? I'll hold it."

I watch Linda move out to the starting line, and my stomach tightens for her, my mouth is dry. I am 30 years old, eight months a columnist, and considerably tougher than I will be later on. I don't care if she wins or loses, only that she will be satisfied with her performance.

The starter's gun snaps, and Linda gets a good start. Her hands move rhythmically on the outer steel rims of the big back wheels in short, choppy strokes that bring the wheelchair to early speed. The eight-inch front casters of the chair have been tightened so the chair will not veer out of its lane during the race, and the brake has been removed so Linda will not inadvertently engage it during her follow-through. Half-way down the course Linda begins pumping steadily, long, coasting strokes that carry her into the lead. A young woman a lane away founders in a rut, two others lose strength, and Linda flashes across the finish line a winner. My eyes are wet, with perspiration, I hope.

Ella laughs and claps as Linda, flushed and feigning surprise, rolls back to where we are waiting for her. Her hands shake as she lights a cigarette. She takes her pocketbook back, and Ella's, too, as the slim young blonde woman rolls out for the next heat of the 60-yard dash. We watch her in silence.

The National Wheelchair Games were twelve years old at the time, and they rarely rated much more than a paragraph or two in most papers. I'm not sure what had brought me out that first time—curiosity, sentimentality, the drive to be different, or a reaction against all the gross spectacles I had been covering, the Indy 500, the Super Bowl, the Kentucky Derby, the America's Cup Yacht Races, those swollen carnivals that had made pimps of the best of us. And so I had driven out to this shoe-string two-day tournament to reclaim my soul and write some honest emotion and do the crips a favor.

I had wandered around for an hour or more before I found Ella and Linda and Hope Chafee, a 23-year-old chemist. The atmosphere of the Games had surprised me: The noisy, nervous, confident, intense, flirting athletes might have been warming up for any of a hundred track and field meets I had attended, except, of course, for the chairs and the crutches and the stumps. But such qualifications were mine, not theirs. Magnanimously, I was willing to accept them as athletes, *handicapped* athletes, to be sure, while they saw themselves as archers and weightlifters and swimmers and sprinters with opponents to psych out and titles to win. I knew these sports had been developed after World War II for therapeutic purposes—Ben Lipton, guiding spirit of American wheelchair games, told me to come back in a year or two when the Vietnam paraplegics would be leaving hospitals and rehabilitation centers—but the athletes insisted that the Games were now basically social and recreational. It was a way of meeting people and of earning trips to international events. The next Paralympic Games, for example, would be held later that year in Israel, and winners here would make the American team.

Ella wins her heat, and rolls back to us. My pencil and pad are out, I make notes, but my questioning somehow seems flabby to me, cautious, solicitous. It takes forever to find out that Linda and Ella and Hope all met as undergraduates at the University of Illinois, which has one of the country's finest rehabilitation centers. Now they all work, live in regular apartment buildings, bowl and square dance from their chairs, and drive cars, which is essential if a person in a chair is to travel with any measure of independence.

"If you're a good gimp you'll do all right," says the flip Linda. When I wince at the word, which somehow sounds like nigger or fag, she grins and says, "We like to use that word first, before an A.B. does."

"An A.B.?"

"Able-bodied." She makes it sound like whitey or straight, and liberates me. Confirmed as an outsider, I begin to relax and regain my technique. I ask them how they all got to be gimps, the question they were all waiting to answer and get out of the way.

Ella was stricken with polio at 5, Hope at 8. Both are now 23, and they think they had it easier than Linda. Suddenly and mysteriously one morning when she was 13 years old, Linda was unable to rise from the breakfast table.

"Small children make adjustments and friends," says Ella, "and adults, if they don't become embittered, work hard to get their independence back. But teenagers are just at the age when everyone is running off for a pizza, and there's a great tendency to withdraw."

"I had depressions," says Linda, "but not so much over my handicap as over where to go to meet other people like me. I had to function the best I could in an A.B. world."

Hope nods. "You never really know what a wheelchair can do until you see other people doing it."

We talk some more, mostly about the events, about the classifications, which are according to the extent of disability, about records and titles and equipment and, as is also standard with amateur athletes, about the general lack of press coverage. Then they are called for their next heat, and wheel away. I start walking toward the finish line for a better view. A chair whirrs up beside me. It is Ella.

"You know, we consider this sport. We come here to win and have fun. But A.B.s don't really understand this. Even after you give them some big hairy explanation, it comes out sob-sister for most people. Please, one thing, don't go back and write a sob story about us."

I promise I won't.

Two years later, I went back to the Wheelchair Games and met Bob Wieland, a 24-year-old weightlifter. When he was 23, he had stood 5 feet 11½ inches and weighed 205 pounds. In Vietnam his legs were blown off by a booby-trapped 82-millimeter mortar round. He contracted malaria in the hospital and his weight dropped to 95 pounds. But the day I met him, June 12, 1970, he weighed 166 pounds and he had just bench-pressed 300 pounds to win the Games' light-heavyweight championship.

"You think you'd really be charged up for the Nationals," he said over lunch. "I mean, this is the National Championships, wow. But I used to get much more turned on before a college football game. I guess it's because I don't really want to be here. This is a substitute, the best there is, but still a substitute. I'd rather have legs."

Wieland was one of only eight recent veterans among the more than 280 male and female competitors in those 14th Games. The waves of new athletes Ben Lipton had predicted never materialized. The World War II veterans had been older men, they had had a greater sense of purpose, and they had been treated as heroes on their return. Vietnam produced many more amputees and paraplegics than did World War II, but the Vietnam veterans were tucked away out of sight.

"A lot of guys I was in the hospital with refused to face reality," said Wieland. "They drank alcohol and smoked grass and waited for their legs to come back. In the hospital it was all right, you were accepted, but out in society, well, it's not that they don't like you, it's that they don't know what to say to you, and they really don't want to see you and hear about what happened."

Wieland was from Milwaukee. He had been an athlete at Wisconsin State University. He turned down a contract to pitch in the Phillies farm system. He was, he said, "doing well, real well" for himself when he was drafted, and now he was "making the most of living in a different world."

"There are times when you just lie in bed and cry, 'Oh, my legs,' but it's all up to the individual and most guys make it. A lot depends on how stable you were before, on your home life. I have an outgoing personality, and that helped.

"I keep reminding myself that I had twenty-three good years, that I can remember running along the beach and jumping into the water, dancing, going down the basketball court on legs. A lot of the kids here never had it to lose, and I think it's easier for them than the veterans."

Wieland was an only child, living at home, driving a Cadillac Eldorado and collecting about $800 a month in disability pay. Seven months before I met him he had begun lifting weights to build up his strength for artificial legs. An athlete, he had barely mounted the legs when he began thinking competition. The paralympic weightlifting technique requires more wrist snap and more explosive muscle action than the A.B. style because the weight bar is only two inches above the lifter's chest. Even after winning his championship that day, Wieland began planning his training schedule for the coming months. He was sure he could lift more than 300 pounds, and he wanted an international title.

"When I get down, I think about June 14, 1969," he said. He smiled faintly. "My first anniversary. Day after tomorrow. Those 82s can destroy a tank, so I'm lucky to be alive. I say, 'Every day's a holiday.' Well, you know what I mean.

"My stumps are short, the left one is five inches, the right is twelve inches. If they were longer I could walk much better. I'd really be dangerous. But there are guys with no stumps at all.

"I can go out and enjoy the weather. I can have a good time. I'm alive. People tend to let themselves down after an injury. What it all comes to is this: You've got to learn some new moves, and keep yourself together."

You've got to learn some new moves, and keep yourself together. Write that on your locker-room wall.

If Linda Laury and Bob Wieland were products of a broad-based government program of rehabilitation through sports, or even of recreational fitness, there might be some reason to have hope for the physical culture of America. But the wheelchair sports are basically supported by scattered institutions and a few corporations, most notably Bulova, which employs and trains many disabled persons. Despite overwhelming medical evidence of the enormous physical and psychological benefits of such programs, sports for the disabled, the blind, for old people and mentally retarded children, are erratically funded, usually by private agencies, and shamefully neglected by the media, which conserves its time and space for paying customers, and by the functionaries of SportsWorld, who have not been doing all that much for A.B.s, either.

Interscholastic competition has been emphasized to the detriment of general physical education programs. From elementary school on, the child who most needs help getting into shape for the rest of his life is shunted aside for the gifted few who will bring glory and merit raises to their teachers. In many schools where facilities are limited, recreational and intramural programs are routinely sacrificed to varsity sports: A small six-basket gym can be used for either two five-man teams playing full-court or twelve three-man teams. In the constant struggle between "fizz ed" and academic departments for time and space and money, gym teachers know they can usually get more out of a winning team with its overrated effect on school spirit and community interest than out of a recreation program that might truly bring significant progress to many lives.

By the time most youngsters get to a high school gym class and are ordered by a clock-watching coach to touch their toes, the athletic experience, the inspiring, sensual process of shaping and cultivating and extending a body, has become unreal, a dream lost at kindergarten recess. The high school gym period may be all of forty-five minutes, most of it spent checking in and out, changing clothes, and getting into line. Very little of it is fun, and everyone spends the rest of the school day wondering if other people can smell the sweat.

Sports are not necessarily good for you, and championship athletes are not always healthier than non-athletes. Doctors have concluded that American football, particularly on the high school and college levels, may be the world's most injurious sport. The permanent elbow damage suffered by Little League pitchers has been well documented. Big Leaguers in every sport, amateur and professional, have been relying with increasing frequency upon anabolic steroids, phenylbutazon, novocaine, amphetamines, barbiturates, tranquilizers, and cortisone just to stay even with the competition. Often they are encouraged, even ordered, by their coaches and team physicians, to take drugs whose long-range effects are not known. And once retired from active competition, ex-athletes seem to pitch over dead as often and as early as non-athletes.

But that's no reason to just sit there.

Meet Dr. George A. Sheehan, a cardiologist, essayist, philosopher, and long-distance runner whom I met while covering the 1968 Boston Marathon. He finished 179th of 890 starters that year, his fiftieth. In 1971, to start the new year running, I asked him questions that he answered and *The Times* printed.

Lipsyte: Dr. Sheehan, should I start running tomorrow?

Sheehan: I'm not sure everyone should be running: Not everyone has the discipline, nor does everyone find pleasure in it, although I don't see why. It's important to become involved in an activity that properly exercises the cardiopulmonary system. Walking, swimming and bicycle riding will also do that.

Lipsyte: How often do I have to run, and how far?

Sheehan: It takes less time than you think. Three sessions a week, fifteen minutes at a time. Don't use stopwatches or pedometers at first. Start slowly, that's important. If you begin running too quickly, you'll miss the pleasurable feelings. I find that after six minutes I begin to sweat, my respiratory rate slows, I get my second wind and a euphoria that makes the next half hour or so truly enjoyable.

Lipsyte: Okay, what shall I do tomorrow?

Sheehan: Get up forty-five minutes to an hour earlier than usual. Statistics seem to indicate that those who run before work are more likely to stay with it than those who run after work. If it's really cold, wear thermal underwear, a turtleneck shirt, and inexpensive painters' gloves. Good road-running shoes are worth the investment, although Hush Puppies will do. Wear a ski mask: This will also grant you anonymity in the neighborhood. I don't think you should go into this with a great deal of fanfare. Sneak into it. We spend too much of our lives saving face. Don't keep on doing this just because you said you would, or because it's good for you. Find out if you really like it.

Lipsyte: It seems like a boring chore.

Sheehan: This is a real problem. Coaches are always changing courses for their runners to keep up their interest. It's best to run with someone else. Psychologically this cuts distance in half. You should be able to talk while you're running. A number of people have told me they can think more clearly while running, solve problems, gain insights into their personal relationships. I write the third and final draft of my newspaper column in my mind while running. Erich Segal says he wrote *Love Story* while running.

Lipsyte: Is running enough to make me healthy?

Sheehan: It's a great start. Running opens doors to further thought. It can lead to a new set of values. In itself it's changing your lifestyle. A fair number of people with heart attacks simply let themselves go. But for a larger group, I think, the cause was too much stress. The body suffered an overload. It blew a fuse. Just by putting in a physical activity, you're changing your lifestyle, and this may be the first step toward other changes.

Lipsyte: Will running extend my life?

Sheehan: You could run for the next ten years, hating every minute of it, and then get hit by a truck. There's no point in that. You should feel a difference day by day. Too many people are living sodden, marginal lives, they have just enough energy and interest to raise themselves to a level necessary for life. This is a time to live at the top of your powers. You have to think of yourself as a totality, your body reflects your personality, your mind, your spirit. It's a tragedy not to live as completely as you can. If you're not in good physical shape you're not living to the fullest in any capacity. You've got to start to do something to be the best of what you can be.

CHAPTER
8

Designated Heroes, Ranking Gods, All-Star Holy Persons

1

SPORTSWORLD HAS ALWAYS considered its traditional oppression of women as something of a locker-room joke: Sports is a male sanctuary, therefore any woman who tries to invade it is not really a woman. In the 1930s, the same male sportswriters who called Babe Didrikson the greatest all-round athlete in the country were also quick to describe the down on her upper lip, the prominence of her Adam's apple and the angular contours of her "boyish" body. When she turned professional and began to wear cosmetics, style her hair, and dress in a more conventionally "feminine" fashion, the sportswriters were divided; some thought she was merely "glamorizing" herself to attract more commercial endorsements, while others congratulated her on finally growing into womanhood. Innuendoes about her sexuality followed her into marriage with George Zaharias, a huge professional wrestler.

As a performing athlete and as a winner, Babe Zaharias was in a class with Jim Thorpe and Babe Ruth, but sports herstory has yet to be written in which her confidence, courage, and accomplishments are given the same exposure as those of hundreds of lesser men.

From the late nineteenth century until the 1920s, women's sports were on the increase, probably reflecting the burgeoning women's movement. ("Many a woman," wrote Elizabeth Cady Stanton, "is riding to suffrage on a bicycle.") Calisthenics, riding,

boating, swimming, tennis, skating, and basketball were introduced at the women's colleges. In 1912, women began participating in the Olympic Games.

The gains were not only wiped out during the sports boom of
the twenties, but regressive legislation was passed that elimi-
nated most state basketball tournaments for high school girls and
severely restricted the types and extent of competition available
to women. The reactionary and male-dominated Amateur Athletic Union took over women's sports in 1922. A year later, the
Equal Rights Amendment was brought before Congress and
stifled in committee.

In those years, as the women's movement itself was checked,
the vital separation was made: SportsWorld for the men, House-
World for the women; SportsWorld to prepare men for industrial
production and warfare (draft officials had been shocked by the
percentage of men physically unfit for World War I combat),
and HouseWorld to contain the energies and progressive tenden-
cies of women who had just won the right to vote; SportsWorld
to provide a safety valve and a male sanctuary and a manipula-
tive entertainment, HouseWorld to create stability and a breed-
ing shed for capitalism.

Mildred Ella Didrikson was born in 1914 and raised in Beau-
mont, Texas, one of seven children. Her parents were Norwegian
immigrants, her father a ship's carpenter, her mother a housewife
who had been an outstanding skater and skier in Norway. They
encouraged all their children in athletics, and built a gymnasium
in the garage and backyard. Babe was an athletic prodigy. By 15
she was a schoolgirl basketball sensation, as well as a superior
student, a harmonica player, a gold-medal typist, and a prize-
winning dressmaker. In 1930 she was recruited out of high school
to play on the employees' basketball team of a Dallas insurance
company. She led them to a national championship, and was
named all-America three years in a row.

Babe ran, swam, dove, and played softball on high competitive
levels. The company sponsored her first real flyer at organized
track and field events, the Olympic tryouts in Chicago. She won a
place on the American team, and at the 1932 Games in Los Angeles, she won two gold medals, in the javelin throw and the
hurdles. After breaking the world record in the high jump she

was disqualified because her western roll technique had not yet been officially recognized.

In his 1938 *Farewell to Sport*, Paul Gallico wrote off her phenomenal athletic success as "simply because she would not or could not compete with women at their own best game—mansnatching. It was an escape, a compensation. She would beat them at everything else they tried to do."

In the early fifties, when I first read that, I believed it. Years later, my consciousness partially raised, I accepted it as routine sportswriter sexism. Only recently, rereading Grantland Rice's *The Tumult and the Shouting* and Babe Zaharias' own 1955 autobiography, *This Life I've Led*, did another explanation present itself. Once, during a round of social golf, Rice promoted a foot race between Babe and Gallico, who was a fine and vain athlete himself. Babe ran Gallico into the ground.

Between 1935, when Zaharias began playing golf seriously, and 1956, when she died, she won nearly every prize and title in the women's game. In a 1970 letter to me, her widower wrote, "She told me when things were tough, George, I hate to die. I said, why—she said, I'm just learning to play golf."

Of such stuff SportsWorld creates hymns and gospels for men. Zaharias was operated on for cancer of the lower intestine in 1953. A permanent colostomy was necessary. Three months later she was playing tournament golf, and in 1954 she won the National Womens Open. She talked about her operation publicly "because I believe the cancer problem should be out in the open. The more the public knows about it the better."

Also in his letter, George Zaharias wrote, "After she won the Womens British Open golf championship—1947 press party at Toots Shor's—with all the great sportswriters including Grantland Rice for openers. Fred Corcoran, who was 'Babe's manager asked her what her plans were. 'Babe' said Guess I'll play in the U.S. Open. No other question was asked. All the writers hit the door. All the papers had it 'Babe' to play in the U.S. Open. It didn't take Joe Dey long, the very first edition the name was changed to the U.S. Mens Open. Check it."

I never did. The story may be apocryphal, but it rings with a sad truth—nothing seems to panic the functionaries of SportsWorld faster than the threat of a woman athlete beating a man in fair combat. We are constantly assured that it can't happen, for biological, psychological, and sociological reasons, and that if it somehow should happen, then the woman would be more than a woman and the man less than a man. Babe Zaharias, being a woman, was obviously frustrated, abnormal, perhaps genetically confused, according to many of the commentators of her day, to display such toughness and competitive fire.

In *Rip Off the Big Game*, Marxist commentator Dr. Paul Hoch has equated America's sexual apartheid in sports with South Africa's racial apartheid—both were established in England's all-white, all-male public school training grounds for elitist rule.

Dr. Thomas Boslooper, a New Jersey clergyman and author of *The Femininity Game*, has said, "Men can keep women in a secondary position by keeping them weak, and the best way to keep them weak is to keep them physically inactive."

For all her talent, fierce ambition, and friendly press relations, Babe Zaharias had continual financial problems until her 1938 marriage. She turned pro, although the best golf was then in the amateur game. She was always going back to type for Employers Casualty Company. She even toured for a while with the otherwise all-male House of David basketball team.

The best advice she ever got in sports, she says, was Babe Ruth's "Get yourself an annuity," but until George Zaharias appeared to give her financial and emotional support, she had trouble surviving on a day-to-day basis. And it was only through George that she was able to quit pro golf long enough to reclaim her amateur standing and develop her game to its potential.

George Zaharias had been stimulated to write to me by a column of mine about a golf match between Doug Sanders, a touring pro best known for the size and variety of his wardrobe, and Carol Mann, the best female golfer. Their comparative statistics are noteworthy. At the time of their match, Sanders had won seventeen tournaments and his accumulated prize money, $550,000, placed him eighth among men, while Mann, the No. 1 woman, had won twenty-nine tournaments, but only $203,000. By SportsWorld logic, the discrepancy in their earnings was proof of the superiority of the men's game rather than the inequality of winners' purses.

By playing Sanders, Mann hoped to generate the favorable publicity that could lead women's golf into better television contracts, richer endorsements, and more serious press and fan attention. No one actually expected her to win. Maureen Orcutt, a famous amateur golfer who worked in *The Times'* sports department, expressed the conventional female line: "It would be wonderful if Carol won, but Doug just won't let her." Had Carol won, of course, the entire project would have been reinterpreted; after all, the male line would go, isn't there something queer about a man who travels with twenty-five pairs of shoes? And this 6-foot 3-inch Carol Mann—has anyone scraped the inside of her cheek for chromatins lately?

Sanders won the match by twelve strokes, but Mann made her point—a man and a woman can compete on equal terms without washing the greens in blood, tears, or excess hormones. For the summer of 1970, a watershed season in SportsWorld's version of the battle of the sexes, this was a rather new and important point.

A few weeks before the Sanders-Mann match, a 27-year-old schoolteacher, Pat Palinkas, became the first woman to play men's professional football. In a minor league exhibition game in Orlando, Florida, Palinkas was sent in to hold the ball for her husband to place kick. But the snap from center was off-target, and Palinkas bobbled the ball. Before she could recover and set for the kick, a 240-pound opposition linebacker, Wally Florence, crashed through and knocked her down. He said, "I tried to break her neck. I don't know what she's trying to prove. I'm out here trying to make a living and she's out here prancing around making folly with a man's game."

At first, my sympathies were with Palinkas, this doughty little 122-pounder who sprang up unhurt to inspire her Orlando Panthers to victory. Why shouldn't she be allowed to play, to find the limits of her skill and talent, to gain the fame and fortune that SportsWorld bestows upon its stars? Man's game, indeed. Florence (as symbolic a name as Mann) couldn't even knock her down for keeps.

Later I thought about Florence as victim. I called him a few days later at Project Cool, a ghetto vocational training agency in Bridgeport, Connecticut. He was a Big Brother in charge of keeping the Little Brothers off Downtown Whitey's back. Florence needed some cooling off himself. "I wanted to show her this is no soft touch," he told me. "I wanted to smash her back to the kitchen."

Florence had earned his scars and stripes. He had played at Purdue, he had been cut by the Giants and Jets, he had been dropped by several minor league teams before hooking on with the Bridgeport Jets. He was 27. This was his last chance to get his game together for a final shot at the big leagues, and now, before the regular season even opened, he was a national joke.

The wealthy businessmen who toyed with minor league football franchises were bush-leaguers ogling Wally Florence because they couldn't afford O. J. Simpson. But they weren't losers like Florence because they had the power to send in Pat Palinkas to hype the box office, and because they knew that the codes of SportsWorld, the locker-room slogans about manliness and discipline and integrity, were theirs to bend or change.

Only fools like Palinkas and Florence and me were expected to take the rules seriously because we had to make our ways in a system we neither created nor controlled. If Palinkas had to ridicule Florence's dreams, and if Florence had to mock-rape Palinkas, and if I had to turn them both into symbols, well, that's the way of the world. Unless the three of us could get together and take over the league. A tidy microcosm, this.

The Sanders-Mann and Florence-Palinkas match-ups were only two of the male-female skirmishes that summer. Women jockeys were riding at major racetracks, threatening the pathetically macho male jockeys who had escaped into the one sport which gave a small man refuge from a world of bullies. Some male jockeys actually stoned and fire-bombed female jockeys' dressing quarters. Male reporters were less physical but no less threatened and hostile keeping accredited women reporters out of their press boxes. It was no victory at all when Elinor Kaine, denied a seat in the Yale Bowl press box, was eventually seated in an auxiliary area. She had been covering football for years with greater intelligence, energy, ingenuity, contacts, and background than most of the men who took their seats as a birthright.

2

"To me," wrote Billie Jean King in her 1974 autobiography, "Women's Liberation means that every woman ought to be able to pursue whatever career or personal lifestyle she chooses as a full and equal member of society without fear of sexual discrimination. That's a pretty basic and simple statement, but, golly, it sure is hard sometimes to get people to accept it. And because of the way other people think, it's even harder to reach the point in your own life where you can live by it."

As the Feminist Statement from a woman who has been promoted as SportsWorld's model WOMAN to Vince Lombardi's FATHER and Joe Namath's SON, it seems mild, even stale, in the mid-seventies. But to Billie Jean's everlasting glory, she was saying pretty much the same thing back in the late sixties, when I first met her, long before it was considered fashionable or even acceptable.

"Almost every day for the last four years," she told me once, "someone comes up to me and says, 'Hey, when are you going to have children?'

"I say, 'I'm not ready yet.'

"They say, 'Why aren't you at home?'

"I say, 'Why don't you go ask Rod Laver why he isn't at home?'"

At the time it seemed revolutionary, a woman in sports actually equating herself with a man. Ask Rod Laver why he isn't at home? The cheekiness of the broad. Rod Laver isn't at home because he doesn't have to be. Like male sportswriters.

"My husband's the one who thinks women's lib is really great," she said back then. "He feels everybody should be equal. He's loose and limber. I think he knows in his heart and mind he'll be a real big daddy some day. I still think you can be feminine and do your own thing. I agree with most of the women's lib things, but some of it seems far out. But that might be just for attention. Lord knows, you really have to exaggerate things these days to get attention."

Billie Jean always got attention because she was "good copy," the first requirement of celebrity. Sportswriters might call her "outspoken" or even "kooky," but they could count on her always to cooperate, to accommodate yet another interview in which she would answer questions frankly. Her reputation for being "controversial," however, did not come from an early feminist position but from an unselfconscious populism that was so exotic in tennis that those who weren't horrified found it "refreshing." She believed that fans should stomp and cheer at tennis matches, that players had the right to question referees and officials, that the game had to shuck its country-club image and plunge into the arena to survive. In this, she was ahead of her time. The following quote, delivered breathlessly while we watched a tennis match in Madison Square Garden, was advanced for 1968.

"If I was an announcer, I'd try to influence people. I'd tell them how grueling tennis is, I'd get away from this sissified image.

"I mean, after all, they stop the action because a player's got a blister. The fans have to laugh, they've seen hockey players get their teeth knocked out. And I'd go into poverty neighborhoods, middle-class neighborhoods, I'd get those kids out to play. And it doesn't matter what they're wearing.

"Do you know, for my first tournament, I was 11 or 12, my mother made me a pair of white shorts. We couldn't afford to go out and buy shorts then. It was a southern California junior tournament, and Perry T. Jones pushed me out of the group picture. He said I should be wearing a tennis dress. I felt bad for my mother."

Billie Jean has described her mother, Betty Moffitt, as "a creative person. She liked painting and ceramics, and made rugs for the den." She was a part-time Tupperware saleswoman, a sometime Avon Lady.

Bill Moffitt, for whom Billie Jean was named while he was away at war, "loved being a fireman and never even made a big effort for advancement, just so he could continue doing what he liked doing best—working as an engineer on all those trucks and pumping equipment." He could never afford to buy a new car during Billie Jean's childhood.

An active recreational athlete himself, Moffitt began coaching Billie Jean in ball sports at 4. By the time she was 10, in 1954, she was shortstop and youngest member of the girls' softball team that won the Long Beach, California, public parks championship. Billie Jean also played sandlot football. She remembers that most of her schoolmates played tennis and golf at their parents' country clubs, and some of them owned horses. She has always been keenly aware of people acting "snobby" toward her. She remembers carrying her lunch to tournaments as a junior player because of the "outrageous" $2 price of a sandwich at the Los Angeles Tennis Club. Her parents felt uncomfortable there, too.

She has characterized her family as middle-American, religious (Bob Richards, the pole-vault champion, was the minister of their Protestant church), and "pretty basic." She wrote, "Dad was the boss, the breadwinner, the one who made all the final decisions." He was against homosexuals, interracial marriage, unpatriotic expression. He believed in hard work, discipline, and traditional roles. Her younger brother, Randy, went on to become a major league baseball pitcher, but Billie Jean's baseball and football careers were aborted when she was 11. She agreed they were not "ladylike."

Her father suggested she choose from among tennis, golf, and swimming, and when none of them appealed to her he endorsed tennis. "Well, you run a lot and you hit a ball. I think you'd like it."

She began taking lessons at a municipal park from a city instructor, a man in his sixties who was delighted with this big—5 feet 4 inches, 125 pounds—enthusiastic, strong, and "hungry" girl. Within a year she began playing in tournaments, and entered the traditional, outrageous, snobby world of amateur tennis.

There had always been great women tennis players, cherished and honored by the sport even after their playing days. Billie Jean would break no new ground merely by being a female.

Despite her competitive drive—her scrambling style and fierce net play were said to be copied from "the men's game"—she has never been considered the equal of such past champions as Suzanne Lenglen or Helen Wills Moody.

And she was certainly no prole pioneer in the game. Althea Gibson, a Harlem black, and Pancho Gonzalez, a Los Angeles Chicano, were tolerated and exploited as young amateurs long before this self-styled "El Chubbo" in harlequin glasses appeared to cry "Nuts" and gamier expletives whenever she missed a shot.

What Billie Jean had, and may even still have, was a naive faith in the opportunity and justice of the American system. It came from being raised a lower-middle-class WASP in southern California after World War II. Billie Jean's people had always known they were true Americans, that the history books had

been written for them, that the heroes and heroines of movies
bore their names and that all they needed to do was work hard,
be honest, God-fearing, and single-minded, and they could ride a
big talent to the top of the heap. There was no question in Billie
Jean's mind that if she could just hit enough backhands, concentrate hard enough, sacrifice enough candy bars, and get enough
sleep, she could be, as she would say, Número Uno.

And when Billie Jean found out she was wrong, that in tennis,
at least, the officials were more interested in retaining control
than in making money or turning on the nation to their sport,
Billie Jean had the confidence, articulateness, assertiveness, and
self-righteousness to take their sport away from them.

I am not suggesting that Billie Jean, all by herself, snatched
the game from the Lawwwn Ten-Nis bureaucrats and served it
into the Big Bucks. There was Texas money (once again, Lamar
Hunt), and a community of interest that included television,
sporting goods, clothing, construction, cigarettes, Las Vegas. The
tracks of the pro tour had been laid by Jack Kramer and Pancho
Gonzalez and a score of their Australian mates over thousands of
one-night stands. New patterns of leisure hooked up the spectator boom with the participant boom, and they nourished each
other.

But the animus/anima that gave soul to the trend was Billie
Jean. She personalized this bringing of tennis—classiest of sports
—to the people. And she was the only one who could have done
it, male or female. Others grumbled about the hypocrisy of the
United States Lawn Tennis Association, about the humiliation of
having to accept secret payments from the very officials who had
solemnly ruled them illegal, about having to dance attendance
upon wealthy patrons, of playing under poor conditions, of slipping into a dependent life instead of being allowed to sweat and
fight for independence and wealth. But nobody who had as much
to lose from the old way and as much to gain from a new way
stepped up and spoke as boldly as Billie Jean.

She said she wanted to turn pro so she could be an honest
person. She said she wanted to hear the fans hoot and holler so
she'd know they cared. She said she wanted to make lots and lots
of money. The fact that she was a woman emboldened the other
women and shamed the men.

Nowadays, with tennis crowds screaming, "Get it, baby," and linesmen no longer as secure as Supreme Court justices and players' costumes as cheery as parfaits, it is hard to recall the stiff white formality of amateur tennis in the early sixties, the library hush around a final match, the awesome pomposity of the beribboned officials. Tennis seemed grim, except when it was hilariously fantastic.

Imagine Lipsyte, a cub reporter, stalking the corridors of the Mayflower Hotel in Washington, D.C., while the USLTA delegates he had been sent to cover moved from secret conclave to executive session, plotting counterattacks against Jack Kramer's pro raids, staging high-tea coups against each other, rewarding friends with sanctioned tournaments, and constructing intricate new legislation to further restrict their flighty young wards, the players.

I was covering because *The Times'* regular tennis writer, nay, its Ambassador to Racket Games, Allison Danzig, was gravely ill. Danzig, a fine, erudite, helpful man who wrote beautiful rolling 100-yard sentences, was missed—for years he had certified these conventions with his presence, and after matches players always approached him deferentially and asked for an analysis of their strokes—but politicians among the delegates were letting me know that if I became "the new Danzig" his perks and news sources would be mine. The Timesman is dead, long live the Timesman, an early lesson of inestimable value.

But stalking the corridors, most un-Danzigian, I noticed a mop-sink closet adjacent to one of the meeting rooms. I stepped in briefly, hoping to eavesdrop, but I could hear only the mumbling of voices through the wall, no distinct words. As I stepped out again, a USLTA regional vice-president saw me, and cried, "You heard it all?"

"Yeah, sure," I grumbled, and went upstairs to my room. I called the airline to reconfirm my flight home. As I replaced the phone, a national vice-president who also was a *Times* advertising executive burst into my room.

"You phoned in your story," he accused.

"What story?"

He brushed me aside, picked up my phone, and called *The Times* sports desk. He ordered my story killed. He must have interpreted the puzzled silence on the other end as abject surrender because he slammed down the receiver with a triumphant flourish and looked down at me with benign majesty.

"You're young. You'll understand someday." He was very tall, very thin, very old. He had great flapping arms. "There are some things far, far more important than a newspaper story. Tennis. Sports. The future of young people. Our country."

Much later, when I thought about it, I became furious, at his arrogance and my passivity. He was tampering with Freedom of the Press. I should have killed him for trespassing. Even later, when I found out the big story was an obscure, internecine dialogue of little significance or interest to *Times* readers, I could still get angry with a flashback. Today the USLTA, tomorrow the White House. But at the moment, I was simply dumbfounded. The national vice-president paused at the door on his way out.

"Naturally," he said, "I'll have to mention this to Allison."

Apparently he did because Danzig made what was considered a miraculous recovery and returned to reclaim his beat.

Imagine Billie Jean in such company.

"They love you when you're coming up," said Billie Jean of those ranks of vice-presidents. "But they don't like winners. And they especially don't like me because I talk about money all the time. I'm mercenary. I'm a rebel."

Yet her rebellion was not against society, or even against tennis. It was against the crumbling traditions of a game about to be refurbished, an ancient family business on the verge of a corporate take-over.

The rebel got married because it was obviously the thing to do in 1965 when a 21-year-old woman fell in love and wanted to establish herself as a person outside her mother's kitchen. She "stayed home all that fall and winter because I thought it was really important to be a good wife." It was her husband, Larry, then a law student, who was sensitive enough to send her back into the arena and encourage her to seek her salvation.

"Being a girl was not the only thing I had to fight," she told Frank Deford in a 1975 *Sports Illustrated* profile. "I was brought up to believe in the well-rounded concept, doing lotsa things a little, but not putting yourself on the line. It took me a while before I thought one day: who is it that says we have to be well-rounded? Who decided that? The people who aren't special at anything, that's who. When at last I understood that, I could really try to be special."

And she became special in the same ruthless way everyone else becomes special—she let her marriage slide into a sporadic relationship, she traveled continually for instruction and tournament experience, she underwent extensive knee surgery, she blotted out anything that might distract her from becoming No. 1.

And she became No. 1, justifying, in SportsWorld at least, the disruption, the sacrifice, the pain. And when President Nixon called her up it was to congratulate her on becoming the first woman athlete to earn $100,000 in a single year.

That was 1971, the year of the women's breakaway tournament circuit, sponsored by Virginia Slims (she tends to sneer at those who suggest she should not be associated, however indirectly, with cigarettes) and the year of her abortion, which she later made public ("I was only about a month pregnant; I didn't feel I was killing a life or anything like that. But the real reason for my decision was that I also felt it was absolutely the wrong time for me to bring a child into the world.").

But, of course, it took a man to finally authenticate Billie Jean. On September 20, 1973, in a grotesque extravaganza in the Houston Astrodome that brought tennis into the show-biz division of SportsWorld, Little Myth America beat Bobby Riggs, a male of comparable size, but considerably less championship experience, twenty-six years older, and far, far less admirable by any humanistic measure.

When it was all over, when this Rigged-up superstar was acclaimed the Joan of Ace, when this flat-chested, stubby girl in glasses (as she describes herself), whose father still called her "Sissy," was besieged by toothpaste, deodorant, suntan oil, and hair curler manufacturers, when it was implied that she had hung a pair of balls on every American woman who wanted them, only Billie Jean made sense. She said:

"This is the culmination of nineteen years of work. Since the time they wouldn't let me be in a picture because I didn't have on a tennis skirt, I've wanted to change the game around. Now it's here. But why should there be a rematch? Why any more sex tennis? Women have enough problems getting to compete against each other at the high school and college levels. Their programs are terribly weak. Why do we have to worry about men?"

3

On opening day of the 1974 baseball season the management of the Cincinnati Reds were asked by Henry Aaron to announce a moment of silence to mark the sixth anniversary of the assassination of Dr. Martin Luther King. The Reds' management refused.

"For some reason," said Aaron, "they found that their schedule wouldn't permit it. They already had the program all set. But it would've been appropriate. We were all very disappointed about it. I'd spoken to Jesse Jackson about it before the game."

But the show, so they say, must go on. After the milling herd of sportswriters had left the field, after the perorations and the posturings of Commissioner Kuhn, after the ceremonial first pitch by Vice-President Ford, Aaron, with his very first swing of the season, hit the 714th home run of his major league career. He had tied The Record.

"Later, in another place," wrote James Reston, "the man called Babe, whose name was taken from the Biblical character Ruth, told Arthur Daley of *The New York Times*, who was with him in that place, that it didn't mean much to him now and that actually he was very pleased."

Reston continued, "Meanwhile, there was a transformation in the great Republic. People began to believe again in the possibility of heroes and institutions. . . . Even Washington, which has lately been staggering and blundering in both politics and sports, suddenly realized that all the problems of life might be a little easier if only you had somebody called Henry—Kissinger or Aaron . . ."

Reston, once the Reds' traveling secretary, later an Associated Press sportswriter, then announced the latest conventional wisdom.

"So the idea began to get around in Washington that maybe the system wasn't a fraud after all, maybe there were some heroes and some triumphs that could be equaled or even broken.

. . . Everybody felt a little better after Henry hit it over the fence."

Ah, baseball. Our National Pastime.

Several days later, back in his home park in Atlanta, Aaron fanned the flames of democracy by breaking the record. But, once again, satisfaction eluded him.

"When I hit 715," he said, "I thought it would settle down into a nice peaceful season. But while I got rid of the sportswriters, I picked up the politicians. Everywhere I go they asked me to do this or appear here. It really became pretty difficult to keep my mind on my job."

By that time Aaron was counting days. At the All-Star break the Braves' manager was fired and Aaron, 40 years old, in his twenty-first season with the club, expected to be asked to replace him. He would have become baseball's first black manager, a responsible position with historical significance worthy of his talent and achievements. But the Braves' management said nothing to him, and hired someone else.

"I always thought I'd be involved in making decisions on players and working in player development, things like that, baseball things," Aaron told Dave Anderson after the 1974 season ended. "But when we began having meetings late in the season, they started talking about how they wanted me to work with the LaSalle Corporation as an ambassador for their sporting-goods division."

LaSalle was the Chicago-based conglomerate that owned the Atlanta Braves. The salary offered was $30,000, less than 20 percent of what Aaron had made in 1974 as a player. It was $9,000 less than Stan Musial had received ten years earlier when the Cardinals moved him from the playing field to the front office.

"They just wanted me to shake hands for the LaSalle people," said Aaron. "I didn't want to shake hands for them. I shake hands for Magnavox, and they pay a lot more money."

So Hammerin' Hank, who had made everybody feel a little better, was traded to Milwaukee to be a designated hitter and to train for a front office job, yes, that same Bad Henry who was talked about in Heaven and Washington, who had transformed the Republic, who had started people believing again in the possibility of heroes.

But that, of course, was exactly what Henry hadn't been able to do. He hadn't even been able to make us believe in the possibility of him. In 1974, America wasn't buying heroes, even from SportsWorld, the only hero-shop left in town.

Once we had carelessly scooped out our heroes from the soldier-statesman-athlete pool. But in 1951 the military dried up when President Truman dismantled Douglas MacArthur, posthumously demoting Mad Anthony, Stonewall Jackson, Custer, Sergeant York, and Patton. Soldiers would never again be given their moments in the sun, much less their seven days in May. By the late sixties, the media had somehow turned the Medal of Honor into a psycho's badge. Vietnam veterans and prisoners of war came home in 1974 to the perfunctory welcomes reserved for losing teams in state championships.

The murders of the Kennedys, Dr. King, Malcolm X, and the crippling of George Wallace made it impossible for us to attach ourselves emotionally to public men. To avoid vulnerability, our politicians stepped out of range, and we became cynical. Just in time for the Nixon-Agnew Black Sox administration.

That year, my novel *Liberty Two* was published, and I sometimes thought (feared) that life would follow art, that an astronaut who saw himself as Carlyle's vision of the heroic original man—a messenger sent from the infinite unknown with tidings for us all—would seize fire and run with it, would try to lead America into a New Era.

But the astronauts were not up to it. Most of them were unimaginative, seasoned pros, like Henry Aaron and Gerald Ford, or disturbed, private men who had come back from strange places with stranger thoughts.

The past could no longer help us. Despite all the books and magazine articles reviving the memory of the Sultan of Swat, Aaron had destroyed the foundation of Ruth's cathedral; in SportsWorld you can never worship No. 2. Poor Babe. He had hit his 714th home run in 1935, for the Boston Braves, because the Yankees didn't need him as a player any more, and didn't want him as a manager. He was deeply hurt. He lasted only a few months with the Braves. He was a Brooklyn Dodger coach for half the 1938 season, but baseball never found a real place for its saviour and meal ticket. In a 1959 *Esquire* article, Roger Kahn asked, "Was it simply Ruth's intemperance that kept him out of baseball? Or was it the mass resentment of club owners against a man whose personal income pushed baseball salaries up as his own income soared?"

Ruth died in 1948. His birthdate has never been absolutely verified, so he was either 53 or 54 at death. He was becoming an embarrassment to SportsWorld, and once he was gone it was easier to inflate and float the legend. His second wife, Claire, was a willing accomplice, and in the years I attended sports banquets, the Widow Ruth and the Widow Lou Gehrig, who were apparently not that friendly during their husbands' playing days, were as ubiquitous a dias duo as Joe Louis-Billy Conn and Dempsey-Tunney.

The athlete is a hero at sufferance, controllable and disposable. Dead ones, like Ruth, are even better than old ones who could, presumably, commit racial slurs or be caught fondling children in YMCA bathrooms, or, worst of all, complain. The hero as object gives us role models we can manipulate, notches in time as nostalgic as old hit tunes, and diverting amusements. Sportswriters, presumably speaking for their constituents, the fans, react badly against holdouts, strikes, and lawsuits by players, because it unmakes the magic: Fans do not really want players to humanize themselves too much. Pictures of wives and kids in the yearbook, okay, but the sportswriters thought Ron Swoboda went too far the year he said he was ashamed to face his wife after the paltry raise the Mets had given him. He was ashamed to face his wife. Who isn't? Who needs a National Pastime to hear that?

The Babe's partner in glory that marvelous 1927 season, Charles Lindbergh, died in the summer of 1974. After several generations of bad press he was making a comeback as a hero of conservation. But I don't think he would have made it; the superlatives necessary to distinguish Lindbergh from contemporary celebrities had been devalued in his lifetime, and they no longer packed the power to convince us. On the day Lindbergh died, Harry Reasoner described him on network news as "a legend in his lifetime." Although I'm still not sure exactly what the phrase means, it seemed fair enough when applied to Lindbergh.

But later that night, on the same network, Frank Gifford referred to the Cincinnati Bengals' football coach, Paul Brown, as "a legend in his own time." What chance would the Lone Eagle have against all those other living legends, those men larger than life, those TV immortals?

As for Coach Brown, if I think of him at all it is because he once ejected Leonard Shecter from a training camp news conference. Shecter had written magazine articles on Lombardi, Rozelle, and Al Davis that Brown considered "hatchet jobs." They were certainly not the usual amiable fictions that pro football had grown accustomed to, vigorously encouraged, and often planted.

"I'm not interested in anything like that pertaining to our football, so out," cried Brown, throwing open his office door.

After a brief argument, Shecter left. Coach Brown was quite right; he would never become a legend in his own time with highly skilled, dedicated, passionately honest journalists writing stories about him.

That was in the summer of 1971. Shecter was already dying of leukemia, and would soon devote all his efforts to his last major work, *On the Pad*, the memoirs of a crooked cop. His contribution to sports journalism had already been made, and it was substantial: ground-breaking columns for The *New York Post*, the publication of articles about and by Jack Scott and Dave Meggyesy as sports editor of *Look*, *Ball Four* and its sequel, *I'm Glad You Didn't Take It Personally*, with Jim Bouton, and *The Jocks*, his seminal 1969 statement, which, like the body of his work, could be erratic, self-consciously dyspeptic, often sentimental, but established standards for integrity and shit detection that raised the level of the craft. He died at 47, in 1974.

How we needed him that year, at the very least to provide some balance to the consistent self-service of the SportsWorld hacks, and even worse, the non-sportswriters who were using sports-related news to teach ideological lessons.

Do we cheer or jeer for Frank Robinson, major league baseball's first black manager?

Hooray, cried capitalism's cheerleaders. The door has been opened. Baseball will show America, and America the world that we can live and work together in peace and harmony. And still win.

Boo, cried the critics, we're not about to be taken again by the old ballgame. All the problems of life aren't a little easier because of somebody called Frank. The country's in a recession, except for young black men who are in a depression, and if they all get the idea to start swinging bats it'll serve you right.

Thoughtful sportswriters, however, stuck to the specifics and made telling points. Leonard Koppett in *The Times* pointed out that "To compare Frank Robinson's 'breakthrough' . . . with Jackie Robinson's . . . can be cruelly misleading and can obscure the true situation. Until and unless other actions are taken by baseball authorities on a large scale—in giving black players a chance to manage teams in the minor leagues—the appointment of Robinson as Cleveland's manager won't have much effect on the total picture." Jackie had broken a clearly defined color line, and truly opened the door for hundreds of American Negro and dark Latin players. But Frank, an established superstar with five years of experience managing in the Puerto Rican winter leagues, not only did not break an avowed barrier, but was hired six weeks after Commissioner Kuhn used a *Times* interview as a trial balloon calling for a black manager.

"I don't think that baseball should be exceptionally proud of this day," said the Commissioner after the announcement of Robinson's appointment. "It's been long overdue, and I'm not going to pat myself on the back for it."

Robinson handled himself shrewdly through it all, justifying his selection. While he might be willing to say he had been held back because of his race, he was certainly not about to announce he had gotten the job because of it. Of course, observers pointed out that Cleveland had a large black population that wasn't represented at the ballpark. Frank might not open doors as had Jackie, but on a smaller, local level, he might open ticket gates.

It was an interesting, tricky story. I remembered when Satchel Paige had appeared with Commissioner Kuhn at Toots Shor's noisome restaurant in 1971 to be displayed as "the first player to receive special recognition for outstanding achievements in the Negro baseball leagues." A likeness of Paige would be hung in what seemed like a Jim Crow section of the Cooperstown Hall of Fame.

Athletic halls of fame tend to be eerie crypts; the powerful and

gifted youth who stretched our possibilities is symbolically en-
tombed here with his hat and number and statistics, while this
short-breathed, weepy, grateful middle-aged imposter accepting
congratulations seems as much a stranger to glory as you and I.
Paige was even further removed: He had been introduced to
most of America as a legend, and now he was being recognized in
an apology.

It was an awkward afternoon. A dais was filled with members
of the special selection committee—some black stars of the
Negro leagues, a white Negro league owner—and they glowered
and looked sad as white and black interviewers asked Paige if he
felt "bitter" about his exclusion from major league baseball
through his prime, if he was unhappy at being "enshrined" in
separate facilities.

Paige stood uncomfortably at the microphone, and the pleasure of his moment seemed to drain out of him. But he was tough
and no fool, and he finally managed to bend his answers around
the questions with a sly humor that depended a great deal on
jokes about his age, which he said was 64, and the repetition of
one or another of his famous maxims, such as, "Don't look back,
something might be gaining on you." After a while, we relented,
and the ceremony smoothed out. I was standing in a corner, just
watching now, and Larry Doby beckoned me over. Doby had
been the first black player in the American League, always in
Jackie Robinson's shadow, and now he was a batting coach at
Montreal. He wanted very badly to be the first black manager,
and I had written about that back in 1964.

"You know," said Doby, "I think you were right to ask your
questions and all, but I think everybody should rally around this
decision as a good thing, and not look for the bad in it. The
people who did wrong are not here. The only thing I'd be against
is a separate wing in the Hall of Fame. Everyone should be together now."

I raised a mild argument, mostly to draw him out. Baseball is
just trying to pay some back dues, I said, and the price seems cut-
rate.

Doby nodded and began to speak softly. I didn't get his exact
words, at first, but the message was profound. If there was any
injustice in all this, said Doby, it might just be in transmitting the

idea that Paige and other Negro leaguers are pathetic figures of history, and that there was true joy and fulfillment only in the white leagues.

"We had our good times," said Doby. "The Negro league players were dedicated athletes playing a game they loved. There was laughter and songs in the bus, new people, fans in every town. When you come down to it, all the major leagues offered was more; more money, more bars, more women, more friends, more opportunities."

But the sharp questioning that day apparently provoked a re-evaluation, and that summer Paige was inducted into the regular Hall of Fame. Despite his lack of formal qualifications, his bronzed plaque was hung in the same neighborhood with Ty Cobb and the Babe and Jackie and Ted Williams, who, at his own induction five years earlier, had called for honors for Paige and Josh Gibson "as symbols of the great Negro players who are not here because they were not given a chance."

I thought of Doby again when Frank Robinson got the call in 1974. Doby was the logical choice; he had broken in with Cleveland, he was coaching there at the time, and he had managed several seasons in Venezuela. But, perhaps for all his patient preparation and waiting, for all his diplomacy, Doby was just too radical. After all, he had denied the intrinsic superiority of the major leagues over the Negro leagues. He even dared to suggest there was success and happiness outside the dominant culture.

Who did he think he was, Muhammad Ali?

On the very last day of 1974, baseball tried once more to sell us a hero. Catfish Hunter. $3.75 million. But we had been that route before, and too much had happened since. We would go to the ballpark to watch $3.75 million pitch, our contribution to the investment, but it was too much to ask of us to take this man as a symbol of economic recovery and spiritual hope.

After all, Catfish had belonged to Charles O. Finley, and were we really supposed to believe that Foxy Finley lost this best pitcher in baseball by reneging on some tax-shelter payments?

And the buyer was George Steinbrenner of the Yankees, who had just been convicted of making illegal contributions to Nixon's campaign. He had helped buy an election; why should we become excited because he was trying to buy a pennant?

4

I am watching the black stick fingers of Luis Sarria play over the sweat-slick brown flesh of Muhammad Ali. The heavyweight champion is on his stomach on a rubbing table in a small dressing room of the Fifth Street Gym in Miami Beach. Eight of us, press, fans, friends, stand against the peeling gray walls to give Sarria elbow room. The old trainer's fingers knead the muscles of Ali's thighs, then walk up to his waist, and sink in. The flesh here is still firm, but plumpish. Sarria prods and strokes. He knows Ali's body better than his own: He has been over every inch, massaging, sponging, drying, slathering Vaseline on the face and head and shoulders before a sparring session, holding the ankles for sit-ups afterwards, rubbing out kinks and stretching muscles for fifteen years now, since 1960. And I have watched Sarria handle this body for more than eleven years now, since February 18, 1964, when I stood in this very same room and wrote down everything I saw and heard in a spiral notebook with a ballpoint pen, just as I am doing now. Then, Cassius Clay called himself "the double-greatest." Since then, he says, he has come to realize that Allah is the greatest. Now, Ali modestly refers to himself as "the king of all kings."

Then, lying on the rubbing table, he told the sportswriters around him that his promotion of the coming Liston fight had given us "something to write about," and had made "your papers let you come down to Miami Beach where it's warm."

Now, on April 28, 1975, the dressing room door opens, and a middle-aged man in a dark suit steps in, hesitantly. He stares at Ali's large, rounded rump, and clears his throat.

"Champ, I'm a federal court officer and I've got some papers for you."

Ali turns over on his back and covers his groin with a towel. "I ain't taking them."

The court officer, startled, looks around for a friendly face, and finding none loses his poise. The room is small, oppressive, and the door bangs shut as a hard-faced black man slides in behind the court officer, who chokes out a laugh. "It's only for $20 million, champ."

Ali smiles and reaches for the papers.

The court officer relaxes, I think I can hear the air sigh out of him. He says, "I didn't want to give it to you out there in public, champ."

"That's okay, the press is here. *The New York Times.*" Ali passes the papers to me and raises up on an elbow to watch me unfold them, legal notice of the libel suit instituted by Anthony Perez, Jr., the boxing referee Ali had called, among other things, a "dirty dog."

I make some notes from the papers, then return them to Ali, who says, "See how I take care of you, Bob? When you're around me you always got something to write about."

My immediate assignment was an article on Ali for *The New York Times Sunday Magazine*, my fourth article on Ali for that magazine. Beyond that, however, was my hope that the trip, my first reporting commission since I had left the paper three and a half years before, would help me knot up the loose ends of this book: Two threads—Lipsyte as Observer and Ali as Object—would be entwined, neatly, simply, conclusively, in a Sports-World macrame. Which proved how badly I needed that trip.

I had not gone to Zaire for the George Foreman fight, but seeing it on film had stirred old juices. Ali had looked mythic that night, as Bundini, poet and confidence man, had predicted: "God set it up this way. This is the closing of the book. The king regained his throne by killing a monster and the king will regain his throne by killing a bigger monster. This is the closing of the book."

Flying toward Miami on Saturday morning, April 26, 1975, I feel my stomach, freed from its moorings, float up gently toward my throat. Occasionally, as the plane lurches, it briefly blocks my air supply. This is an old and welcome sensation, the prelude to every assignment that was ever important to me. I am edgy and up for the game. I am most concerned about access: Interviewing Ali directly is generally a waste of time, I need hours, days, to just hang around him, listen to him talk with other people, watch him perform. I have talked to him only once in nearly four years, a brief encounter in the lobby of the Plaza in New York this past January. It took him a moment to recognize me through a beard he had never seen before, then he touched it and asked why I had grown "that dirty thing." When I told him that writers don't have to be as pretty as fighters he stalked off muttering that he had to take a shower before his banquet appearance.

His speech that night was both boring and sleazy—he was accepting *Sport* magazine's athlete-of-the-year award and promoting his fight with Chuck Wepner—and I felt very glad I no longer had to cover him. I had been away from him so long I had forgotten that his public posture and his image in the press were often far removed from the truth of him as I had once perceived it. Three months later, arriving in Miami, I am beardless but not without my doubts.

Angelo Dundee is talking: "Muhammad in decline? Sure, he is. But it's a very gentle slope. Boxers decline slow. Bangers like Frazier go fast. Joe's shot city already. Muhammad was reaching his peak for the Foley fight in '67, that was a real artist at work, but he never got as good as he might have been. Three and a half years off was just too long. But then you've got to ask yourself, who but a super human being could have come back at all?"

I had met Angelo at the Miami airport, as arranged, and now we are flying to Orlando, where Ali will box a charity exhibition tonight. Our party includes two sparring partners, John L. Johnson and Levi Forte, and Ali's new lawyer, Albert P. Griffin of Philadelphia. My stomach is firmly moored again now that I am plugged into the assignment. Butterflies always disappear after the first shot, the first tackle, the first question.

Angelo has worked with Ali since 1960, and has held his position as master coach, through high tides and low, because he has never allowed himself to become professionally or psychologically dependent on Ali. He has managed Luis Rodriquez, Willie Pastrano, and Jimmy Ellis to championships, and he doesn't much care if Ali introduces him as his manager or trainer or cutman or friend. Angelo is 53 now, although he appears younger; he is trim in a chunky, athletic way, and his thinning gray hair is

adroitly combed to cover his scalp. He is known throughout boxing as a sharp hustler who came out of south Philadelphia in the
1950s with his older brother Chris to corner the market on Cuban
and South American fighters, the base on which they built a
substantial promotional and managerial prizefight empire. Cassius Clay was dropped in Angelo's lap by the Louisville Sponsoring Group because he had the experience, the gym, and the
organization to maneuver him through early buildup fights.

Angelo is so friendly, generous, and helpful to journalists that
his own press remained favorable even when Ali's was generally
hostile. Angelo steadfastly refuses to discuss Ali's religious or
political life, and is very modest about taking credit. "Face it," he
likes to say, "on important things the guy stands alone. I can't
fight for him, and I can't fuck for him." One big brown eye winks.
"Course if I had a choice, I'd rather fuck for him."

In Orlando we take several rooms in the Ramada Inn and settle
down for the afternoon to watch two sports spectaculars, the
Jimmy Connors-John Newcombe tennis match in Las Vegas, and
the George Foreman-Five Opponents boxing show in Toronto.
They are on simultaneously, and Angelo characteristically ap-
points himself dial manipulator.

Connors is the Cassius Clay of tennis. His performing and promotional talent has made these challenge matches possible. At
the same time, there is a concern that just as big TV fights wiped
out the grass roots boxing clubs, so will these million-dollar
tennis matches ruin the tournament circuits. Watching Connors,
the concern seems genuine: Why should the spectator settle for
anything less?

"Connors is a killer," says Angelo, "he's got timing, guts, he
knows just when to come in and dig. Would've made a helluva
fighter."

We can't say the same for Big George. He looms on the screen,
but the menace is gone, like Liston after the first Clay fight.
We've seen him badly beaten.

Suddenly, the gold-dust twins of SportsWorld, Howard Cosell
and Muhammad Ali, fill our Big Window. They are wearing
vanilla jackets with the American Broadcasting Company patch
over their hearts. It is a $15,000 gig for Ali, who has been prom-
ised a private Lear jet to fly him down from Toronto in time for

the Orlando show. Ali tickles Cosell's dewlaps, mugs and winks, shouts directions to each of Foreman's opponents, and informs an international audience that there is no comparison between this sad farce and the charity show he will put on tonight in the Orlando Sports Stadium. Cosell wears a mask of patient suffering, and is typically unflappable. But Big George keeps glancing down at Ali; he cannot concentrate on his opponents when his greatest rival is tormenting him from ringside.

"Muhammad is blowin' his *mind*," cackles Angelo. "Oh, is he havin' a *ball*."

So are his sparring partners, Levi and John L., who have been shaking the motel room with their laughter, their stamping and knee-slapping. Levi once lasted ten rounds with Big George, despite three cracked ribs, before losing a decision.

By the time the show is over, Ali has left for the Toronto airport, and Big George's mind is long gone, too. Two of his opponents stayed the three-round limit, and George's ring conduct was deplorable. He attacked several opponents after the bell, wrestled with them, scuffled with their handlers, and provoked Cosell to call the show "a zany, non-advertisement for boxing" and a "charade" and "depressing."

This is why Cosell is a genuine superstar. He is the only broadcaster in America who can be the promoter, the reporter, and the critic of an event packaged and merchandised by his own network. ABC produced a bomb, and Cosell absolved them of responsibility by turning around and blaming Big George, the nature of boxing, and the appetite of the public. Cosell is the franchise. He may also be the most valuable property in American sports.

The dressing room door bangs open to admit the king of all kings.

"This jet age is something else," says he.

He barely acknowledges the men in the room. He immediately strips. We scrutinize him with unselfconscious interest. Boxers are intensely absorbed in their bodies, yet discuss them with a curious detachment, like drivers talking about their race cars. Ultimately, defeat will be blamed on a failure of the machine/

body to respond to the demands of the driver/brain. Muhammad's body is the most superb machine any of us have ever seen.

He dresses briskly, efficiently. How many thousands of times has he stepped into his jock-strap, one, two, slipped on white socks, laced up his high white boxing shoes, pulled on his leather-and-metal protective harness, pulled on white trunks? He stands like a race horse, quietly with nostrils flared, as Angelo smears him with Vaseline, then snorts and chuffs as he warms up shadowboxing and running in place. Waves of body heat ripple off him and cook the dressing room in the Orlando Sports Stadium. A local reporter in the room asks him if he thinks George Foreman's performance this afternoon will hurt boxing.

"Boxing never die," he says, dancing from foot to foot, bobbing, snapping his head back and forth. "Only need two people, and people always be fighting, fussing.

"Wrestling is fake, I've got boxers now acting like wrestlers, but the reality is there. George Foreman supposed to be fighting but he's looking around to talk to me. It's like the Christian spirit around the world. You could be somewhere on a Sunday where they don't practice Christianity, and all the stores are open, but you feel different because you know it's Sunday. The spirit of Muhammad Ali is there in boxing, even if I'm not in the ring."

Newsmen look at each other, slightly bewildered. One of them asks if he believes in Jesus.

"I can't believe a woman had a baby without a man."

It does not seem like a promising avenue, and the talk veers. Someone has heard that Ali will star in a movie about himself. He stops warming up to flash coming attractions.

"This movie will tell people things they never knew.

"Why I don't have my Olympic gold medal today.

"About the shoot-out in Arkansas during my exile.

"Nine-teen-fif-tee-nine. My first woman.

"How I rode with a motorcycle gang for six weeks. With a mask on.

"Things I stole.

"The money I turned down. Companies will be revealed.

"My first wife, how we broke up, the fight we had the night before the Liston fight.

"What happened in the desert in Arabia.

"What happened in the White House with President Ford, real strange."

Ali looks at me for the first time. "Things you don't know nothing about, Lipsyte." As if I had never been away.

"Are you going to tell me?"

"Have to see the movie to find out. We got a orchestra, hit songs, no *Superfly*, it's going to be big, like *Godfather. The Magnificent Seven*. They could make ten films from my life."

The dressing room door opens. "Ready, champ?"

"The master is ready." He strides out quickly into the darkened arena. Dozens of small boys lead him toward the lighted ring crying, "Ahh-lee, Ahh-lee," and when their chant falters he picks it up and whips them into a frenzied, "Al-lee, Al-lee, Al-lee," until the sparse crowd stands and sends it echoing through the shed, "AL-LEE, AL-LEE, AL-LEE." He mounts the ring as if it were a throne.

Tonight he is fighting for the Orlando School of Black Performing Arts. Like so many of his benefits, there is an impromptu feel to the event, which has been amateurishly organized and promoted. The school director's wife, who attended high school with Ali in Louisville, recently called him to beg he save the school from imminent ruin. That was all he needed to hear. He is a soft touch for certain kinds of appeals, especially ones in which he flies to the rescue of children. A local catalogue store, Leeds, has covered the basic nut of renting the arena and Ali has promised to appear at the store next week and sign autographs. But tonight's show will not raise as much money as it should. Ignoring Ali's suggestion that admission be cheap, the sponsors priced tickets considerably higher than the tickets for a similar benefit Ali will give three nights from now in Daytona Beach, only an hour's drive away. The natives of central Florida are not so flush these days they can afford to blow the $5 or $6 per seat difference.

Even for free, perhaps especially for free, Ali gives a good show. First he boxes three rounds with Levi Forte, a long-time sparring partner and Fontainebleau bell captain. He dances, prances, cowers on the ropes, spins into the Ali Shuffle, a perennial crowd-pleaser, and unveils the Foreman Chop, invented on the spot, a fine mimicry in which he stiffly misses, just like Big George did this afternoon. At the end of the third round he lets Levi dump him on the seat of his trunks.

While boxing three rounds with tall John L. he keeps shouting at the crowd, "Down?," and when it finally responds by cheering and showing thumbs down, he turns on a furious but controlled attack that stampedes John L. around the ring but never quite knocks him down.

Through it all, Angelo flinches and winces in the corner. In less than three weeks Ali is scheduled to defend his heavyweight title, and here he is boxing without headgear. At least he is wearing a protective belt—Ali has been known to leave it in the dressing room because it spoiled the line of his figure.

"Let me speak." Ali pulls down the ring mike. "I want you all to know my next fight is going to be on home TV. You can sit right in your living rooms with your cheeseburgers, hamburgers, french fries, and see *me*. I'll show you the true champ."

There are a few friendly jeers, and he shakes his head. "It's hard to be humble when you're as great as I am. You could be the world's best garbage man, the world's best model, it don't matter what you do if you're the best.

"Why, I'm so fast I could hit you before God gets the news. I'm so fast I hit the light switch in my room and jump into bed before my room goes dark. Now, I'm going to show you how fast I am."

He calls into the ring Solomon McTier, a local heavyweight who once trained with him. "Put up your hand." He pumps six jabs into McTier's palm, then tells the crowd, "I can throw six punches before you count one, two. That's how fast I am. Now let's hear you count, one, two."

He builds them skillfully. From each corner of the ring he signals, "One, two," until the crowd is up and alive, laughing and hopping. Now he raises his hand for silence. The crowd holds its breath as he steps to the center of the ring and cocks his fist in front of McTier's palm.

"Now you better watch real careful. So fast you might miss it." His eyes are dancing. "Ready? . . . Go."

"ONE, TWO."

He has not moved a muscle. "Want me to do it again? You missed it. You must of blinked."

He leaves them laughing.

We board a 1:58 A.M. flight to Miami. I have been in Florida a little more than twelve hours now, and it feels like a week. The two chronic conditions I remember most vividly from newspaper days have recurred—sweaty armpits and gritty eyelids. They are not entirely unwelcome.

Ali flops into the first seat in the first-class cabin and motions me to sit beside him. I block the stewardess' view and show him my economy class ticket.

"Don't matter," he says impatiently, "you with the champ."

And so I am. The ticket is never checked. Ali orders coffee, empties in six packets of sugar, and gulps it down.

"You ever hear my lecture on friendship?"

"No."

"It's not so heavy as my lecture on the heart of man, but it's real good." He opens a slim black attache case on his lap, and lifts out a thick, dog-eared deck of white five-by-eight-inch index cards. The lecture is written out in black script, and when I lean over to read it he pulls the deck away. "I'll say it slow so you can write it down."

"I've got a tape recorder with me."

"That's good. Then you can concentrate on listening."

My mike hand is steady but my mind wanders during the next half-hour, no mean feat when Muhammad Ali is delivering, at concert hall force, his lecture on friendship a foot from my ear.

"Whenever the thought of self-interest creeps in, that means a destruction of friendship. Every little thought of profiting by it means destruction. This is what I'm doing, things I'm doing today. It can never develop into a real friendship, it can only develop into a business relationship. It will last as long as the business relationship lasts. Like me and Cosell. I lose he goes to somebody else."

I am thinking of questions I will not risk asking while we are just beginning to rebuild our old rapport. Questions about money, sex, politics, and religion. Given time enough and access, some will be answered without having to be asked. What is he thinking about those Vietcong now, in the closing hours of that war? How much of the millions Ali has earned in recent years will he actually keep? This is the kind of question journalists ask to satisfy their editors that they are covering all the bases. Even if there is an accurate figure, Ali will not know it and his tax lawyer will not tell it to me.

How has the recent death of Elijah Muhammad affected Ali's relationship with the Nation of Islam? The Muslims hanging around his Orlando dressing room were pussycats compared to the hardcases I remember, and they seemed extraneous to the scene. Ali barely acknowledged their presence, he was so busy kissing babies and entertaining the newspaper and TV interviewers. As a matter of fact, looking around the airplane, I realize that there are no other Muslims in Ali's party, which has grown to eleven, including a tall, beautiful young woman in an orange dress who may or may not be his companion. I had made discreet inquiries about her, but Angelo and Howard Bingham, the photographer, and C.B. Atkins, the booking agent, stonewalled me. I let the matter drop. Other sportswriters had told me—and several had suggested in print—that Ali was no longer the self-proclaimed "clean-livin', nonfornicatin'" Galahad. Sooner or later I will find out for myself.

"What you think?"

With a start I realize the lecture is over. I blurt the first word that comes to mind and seems appropriate. "Heavy."

"No, it's not heavy at all. It's simple. People understand it right away. I'm going to give it this afternoon at the mosque."

"Are you preaching this afternoon?"

"We say ministering."

The captain announces the start of our descent toward the Miami Airport and Ali looks out his window into the light-pricked early morning darkness. "We're all like little ants. God sees all these little ants, millions of them, and he can't answer all their prayers and bless every one of them. But he sees one ant with a little influence that the other ants will follow. Then he might give that one ant some special powers.

"I'm like a little ant. Lots of other little ants know me, follow me. So God gives me some extra power.

"I pray to Allah before a fight, let me win tonight so I can keep representing my people. Let me win tonight so I can keep walking through the streets helping my people. God, let me fight for *you*.

"God, with this title I can do it.

"No one can whip me as long as I feel this way."

"But you've lost fights," I say. "How come? Was it a lack of sufficient faith?"

"It was a punishment. Things I did, playing too much, didn't train right."

"What things did you do?"

"Nobody's business but me and Allah," he says firmly and looks away. But to change the subject and make up he fishes out a small white envelope and spills seven paper geometric shapes on top of the attache case. "Can you put this together into a perfect square? I can."

All the way down to Miami I try, and fail. When I ask him to show me the trick, he shakes his head and puts the puzzle away.

At the airport, the tall, beautiful young woman in the orange dress is dismissed by Ali with a curt "I'll call you." Cabs roar up. Ali yells to the others, "I'm going with the reporter," and we both climb into the rear of a cab. John L. gets into the front, turns, sees us, apologizes and starts to get out, but Ali invites him to stay. We are going to the Fontainebleau, John L., a few miles further up the beach.

"How old are you?" asks Ali.

"Thirty-one," says John L.

"You old."

"You older," says John L. "You thirty-three."

"I got gray hair. My hair's getting thin in the back. You see it? Pressure." He nudges me. "You know why I came down here to train?"

"As a matter of fact, I wondered why. You've got some setup in Pennsylvania."

"Got $300,000 in that camp. And everybody on me up there, day and night, got to give 'em money, got to worry about their problems. Had to get away from that. Fuck 'em. Got to take care of my own family, my brother's family. I got $1.5 million for the Wepner fight and I only cleared $240,000. I'm getting $1 million for Lyle, I'll clear $300,000. Just from saving money on all my helpers. Fuck 'em.

"I can use that extra money to buy schoolbuses for children. Sewing machines for women they can save money making their own clothes. Air-conditioning for the mosque in Miami. If I'm going to give my money away, I'll do it the way I want.

"Can't drive but one car at a time, I eat only one meal a day. Clothes. You see I don't care about clothes. When I first came down here I saw this millionaire, I wondered how he could wear such cheap suits and drive a Chevvy. Now I understand. *He* knew he got it.

"Now, *I* know *I* got it. Look at these shoes, only ones I got and they need a shine. These pants, too big on me so that's why I roll the waist. This jacket I took off Howard Cosell this afternoon. No tie. I *know* I got it."

He points to John L. in the front seat. John L. is staring straight ahead. "Now him. I gave him a hundred dollar bill and he's real happy. Hundred dollar bill make him happy, that's why he's got to wear that special suit and those high heel shoes."

As the cab pulls into the Fontainebleau driveway Ali turns his pockets inside out for money. He finds three single dollar bills which he gives to John L. to pay for the last leg of his ride home. He says to me, "You got five?"

"I do." The fare is twice that, and I pay it as the king of all kings, the man who *knows* he's got it, waves goodnight and with remarkable energy bounces up the steps of the hotel.

The pot-bellied, balding man at the door of the Fifth Street Gym says, "Hey, cost you a buck to get in," as I brush past him.

"I'm press," I say. It's the principle.

"Press my pants. One buck."

"Lou Gross, don't you recognize me? I remember when you used to bang on Willie Pastrano's bathroom door, 'Willie, if you don't get off the can this minute you'll die of piles.'"

Lou Gross backs up to study me. "Bob Lipsyte? Whatever happened to you? Why'd you quit? How ya makin' out? I didn't recognize you, you gained weight and lost some hair." Good old diplomatic Lou. He could never get Willie out of the bathroom, either. Lou steps forward and lowers his voice. "I got a real good lightweight I want you to meet."

Everybody's got a real good lightweight, with a nickname like Spider or Termite or Chi-Chi, and it seems as though every one of them, hair still damp from the dressing room shower, is waiting at the ring to watch Ali work out. This is his true throne room, this determinedly shabby second-floor gym. Since 1960 he has been prince and heir-apparent and king and ex-king and king again here, among men who share an aspect of his life that I suspect is far more important to him than he would have the world believe. Yesterday, explaining to me why he keeps fighting, Ali said, "People listen to me because I'm champ of the world, that's why I keep fighting, so I can keep doing Allah's work. I'm on a divine mission. I was born to do what I'm doing. I'll be told when to retire."

I believe he is sincere, yet I cannot forget that Ali has been absorbed in boxing for more than twenty years, since he was 12, and I have never seen him so comfortable as when he is boxing or talking about boxing or surrounded by boxing people. When he is talking about God or money or friendship he is often less than compelling, but when he is explaining a ring strategy there is no doubt you are listening to that rare craftsman who understands his work so thoroughly he can make it clear and simple.

Ali: "Now, boxers always been told, 'Don't get caught in the corner, don't get trapped on the ropes, spin off the ropes.' That was a cardinal rule. I'm changing all that. I say, lay on the ropes. You cover up, your arms and elbows protect your body and your ribs, your gloves protect your face. Only place you can get hit is your arms, shoulders and the top of your head. Let them hit you. Let those suckers punch themselves to death. You keep peeking out your gloves to see what's happening, but you don't put your hands down. Keep 'em up and lay on the ropes to draw him in. Now, if it's a real *heavy* hitter, you take a chance for a round or two that he won't hurt your arms so much you won't be able to punch later on. You got to be like a jet pilot, ready to change your course if the weather shifts. Lay on the ropes. Bounce against the ropes to take some of the shock of the punches. It takes more strength and energy to dance around, to dodge and duck punches than it takes to just lay on the ropes and block those blows. You get older, you got to think of those things. Meanwhile that sucker is punching himself to death. Now he's so tired after a few rounds, you just go and take him out. Whop-whop-whop. UH. 'Course a real smart fighter's not going to let you do all that; he's not going to let you draw him in so easy. And I'm not saying every fighter should lay on the ropes. You got to know what you're doing. I know a few shortcuts."

The dollar-a-head afternoon crowd applauds as Ali bounds into the training ring. Those who have never seen him before in the flesh are stunned. Because his proportions are so perfect, he is much larger, more powerfully built, than one might conclude from television and still photographs.

While he shadowboxes, jumps rope, exercises, I tour the gym. For years, his spillage has supported this place, but it does not reflect him. Most of the memorabilia on the walls, which are peeling again despite a recent paint job, are either photographs of Angelo and Chris Dundee with their arms around Joe Louis or Jack Dempsey or war buddies, or plaques honoring the Dundees for public service from the local Pony League, the Optimists, B'nai B'rith. In one corner is a faded poster for Ali's January 20, 1970 "computer fight" against Rocky Marciano, a grotesque film ostensibly edited from hours of sparring between the two men. (Ali, then deep in his exile, was "knocked out" in the version I saw. Chris Dundee was the "referee." When the film was released, Marciano was already four months dead.) In another corner is a large, bright oil painting, titled "Youth vs. Experience." The artist had presented it to Ali in Orlando the other night, and Angelo had lugged it back on the plane. It depicts Ali beating Foreman in Zaire. Ali is Experience. Incredible! Only yesterday we were standing in this room with the Beatles.

There is a stir near the door. Jimmy Ellis strides in behind his million-dollar smile. A bright red sports jacket cannot hide his girth. He has come down from Louisville to get into shape for the last few fights of his notable career. Angelo will so maneuver him that he will earn a few paydays and go out a winner. Ali has quit rope-skipping to inspect his former sparring partner and home-town friend.

"Look good."

"Been running," says Ellis.

They separate to be the center of different crowds. The boxers, managers, and handlers surround Ellis for banter and gossip. The civilians press against Ali, who stands at the rope that separates the audience from the boxing folk. Leggy black girls with flash Instamatics take turns posing with him; few can resist kissing him when they are close enough. Sometimes he kisses them back, on the cheek or neck, the least he does is cry "Wooooooo" and pretend to swoon. Vacationing white collegians, male and female, are more reserved, but stare at him with a hot covetousness that seems nearly universal. It was a sportswriter, Jim Murray of Los Angeles, who summed it up best with the frequently quoted, "I'd like to borrow his body for just forty-eight hours, there are three guys I'd like to beat up, and four women I'd like to make love to."

Tourist couples thrust small children into Ali's arms. He hugs them and kisses them. "You remember this your whole life, your mommy and daddy remind you if you forget, and show you the picture. You was kissed by the champ."

He notices my flying pen and delivers an aside: "One time Joe Louis came to Louisville and he leaned against a telephone pole on my street. Didn't mean nothing to him, how many poles you think he leaned on? But my momma *never* forgot. She still can't pass that telephone pole without telling us Joe Louis leaned on it. Nothing to him, big thing to her."

Reluctantly, Ali lets Sarria lead him into the dressing room for table exercises and a rubdown. Eight of us, press, fans, friends, follow and stand against the peeling gray walls to give Sarria elbow room. Ali hates these sit-ups and leg-raisers and trunk-twisters, but he is overweight and at least as concerned about the aesthetics of the belt of flab around his waist as he is about the drag it might cause in a fight. The talk is desultory, but it gets Ali through the exercises.

"Hey, man, dig this," says a young white man who is dressed and coiffed and bearded to resemble General Custer. "Every morning, God wakes up and looks down and He says, 'Wow! Muhammad Ali! My masterpiece! Did I really make that? How did I ever pull that off?' "

Ali laughs and shakes his head and introduces me to Bernie

Yuman, the 25-year-old manager of a rock group. Ali says, "When he was a little kid I took him and three friends for a ride on my motorcycle. Be a lesson to you. You never know what you're gonna get back when you invest in children. Might even grow up to be a lawyer. Defend you. It happens."

"Ali!" booms C.B. Atkins, the booking agent, who has his arm on a stout black man in a flowered shirt. He introduces him as a promoter from Honolulu.

"What's it like there?" asks Ali.

"Paradise, man," breathes the promoter.

"Fine ladies?" Ali winks at me.

"Everything."

"Lots of us there?"

"More all the time."

The door opens and closes mysteriously. Then I notice a tiny boy wearing a Disney World cap with Muhammad written on the brim in yellow script. Ali's 2-year-old son, the youngest of his four children. Little Muhammad marches to the table, watches Sarria massage his father's leg, then grabs a foot for himself and tickles it. Ali tries to reach him, but Muhammad dodges and hangs on to the foot.

"Love the way you put down Cosell," says someone.

"Yeah," says Ali. He mimics himself. "Cosell, you ain't the mouth you used to be."

There is a great deal more cackling, knee slapping, head shaking and foot stomping than the line deserves.

"Nice of you to take a knockdown for old Levi," says someone else.

"He really knocked me down," says Ali unconvincingly.

"Picture was in all the papers," says C.B. "When you get knocked down it is *news*."

"News," echoes Ali. He shoots a finger at me. "That right?"

"That's right. The editor of *The New York Times* called me this morning and said, 'Forget about Ali, he's old hat. Give us ten thousand words and five pictures on Levi Forte, the Fighting Bellhop.'"

There is a moment of silence, then Ali's tentative, "That right?"

I wait a beat before I say, "Just kidding." I wonder if I really saw an instant of panic in Ali's eyes.

It is now that the man in the dark suit, the federal court officer, enters to serve his papers, and disrupts the mood of the room.

Ali showers in a rusty stall so narrow he must step outside to soap himself. It is a stall for Termite and Chi-Chi, not for the 6-foot 3-inch, 225-pound heavyweight king. But Ali has showered here since 1960, and he is here now not only to escape all his helpers, fuck 'em, but to renew himself at the fountain of his magical youth. If I feel younger in this room and remember my first international front-page assignment, how must he feel?

Ellis slips into the room and watches Ali towel off and dress. His red jacket, jewelry, and glistening shoes seem gaudy as Ali pulls on the same brown pants, the same scuffed black slip-ons he wore in Toronto and Orlando. He puts on a short-sleeved red shirt and buttons it outside his pants to hide the rolled waist. It doesn't really matter what he wears.

"There's a country, I can't name it here," says Ali softly to Ellis, "wants me to defend my title there. I can pick my opponent. Anybody I want. You could get yourself a couple hundred thousand. Okay?"

"Okay?" Ellis' eyes pop. His smile lights up his face. "*O-kay!*"

Ali nods and walks out to tape an interview for Italian television.

Angelo is holding court in a corner of the gym. "You know, he's still a nice kid. The easiest fighter I ever had. Unspoiled from the beginning. He changed around the whole charisma of boxing but he's still the nice kid I used to give a deuce to stay loose."

"Why is that?"

"Because he *likes* boxing. That's the key. He *likes* the sport. You know, the nicest times we have is after road work, 5:30, 6 o'clock in the morning, that serene time after he's finished running when we can just sit around and talk boxing."

"Can he really get Ellis a title shot?"

"Wouldn't that be something?" Angelo shrugs. "Why not? He's the champ, isn't he?"

Our plane is taxiing for takeoff. Ali, beside me, is wearing the same scuffed black shoes, rolled brown pants, and red shirt. I notice his seat belt is open and remind him to buckle it.

"Don't need to," he says.

"Why?"

"Nothing happen to me."

"How come?"

"I'm under divine protection."

I am very relaxed, my notebook is fat, my assignment will be over in less than twelve hours. I take a calculated risk, and say, "In that case, Muhammad, would you mind if I unbuckle my belt, too, and just hold your hand till we get to Orlando?"

Ali laughs. He's come a long way. His religion, which he once described as fitting the American black man like a glove, seems to rest far more lightly and comfortably on him now than it did in the late sixties when he spat out Muslim dogma in undigested chunks. He has absorbed his religion, blended it into his own style, packaged it for easy—well, easier—listening. He is firm enough in his convictions to laugh patronizingly at a non-believer. Once, he might have bridled at my lame joke. Had I dared make it. He's very smooth now, even subtle sometimes. Last night, driving back to the hotel after attending a Miami high school athletes award night, he said:

"Things that are solid, black people don't think about that. They just come up and dance and sing and go to church and shout. We never thought about doing nothing for ourselves, we depend on white people to grow our food and make our clothes. We are now *thinking*! The Honorable Elijah Muhammad, our leader, has woken us up and got us looking, going to the earth. Look at that beautiful plaza there. Ain't that nice, wouldn't that be nice if that was downtown Washington and the black man owned the land and owned the building and employed his own? Everybody could stay in it but we could say, 'This is ours.' Say, if I can get Sammy Davis and Flip Wilson and Bill Cosby and the Jackson Five, the Fifth Dimension, Diana Ross, the Supremes, the O. J.s, the Spinners, Muhammed Ali, we could go to Madison Square Garden and put on a concert for ten days and fill it every night and *buy that building*. We'd just have to work free for ten days. We'd draw the people; they all like me. Used to be a sign on Miami Beach says No Dogs, Niggers, and Jews Allowed. Jews got mad and united and bought the damn beach. So this is all I'm trying to do. I'm not God and I can't save it. But I just want to take my little title, I won't be here too long, soon somebody else'll have it, but now that I got the press I want to do something good."

The stewardess brings us coffee. He watches me drink.

"How can you drink it black?" he asks.

"Black is pure and strong."

He pours lightener into his own cup, and says airily, "See, I'm integratin'."

There is much about him now of the old Cassius Clay and the early Muhammad Ali before his title was stolen. He is making predictions again, spouting rhyme, taking enormous pleasure in staging little surprise parties for the world with himself as guest of honor and gift. Nothing seems to delight him more than to suddenly appear—on a downtown street, in a residential neighborhood (black or white), in stores, arenas, restaurants, hotel lobbies—and watch people stop . . . turn . . . double-take . . . mouth, "Is that really . . . ?", and then, convinced it really is, stampede toward him. He is eminently accessible, rarely turns down a request for an autograph or a handshake, even while eating, and will gladly make a speech for one old lady or two Cub Scouts as readily as for millions on network television. Lest a fan's lifetime dream be spoiled, Ali is usually alert for capped lenses or improperly mounted flashcubes. He often seems as boyish and brimming as the old Louisville Lip, wading through crowds with open arms, touching, hugging, kissing, respectful of old people, gentle with babies, sly with foxes, even mellow with the ultrastylish pimps and whores whose swagger and flash once backed him into defensive postures of contempt. I sense Ali is still more respectful toward whites than blacks, the powerful than the poor, but the gap is not quite as wide as it once was, mainly because he is looser with non-Muslim blacks than he was in the late sixties. Watching him gain nourishment from crowds it is hard to remember how somber he was those years, sometimes bitter, always searching for a moral lesson from his legal, marital, social, religious problems. Allah was testing him, he said then. Now, he is champion again: "That's top of the world," he says. Late one night he qualifies his joy.

"The training is so hard when you really don't have to train. I don't *have* to be up in the morning. Sign up for $1 million in the bank. But if I lose I'll have to start getting up to make a comeback and get serious. Ken Norton won, Joe Frazier won, and I sacrificed. I was real serious. Real strict. Real slim. The last two rounds I came back cookin'. When things are going my way I have a tendency to say, 'Aw, I got it made, I don't have to train that hard. I can beat this chump in half condition.' I enjoy it more when I'm making a comeback, but I'd rather be the way I am now. You never know if you're going to get that chance or not, that chance to come back."

Flying, we look through the current *Ebony* magazine in which he is featured in three separate articles—one about the country's highest-paid athletes (he is No. 1), one about its most important black leaders (in alphabetical order), and one about the death of Elijah Muhammad.

I ask, "Does your religion believe that Elijah is now in heaven with Allah?," although I know the answer.

"He's just in a grave. No pie in the sky when you die. But his spirit is still with us. He was the wisest man in America."

"How will the Muslims survive without him?"

"His son, Wallace, is even wiser."

"How can that be?"

He looks at me with surprise. "You think Allah's going to let us slide backwards? We got a even wiser leader now. Wallace, he can recite the whole Koran by heart. In Arabic. We're in a new phase now, a resurrection. Elijah taught us to be independent, to clean ourselves up, to be proud and healthy. He stressed the bad things the white man did to us so we could get free and strong. Now we're in this new phase, and Wallace is showing us there are good and bad regardless of color, that devil is in the mind and heart, not the skin."

We are making our descent when Ali takes out the small white envelope and spills out the seven geometric shapes on his attache case. "You want to try again?"

"No. I can't do it. And I don't think you can do it either."

"You right. I can't. I'm going back to Cleveland where I got it, and make them show me how to do it. Then I'm going to go around and bet people one dollar to my ten they can't make a perfect square. Gonna raise a lot of money for charity."

"You ever think there might be a piece missing? Maybe you

just can't make a perfect square from the pieces you have. Maybe
it's all a plot to wreck your mind."

"No, there a way to do it." He does not sound absolutely convinced, however. "I just got to find out." But he puts the puzzle
away.

Ali is receiving well-wishers and petitioners in the stern of a
motor home parked outside the Leeds catalogue store. He has
just finished a jive-and-autograph session inside, a leftover obli-
gation from Saturday night's benefit exhibition, and he is briefly
enervated; at least he is not twitching, jabbing, rolling his head
to drain off excess energy. He sits quietly on the long bench
under the rear window, polite and impassive, as local blacks pay
their respects or press a cause. Local whites, like the Daytona
Beach banker who has organized this motor home trip, and
blacks with national reputations, can somehow always get through
to Ali on the telephone.

A young woman approaches and presents a legal-appearing
document, which Ali pretends to study, then hands to me. I do
not appreciate becoming an instant courtier, but Ali is no reader.
I explain that it's an eviction notice. She is $124.79 behind in her
rent. I hand the notice back to Ali.

"I'm not asking you for the money," she says. "Can you give me
a job?"

"I don't have no jobs. I got ten people I really don't need right
now and I'm not paying them," he says. "I'm a Black Muslim. You
know us. I take care of my people. I can't worry about the world.
That's what the government's for. How much money you need?"

"I'm looking for a job." She snatches the eviction notice from
his hands. "Can you create a job for me?"

"If I had a job, you got a job. Okay, sister. Thanks for coming
by."

As the motor home inches through the crowd, Ali points out a
black family, the father in a dark suit, the mother in a white
dress, the children scrubbed and turned-out as if for church.
They wave decorously, with a proprietary pride, as if this is the
royal carriage. "See there," says Ali. "Muslims. So clean and
peaceful. You can tell they're Muslims. Eyes so bright, healthy-
looking, neat hair, respectful children."

On the highway to Daytona Beach, Ali moves up front to be interviewed by two local newsmen. I relax on the back bench between C.B. Atkins and Howard Bingham. C.B. is a large, handsome, stylish middle-aged man who used to be introduced as the ex-husband of singer Sarah Vaughan. In the last few years he has gained a more immediate identification as Ali's "business manager," which he is not; rather he has been spending less time with his Chicago booking agency to stalk the big ten percent of a multimillion-dollar Ali deal. When I ask him about business, he says it's easier to negotiate with a sheik than with a nightclub owner.

Bingham has been Ali's most constant non-Muslim companion since 1962 when the 20-year-old contender Cassius Clay appeared on a TV talk show in Los Angeles. Bingham, a 22-year-old photographer for a black weekly newspaper, covered Clay's press conference, then spotted him on a streetcorner eyeballing girls. They roistered around the city together and later drove cross-country to Miami in Clay's new Cadillac. Bingham is now 35, on his own a successful magazine, record-jacket, and movie still photographer. His wife shops with Belinda Ali, his little son plays with Muhammad, Jr., but Howard occasionally waxes nostalgic for the days when everything was "fun." Life apparently still has its moments: Howard recalls with relish how, after their recent flight from Jamaica bumped down hard in Chicago, Ali commandeered the pilot's intercom to announce to startled fellow passengers, "I'm real sorry, folks, it was my first landing, the best I could do."

I'm sweating. The air-conditioning in the motor home is failing. C.B. and Howard open the side windows and strip to the waist. They try to doze. As seasoned Ali sidekicks they have learned to pace themselves, to snatch their comforts and their food when they can. I'm grateful. At lunchtime they dissuaded Ali from stopping at a McDonald's. They wanted a cool downtown restaurant with amenities. But Ali was in a hurry, he was hungry *now*, and they compromised with a roadside Ponderosa Steak House. For all Ali's talk about good food carefully prepared by his Muslim cooks, he is nutritionally inconsistent. He has been eating hotel food in Miami and fast food on the road; when pressed to justify this odd disregard for the engine of his machine, he talks calories, not chemicals.

Since I'm a short-timer now and do not have to pace myself, I move up to the front of the motor home. Ali is haranguing the local newsmen, reminding them how he has always been ahead of his time. Didn't he change his name before Kareem Abdul-Jabbar made it fashionable? Didn't he put down the Vietnam war before the people woke up to what was happening? The newsmen, jammed into the dining booth with Ali, really want to talk sports but are in all ways trapped. Ali asks if they want to hear his "Recipe To Life," and they feign enthusiasm. The Daytona Beach physician who owns the motor home and is driving it raises his drink and the banker who heads this Boys Club rescue mission looks up from his checklists. Ali is in high humor, and when I flip on my tape recorder he gestures for the machine.

"The Recipe To Life.

"Take a few cups of Love.

"One teaspoon of patience.

"One tablespoon of generosity.

"One pint of kindness.

"One drop of laughter.

"One sprinkle of concern.

"And then, mix willingness with happiness,

"Add lots of faith,

"And mix well.

"Then spread it over the span of a lifetime,

"And serve it to each and every deserving person you meet."

Either the doctor or the banker says, "Beautiful," and Ali repeats his recipe slowly so the newspapermen can write down every word. I am slightly amused by their discomfort. My tape recorder and longer deadline make me temporarily superior; and then, I paid my dues.

"All the stuff that I write is real spiritual," says Ali. "I mean, it moves people. It's real plain." He nods with satisfaction at the pile of pages each has already filled. "You'll have enough to write ten articles about me. Big hit stories."

"I'll have a big hit story out of it," says one of the newspapermen. I cannot tell if he is serious, but I hope not.

"I wrote something once. It says,

"I once had a friend named Billy, who was told by his friend, 'Mary, your girlfriend, is not beautiful. What do you see in her?'

"Billy said, 'To see Mary you must follow my eyes.' So when

we judge people do we see them with the eyes of love? If we can't see it this way, which we cannot, we have no right to question why some are rich and some are poor, why some are successful.

"People say, 'Why does he get so much a fight, why does he get so important?' And then, after they meet me, they say, 'You just don't know him, there are so many sides. He's not an ordinary boxer. Joe Frazier, George Foreman couldn't talk to you with nearly the skill he talks. No ballplayer can lecture colleges.'

"Elijah Muhammad so wise he made Malcolm X what he was. His son Wallace D. Muhammad so much wiser. I'm under these wise black men. I study and read and overhear 'em talking. So when I come out here I'm like a . . . a little god mentally.

"Like I wrote a poem that explains truth. It says,

"The face of truth is open,
"The eyes of truth are bright.
"The lips of truth are never closed,
"The head of truth is up right.
"The breast of truth stands forward,
"The gaze of truth is straight,
"Truth has neither fear nor doubt,
"Truth has patience to wait.
"The words of truth are touching,
"The voice of truth is deep,
"The law of truth is simple,
"All you sow you reap.
"The soul of truth is flaming,
"The heart of truth is far,
"The mind of truth is clear,
"And shines through rain and star.
"The facts are only in shadows,
"Truth stands above all sin,
"Great be the battle of life,
"Truth in the end shall win.
"The image of truth is the Cross,
"Wisdom's message its rod.
"The sign of truth is Christ,
"And the soul of truth is God.
"The life of truth is eternal,
"And mortal is its past,

"The power of truth shall endure,

"Truth shall hold to the last.

"I don't care who you are, professor, doctor, lawyer, what race, they understand that. That's the Christian version. The Moslem version, I say,

"The image of truth is Mohammed,

"Wisdom's message his rod,

"The sign of truth is the crescent,

"And the soul of truth is God.

"In both religions they're right if you understand them. Got to understand them. I'm studying the Holy Koran and the Bible now. I could talk from here to Miami and back, all week, talkin' something different if I had the time permitted."

One of the newspapermen says, "Just since you've been associated with this religion?"

"Oh, no, I was always a talker. Talked about nothin'. Can't remember what I used to talk about. One of my sayings says,

"The man who has no imagination stands on the Earth, he has no wings, he cannot fly. Understand that? Writers are men of wisdom, that's why I talk to you. See, the average man I can't talk to. Some of the most wisest men in the world are the loneliest men. Nobody else is on their level. I can only talk to professors of colleges, great poets, newspaper writers, somebody who understands knowledge. The man who has no imagination stands on the Earth. He has no wings, he cannot fly. You need an imagination to be a writer. You'll write about the man as we went along the highway, right? As he talked, as he drank his juice. Columbus had imagination. The Wright Brothers had imagination. I have an imagination. Boxers don't have imagination. The way I was talking about 'Lay on the ropes!' Imagination. 'I am the greatest, he'll fall in eight, go to your TVs.' That's imagination."

The newspapermen seize this opportunity to ask questions about other fights, about tactics and training. Ali answers, but he obviously has been temporarily brought down. His face sags, his voice drops and its rhythms flatten out. There is a sudden diversion. The banker interrupts with a logistical point from his checklist, and by the time it is settled the newspapermen have lost their momentum.

Ali asks, "How's this one?

"Where is man's wealth? His wealth is in his knowledge. If his wealth was in the bank and not in his knowledge, then he don't possess it. Because it's in the bank!" Ali shakes his head and whispers, "Heavy.

"I prove that when they took my title. My knowledge, I went to colleges. Fifteen hundred dollars a lecture. Some weeks I made $6000 a week, four or five colleges. Campaignin', talkin'. My wealth was in my knowledge.

"I'm learnin' something today. I'm noticing things talking to you-all, you don't notice. Every tree is a lesson, every leaf, every shape has a purpose."

There is another point the banker must check, and the newspapermen gain possession of the loose ball.

"What do you think of some of the other great athletes, Arnold Palmer, for example, Jack Nicklaus?"

"I don't follow them, I don't know them. I know their names, but I never watched a whole golf game. I don't admire nobody much, too much. When you find out how great Allah God is, when you find out the greatest men of the Islam faith, the truly great men of history, never wanted to be great.

"The *truly* great men of history never wanted to be great. Nor did they consider themselves as such. All they wanted was the chance to be close to God, the only true great one himself.

"You-all got that?"

It is evening, a balmy, sweet spring evening in Daytona Beach. The motor home is parked at the edge of a high school football field. Ali sticks his head out of a side window. "Where the foxes?"

The crowd laughs. Hundreds of men, women, children, and foxes are pressing against a wire fence that prevents them from engulfing the motor home. They ignore the amateur bouts in the ring fifty yards away in the middle of the field.

"Bring me some foxes," Ali roars.

It is incredibly crowded inside the motor home: Ali, C.B., Howard, Angelo, Angelo's war buddy, the banker, the doctor, the doctor's son, the doctor's daughter, the doctor's daughter's boyfriend, the son of Jake LaMotta, the boss of the son of Jake LaMotta, a writer from New York, the wife of the writer from New York, Solomon McTier, me . . .

The door clicks open and three pretty young women wearing Ali T-shirts—undeniably foxes—climb into the motor home and are woven through bodies toward Ali in the stern. I squeeze into a momentary vacuum and pop outside. The air is delicious.

My enthusiasm is beginning to wind down. My mind, like my notebook, is swollen with Ali. I need to leave him and dump out. I realize for the first time that it is easier to write about him for a daily newspaper, in 800-word chunks, escaping every day to frame a reality and discharge it, than to write for a magazine never knowing when to stop collecting facts. Or do seasoned magazine writers start to think in 5000-word chunks?

The door clicks open. The five women step down. Ali is dressing for his exhibition bouts. The door clicks open again and by the pitch and intensity of crowd noise I know Ali is coming out. Don't even have to look, old pro that I am. Experience, that's us. I move into the slipstream behind two wide cops and whoooosh all the way to ringside without having to shoulder another body. You get older, you got to think of these things. You got to know what you're doing. I know a few shortcuts.

Ali boxes Levi and he boxes John L. He stands between rounds because Angelo has given me his ring stool to sit on. Angelo is so shrewd we will never know whether he was being kind to me or toughening up the champ. When it's over, Ali grabs the mike. "Very unusual, never before in history has a heavyweight champion, two weeks before a fight come out with no headgear before a crowd so small and tickets so cheap."

The crowd, perhaps 3000, applauds its claim to fame.

"I admire your stadium, I like your style, but the equipment's so cheap, I won't be back for a while."

The crowd cheers wildly.

And then the cops are rushing Ali out of the ring. The darkness beyond the stands suddenly blazes with headlights, cars explode and screech into the night. I hear someone calling, "Lipsyte . . . Lipsyte . . ." It is Angelo, packing people into cars. He waves me over, but I've already found a place in a Cadillac with C.B. Trust C.B. to pick the largest and most comfortable car. The others are scattered among several station wagons, compacts, and a Volkswagen. I take a quick count. Only the doctor, Ali, and one of the foxes are not in a car. The motor home swings out and heads toward the airport. The caravan follows.

I have already made arrangements to stay over in Daytona Beach tonight and fly to New York in the morning so I can talk about this book at my publisher's sales conference. My assignment is over. I'm free now to go to my motel. But some old reporter's instinct refuses to give me a goodnight. I have to go to the airport, I have to make sure Ali gets there in time for his midnight flight to Miami. Most of the cars peel off en route: There is plenty of time for a late supper before the flight. But the Caddy follows the motor home, which turns off the main airport road and stops in a dark and quiet spot on the far side of the terminal.

The doctor comes out shaking his head.

I ask, "What's going on in there?"

"I didn't look."

I stroll over. Is the motor home jiggling ever so slightly; is it jouncing almost imperceptibly? Imagination. You need it to be a writer. Goodnight king of all kings, lonely man of wisdom, champion of the world. And thanks again. It's true. You always take care of me. When I'm around you I always got something to write about.

I ask Bingham to say goodbye to Ali for me and I catch a cab back into town.

I don't want to make too much of this, irony, symbolism, but the Daytona Beach *Morning Journal* of Wednesday, April 30, 1975, the one I read flying back to New York, had four Associated Press dispatches on its front page concerning the end of American involvement in South Vietnam, and the only other news was the caption about the Halifax Boys Club benefit under a very large photograph of Muhammad Ali.

5

On January 8, 1970, Jack Scott, then a young teaching assistant at the University of California in Berkeley, planted his red track shoes on a classroom floor, tugged the peak of his baseball cap, rolled his shoulders under a gym shirt, blew a whistle, and barked, "This is Education 191D. There are two rumors about this course. One, it's a mick. Two, it's a trap for athletes. I'm supposed to be a radical guy, and halfway through I'm going to pile on the requirements and make everyone ineligible."

Several hundred undergraduates smiled warily, shifted in their chairs and exchanged glances. Among them was a senior football captain seeking to clarify his athletic motivations, some of his varsity teammates who thought the 3-point course would be a Mickey Mouse breather, several varsity dropouts hoping to reinforce their moral justification for quitting, a number of girls suspected of "chasing jocks," student assistant coaches and scores of non-athletes lured by the prospect of uncharted inquiry implicit in the course's title: "Intercollegiate Athletics and Education: A Socio-Psychological Evaluation."

Most of that first class session, which I attended, was devoted to registration and orientation, but currents of excitement and anticipation were almost palpable; for some of the students the course promised to be an experience in consciousness raising, for others a liberation. During a break, I talked to a big former varsity lineman, who had let his hair grow after he quit. "People at home began to look at me differently. I had been a football hero and now they had to either reject me or rethink their values," he said.

The present captain of the Berkeley team told me that he no longer fully enjoyed the game, that he understood it was "a manhood thing" and an "ego trip," but he couldn't quit. He had to stick it out to prove how tough he really was.

I asked Scott, whom I had met for the first time that morning, why he had opened the class with a whistle blast.

"It's not the system so much as the misuse of the system by coaches that has to be changed," he said, in the reasonable, if pedantic, modulation that has always marked his speech. "When I walked in and blew that whistle, the class looked startled. A teacher blowing a whistle in class, that's incredible.

"Yet 300 yards from here, men who are also supposed to be teachers act and dress like this all the time, curse their students, and impose arbitrary rules about hair, clothes, social life, and no one thinks twice about it.

"I hope this course makes people think twice, then do something to make the university approach to athletics more holistic instead of a fetish for performance statistics, and stop those coaches who are distorting one of the most creative and exciting activities of college life."

In the five years between ED 191D and his national celebrity as a figure in the Patty Hearst case, Scott got a Ph.D. in psychology from Berkeley and a label—"the guru of jock liberation." He was attacked by Vice-President Agnew, Ronald Reagan, Max Rafferty, and a number of nationally prominent coaches, athletic directors, and journalists who saw him, justifiably, as a threat to the old Big Boy network that runs American amateur athletics as securely as West Point graduates run the Army.

In 1973, in a letter to Columbia supporting Scott's application for the athletic directorship, I wrote, "During the controversies that surrounded him in the sixties, Scott's own tremendous love for sports and athletic excellence was often obscured by his critics. Scott was impressive to me because he was the most articulate spokesman for a larger view that saw the athlete as a student—not as a hairy freak to be manipulated by coaches usurping faculty and administration authority. Scott sometimes gave otherwise reasonable men fits—an odd thing, I thought, since he never questioned the basic worth of sports, but rather illuminated its abuse, that curious two-faced approach that saw sports as, at once, a public relations and fund-raising arm, and as a necessary embarrassment."

The incumbent assistant A.D. got the job.

Scott was born in 1942, in Scranton, Pa. He ran track and played football in high school in Scranton and Syracuse, N.Y., held athletic scholarships in track at Villanova and Stanford. He worked for seven months as a laborer on a ballistic missile site in Greenland and eventually graduated, on academic scholarship, from Syracuse University in 1966.

For all his flair for publicity, the controversy he has stirred, and the real impact he has made on sports, Scott himself has remained a relatively unflamboyant figure; he claims he actively works at "defusing any cult of personality" that might grow around him by emphasizing the contribution of his wife Micki McGee, a writer and photographer, and others to the Institute for the Study of Sport and Society, Scott's center for sports reformation and protest that has helped prepare or publish—at varying levels of involvement—Dave Meggyesy's *Out of Their League*, Gary Shaw's *Meat on the Hoof*, Paul Hoch's *Rip Off the Big Game*, and, of course, Scott's own *Athletics for Athletes* and *The Athletic Revolution*.

The last book is required reading in most of the literally hundreds of college courses in sports sociology, sports history, sports psychology, sports philosophy, and sports through theological, black, female, educational, and kinesthetic perspectives spawned by ED 191D. Scott created a whole new academic subspecialty, interdisciplinary, no less, although much of it is Mickey Mouse.

The Athletic Revolution, which was published in 1971, promotes Scott's basic thesis that intercollegiate athletics are intrinsically worthwhile but should be made consistent with some sort of educational philosophy and placed under the same control and guidelines as the academic departments of a university.

This brands Scott a radical in most athletic departments because it subverts the basis of their power. By remaining free from the control of the educational community, athletic departments have become independent duchies answerable—if at all—only to the highest level of administrators, alumni and, if attached to a public institution, legislators.

No wonder that Scott was hired and fired (without working a day) at the University of Washington, for reasons that have never been satisfactorily explained, although the university paid him a year's salary in settlement. Scott lasted less than two years of his four-year contract as athletic director of Oberlin, an Ohio college whose famous libertarian traditions, according to Scott, are rooted in the nineteenth century, where they remained. Again, he was paid off to stay away.

For a while, however, Oberlin was "like a dream come true" for Jack and Micki. "We had a key to the gym. You don't know what that meant, after years of sneaking into gyms to lift weights or run on the track, after scrounging around for a place to work out. We had our own key to a $5 million gym. We could work out whenever we wanted; we could invite friends over for a swim at midnight."

They also had a large house that became a center for Oberlin athletes and for the visiting "athletic counterculture." Scott hired Tommie Smith of the black-gloved Olympic salute as his assistant A. D. and track coach, and Cass Jackson as his football coach. Jackson was the first black head football coach at a predominantly white college. Ever.

"People kept saying, aren't you moving too fast?" recalled Scott later. "What did we do that was wrong? Every time we had a job opening we hired the best people we could, because I wanted the best program I could get. There's so much racism in this country there's a surplus of highly qualified black people. So we hired three blacks. Isn't that the American way, get the best people you can?"

At Oberlin, Scott finally had a chance to practice his preachments. He discontinued admission charges to athletic events. He opened more facilities to women, and broadened the recreational program. He gave varsity athletes veto power in the hiring of their coaches. He also tried to win games.

"I've always resented deeply being put into the camp that says it's wrong to try hard in sports," says Scott. "One of the beautiful things about sports is going all out, playing with total abandonment, your entire being, your mind and body integrated. But when it's over, it's over. It was a game, not World War III.

"I don't think there's anything wrong with feeling a little bad if you lost, if tension got the best of you and you didn't run as fast as you should have. There's a lesson in that, it's part of growing up. And I'm just old-fashioned enough to think getting punched in the nose in a football game isn't so terrible. If that's the worst brutality on the planet we're in good shape.

"And one of the beautiful things about women getting a chance in sports is seeing them learn to work together, to cooperate as men have learned to cooperate through sports, to bump each other, to get in tune with their bodies, to find out about that authenticity of sports. It's one area in life where there's no bullshit. You go out and do it, or you don't, and everybody can see."

I kept putting off visiting Jack at Oberlin, and by the time I was ready he was on his way out with the president who had hired him. When I saw Jack and Micki during the summer of 1974 they were still bitter over the Oberlin experience, but work-

ing hard to reestablish the Institute in New York, hating the
noise and fumes and concrete of the city. They seemed to have
changed; they were more political, more international, more
radical than reformist. They had toured sports facilities in Cuba
and were deeply impressed by the way they felt sports was being
used to tie that country together.

Later, when I trotted out the old concept of sports transcend-
ing politics and ideology, Jack said there was no way that sports
would not reflect the culture of the society that housed it.

"Sports is like education," he said, "it's always going to be in
the service of some ideology. The question is what do we want
that ideology to be. If you live in a consumption-oriented society,
pretty soon most athletes are going to be money grubbers."

That fall, Jack and Micki moved into the Portland, Oregon
home of Bill Walton, whom they had met the year before when
he was an all-America center at UCLA. Jack was working on a
personal account of his athletic career, including his Oberlin experiences, and Micki was working with a coach and athlete,
Lynda Huey, on a book about a woman's experience in sports.
And Walton was having a very rough rookie season in the NBA.

At UCLA, Walton had been insulated from the harsh rub of
the media by Coach John Wooden, as had Kareem Abdul-Jabbar
before him. As an antiwar activist, self-styled socialist, and
vegetarian, Walton needed as much freedom from the press as he
could get, and Wooden's protection gave him a chance to experiment and expand. But it also left him unprepared for the give-
and-take between press and pro. He seemed to resent, or at least
be bewildered by, the enormous attention he received, and he
was either too thoughtful or too arrogant to give reporters the
snappy two-line quotes they needed to make their deadlines. And
then it was very hard to answer in twenty-five words or less why
a 6-foot 11-inch White Hope was marching in farm worker pro-
tests with Cesar Chavez and Dick Gregory, why he carried skins
of distilled water and recordings of the Red Star Singers on road
trips, and how he could knock capitalism after signing a five-year
$2 million contract.

Walton had his answers but they were drowned in the press'
generally hostile chorus. There were more immediate problems.
The Portland Trail Blazer management apparently wanted Wal-

ton to gain weight and become more "aggressive" by eating meat, and when he was sick with influenza early in the season it was blamed on his natural foods diet. He developed a crippling bone-spur, and refused to take cortisone and pain-killing drugs which he felt might cause permanent injury. He began missing games, and a rumor was spread that he was malingering, trying to get out of his contract. Newsmen seemed particularly eager to dismiss him as a young "dupe" of Jack Scott, now depicted as a lurking shadow on the sunny fields of sport.

Talking to Jack on the phone that winter I sensed he was not entirely displeased with this latest notoriety; not only was the press installing him as the most important non-Establishment voice in sports, but he was moving into a new league of social activists. In one phone conversation, he wondered if he could continue "trivializing the world" by writing about sports.

A month later Jack and Micki disappeared to avoid FBI harassment and grand jury interrogation in connection with Patty Hearst. During the five weeks they were underground a rare photo of Jack shaven-headed (he had had a temporary scalp infection several years before) and wearing dark glasses became his media persona, and most everyone who had ever been involved with the couple was interrogated, some in midnight raids. I have no complaint about my own FBI interview; a local agent called for an appointment and came to my home. He seemed genuinely bemused by my opinion that Jack, Micki, the Institute, their athletic circle, had been the most progressive and hopeful influence on American sports in recent history. The agent, like most people, only knew what he read in the papers.

Jack and Micki reappeared on April 9, in San Francisco, as media celebrities. They flew to New York several times in the next few weeks to appear on network television shows, and we had a chance to spend time together again. I was surprised how fit they looked—they had been able to continue jogging "underground," thanks in part to the shaven-headed photo of Jack. In the flesh, he is tall, lean, muscular, but not intimidating; a fringe of blond beard and balding hair frames and softens a square-jawed face. Micki seems to appear either stern or toothy in most pictures; in her presence one is struck more by her athletic litheness and pretty face.

In private and in public Jack seemed concerned that his work in sports would be attacked on the basis of his new involvements, yet he seemed eager that sportswriters recognize him now as someone who traveled in the higher circles of recognized radicals, such as William Kunstler, Gerald Lefcourt, Jerry Rubin, and Daniel Ellsberg, with whom he tended to identify. He teased with snippets of underground lore—"You've got to find the balance between boldness and paranoia"—while avoiding answering direct questions about Patty Hearst, the Symbionese Liberation Army, or the underground, sticking to the line that whatever he had done had been in an effort to save lives. I sometimes thought that there was less there than met the eye, and when I told that to Jack he offered me a smile that seemed pregnant with secrets.

One afternoon in the spring of 1975, nearly five and a half years after we had first met in Berkeley, I read him a paragraph from *Athletics for Athletes*, written in 1969, and asked him if he still stood by it. The paragraph was: "The typical university coach is a soulless, back-slapping, meticulously groomed, team-oriented efficiency expert—a jock's Robert McNamara. It is not surprising that those students—college athletes—who daily spend two or three hours under the tutelage of these men are often the most reactionary group on campus."

Sitting upright in a high-backed chair, Scott began to speak in that familiar even tone. "I think my weakness then was to personalize too much. To hold individual men too accountable for actions that were part of a larger system. It's like trying to scapegoat Lieutenant Calley for the murderous conduct of a General Westmoreland, or a Richard Nixon, or a Henry Kissinger. My early writing came out of my own immediate experience in athletics. The people that I was having contact with were the people athletes encounter—coaches and low-level officials.

"Now I try to look at a social system that creates an environment where an event occurs. You know, it's the social climate that Woody Hayes exists in that makes him a hero when he beats up a photographer on the sidelines, or when he says, after the My Lai massacre, that he wouldn't trust any Vietnamese over 5.

"I was in St. Louis, at a sports symposium. I was in the motel bar with Willie Davis of the Green Bay Packers and this guy started rapping with him. He was a college coach recruiting in the area, after some high school hot shot, right?, and I just kept hoping, Jesus, the guy is drunk, don't let him recognize me, because, you know . . .

"He said, 'Oh, aren't you Jack Scott?' and I said yes, and he said, 'Look, I want to tell you just one thing. I'm 45 years old, I have a family, I have children, I've been here for three days because there's some kid 6–8 down the road here that I'm trying to get to come to my school. He's not going to come but if I'm not here my athletic director would get rid of me. You think I want to be here? Listen, Jack, the things you're writing and talking about, there are hundreds of coaches all across this country understand it, you just don't let anybody tell you different, you just keep doing it.'

"College coaches know what it's like to be fired this way and that. How capriciously they're treated, they're caught in the middle. Alums are telling them how to coach. They know what it's like to have some fat racist alum complain because you have too many blacks on your team or something. Since I've been an A. D. I've seen coaching from that perspective. On one level you're very optimistic, on the other level we cannot be naive. We are fighting the most powerful social system ever developed to co-opt and distort protest and to tolerate and pervert and make innocuous social movements."

We were sitting in a thirty-fifth floor suite of the Essex House hotel overlooking Central Park. ABC-TV, which had flown Jack in for the Geraldo Rivera "Goodnight America" show, was paying the bill. Earlier, from room service, I had ordered coffee and Jack orange juice and a Margarita. He said that he rarely drank, but that Fidel Castro had turned him on to Margaritas. I complimented Jack on the neatest bit of name-dropping I had heard that month.

I asked, "Do you think the professional athlete, even the highly publicized amateur athlete like Mark Spitz, has any social responsibilities as a hero or a role model, outside his specific responsibility as performer in the arena?"

"I would like to believe," said Scott, "and I was always taught in the schools I went to, that every person in a democracy, in order for the democracy to function efficiently and decently, has a responsibility to exhibit some kind of social awareness and so-cial conscience.

"Bill Walton should not have to have written into his pro con-tract that he has a right to practice his political and religious beliefs as long as he doesn't practice them on the court. That's supposed to be part of the first amendment to the Constitution.

"But in the world of professional athletics, especially consider-ing the degree of political repression practiced by those people who control sports for the purpose of maintaining the present social system, Bill has to have his first-amendment rights written into his contract.

"I've never spoken out against the right of a Jack Kemp or a Bob Mathias to mouth what I consider reactionary views. And I think it's pretty interesting that when a Mary Bacon says how the Ku Klux Klan is going to be the saviour of America, few sports writers get upset, but when Bill Walton speaks out against the Ford-Rockefeller-Kissinger gang that runs the country, most of them attack Bill."

I said, "They wonder what he's bitching about. He's got it made."

Scott nodded and gestured out the window. "All of a sudden you're looking out at America from the thirty-fifth floor. You know, it's easy to see why David Rockefeller sees and thinks the way he does. He's spent his whole life looking at America from at least the thirty-fifth floor of . . . he probably doesn't even slum at places like the Essex House.

"You know, you can't be too hard on Muhammad Ali or Billie Jean King when they move into that level of stardom and the flattery that goes with it. America fosters in people the idea that it was your own individual uniqueness that brought you into this position, not the struggle of masses of black people who are at least partially responsible for Ali, or the beautiful sisters who created a climate in which Billie Jean King could have her op-portunities.

"It was the hundreds and hundreds of athletes who were kicked off teams and the sportswriters who've had their careers snubbed out for writing too truthfully that allowed me to have my platform."

The afternoon slipped into evening. From the thirty-fifth floor we could actually watch the blueness of the sky deepen. We were expected soon at a dinner with other sportswriters. Later, we would go to a West Side party of lawyers, athletes, radicals, newsmen, to "celebrate the release from the grand jury and FBI harassment" of Jack and Micki, Jay Weiner, a young journalist, and Phil Shinnick, the former Olympic long jumper now a college instructor. Money would be collected for their attorney fees.

As Jack dressed for dinner, he said, "You know, I run every day because I know the joy I get from running, not because it makes me healthier. I dig it, I get high off it. I know the joys that exist from sport, and I've written about it. But most people don't pay much attention to that; somehow it doesn't fit my image.

"But those of us who really love sports are concerned that it be destroyed from being the experience it could be. So we focus on those things. We want to save sports for what it can be.

"I get a little disgusted with people who want to know why I'm a social activist, who try to trace it back to psychological reasons, the way my parents treated me, the way I was raised.

"Why don't they look around? Look at the objective conditions of this country. If you see what's happening the question is, 'Why *aren't* you a social activist?' "

CHAPTER
9

The Last American Dream

I HAVE NEVER understood why so many sportswriters and fans (or maybe just sportswriters since they tell fans how to feel) seem so resentful of athletes who earn more than $100,000 a year or sign long-term multimillion-dollar contracts. I've always thought that you can't be paid enough for your body and your time. Those are extremely perishable commodities. Very short shelf life.

Sometimes I wonder if those sportswriters identify instead with the insurance tycoons and the real estate moguls and the conglomerateurs and the heiresses who own the bodies of athletes and depreciate them each year on their income tax returns, a privilege denied the people who wear out the bodies.

I do understand, however, that it strains credulity to call major league superstars "exploited workers" so long as there are migrant farm laborers in America. But then, no one holds up grape pickers as heroes of the American Way, as role models to emulate, while most everyone I know thinks it's a worthy dream to get on the cover of *Sports Illustrated*. I am reminded of Coach Mel Rogers' observation that a boy who devotes his life to becoming president of the United States, even if he fails, will pick up enough experience and information along the way to make a successful and fulfilling career. But a boy who devotes his life to becoming center on the Los Angeles Lakers or the Chicago Bears, or a center-fielder on the New York Mets, had better get there if he expects to get anywhere at all.

Yet even if he does get there he's staked no ground he can call his own. He listens for the footsteps of a younger, faster, less expensive replacement, or the snap of his own Achilles tendon, or, potentially the most damaging, the self-righteous anger of the person who has bought and can sell him.

I think of M. Donald Grant, pouchy, well-turned-out chairman of the Mets, at a luncheon announcing the rehiring of Yogi Berra as a coach. Grant said, "Yogi is so dear to us, we hope he's here with us the rest of his healthy days. We pay Yogi a lot of money and we love Yogi every dollar's worth." I could understand Yogi just standing there, panting and wagging his tail, but I could not understand why Grant, presumably a wealthy and influential man, should have to be so patronizing to a former athlete.

Two years later I got my answer. On a night in 1969 when the Mets came within 2 percentage points of first place, M. Donald Grant ran through the clubhouse yelling, "New boys, new boys," the signal for young minor league Mets, brought up for the last month of the season, to form a single line along a wall. When the new boys were in line, Grant bowed in Mrs. Joan Whitney Payson, the Owner, who reviewed them like the Queen Mother trooping the Household Cavalry. Grant walked two steps behind her calling, "New boys, new boys, raise your hands and say your names." At that moment I understood Grant's own posturings and his studied condescension. Of course. Even he was somebody's bobo.

That year the Mets won the pennant and the World Series. One of their stars was Cleon Jones, a black outfielder from Alabama who batted .340. He had good years and fair years after that, and after the 1974 season he underwent surgery to repair his left knee. When the team came north after spring training in 1975, Jones was left behind on the disabled list to work himself back into shape. On May 4, at 5:30 A.M., Jones was arrested by St. Petersburg, Florida police who claimed they found him asleep in a van with a young white woman. Both were supposedly nude. Police claimed they found a marijuana cigarette in her purse. But after the story broke, all charges against both of them were dropped.

Yet Grant brought Cleon Jones and his wife of eleven years, Angela, north to Shea Stadium and exhibited them at a news conference in which he announced he was fining Jones $2,000 for soiling the Mets' image "of having clean ballplayers." He made Jones sign a statement that read, "I wish to apologize publicly to my wife and children, the Mets' ownership and management, my teammates, to all Met fans and to baseball in general for my behavior in St. Petersburg."

I was not there that day and I read the story in *The Times* three or four times before it sank in. The reporter, Gerald Eskenazi, wrote, "Grant bristled when asked what right the club had to fine Jones when, according to law-enforcement authorities, no crime had been committed. 'It was bad for baseball's image,' he snapped. 'It was in the newspapers.'"

Bristle and snap, that was Grant all right. Perhaps his style was individual, but his power was spelled out in custom and contracts. Curt Flood, in his unsuccessful suit to overthrow the so-called reserve clause, had called himself a "slave," provoking much amusement in the sporting press about $90,000-a-year slavery. Where do you apply for chains, went the line. But if Cleon Jones wasn't a slave, why was he standing with his wife for a public whipping? Mrs. Payson owned the plantation and Grant ran it for her. Jones understood. In July, Jones was kicked off the team. In August, Berra, by now the manager, was fired, his "healthy days" apparently over.

Athletes have always understood how the power is allocated in SportsWorld. Mrs. Payson owns Jones, CBS sells the Yankees, Warner Communications buys Pelé. Like most show business performers, athletes realize early that dignity is a luxury not even superstars can afford. And hundreds of marginal ballplayers turn up for breakfasts and banquets, silently scream through endless interviews, play golf with broadcast advertisers, and make themselves available because cooperation with the front office might mean an extra year or two in the big leagues.

"This land of make-believe business was perpetrated by sportswriters," said a lawyer who represents athletes. "The owners never fell for it; they were too busy forming syndicates and getting concession rights. The ballplayers who fell for it wised up the first time they got hurt or couldn't cut it."

Most wise up much earlier these days. The so-called gladiator mentality develops in high school, where athletes are often allowed to play hurt by ambitious coaches. It flowers in college, where new rules will make it even easier for coaches to unload athletes who cannot or will not play out their scholarships. Just

as the pressure for equal opportunity in minority-group education was used by athletic departments as a ploy to recruit black
and Chicano ballplayers who could not have otherwise qualified
for college, so will the current financial crunch be used to control
"problem" athletes and blunt and co-opt the drive for equality of
women in sports.

By the time an athlete reaches the major leagues these days he
is a fairly sophisticated survivor. He knows he needs a lawyer to
combat the owner's lawyers, and a union to combat the owner's
association. He knows his chances for a fair hearing in the press
or on television are spotty at best. "We have nothing to offer
except a few anecdotes," says Steve Hamilton, a major league
pitching coach. "No press rooms where we can entertain and
serve food and drinks like the owners, no facilities or resources to
counteract the gifts, the tickets, the high-level pressure."

Without a friendly press it becomes difficult for athletes to
communicate with fans. And the fans are getting meaner every
day.

All that repressed assembly-line rage, those fears of foreclo-
sure, fears of premature ejaculation, fears of occupational cancer,
those orchestrated fears of women, blacks, the young, the old, are
spilling out of the grandstand onto the field, the ice, the hardwood. Why not? Fans were always told they had bought the
right to cheer and boo, that the sports arena was not a classroom
or a courtroom or an office, it was one place where they could
righteously express themselves. Everything else has escalated—
prices, anxieties, dangers, and crime—why not self-expression?
And if you can't be heard anymore, you have to throw something.

Nothing is simple anymore, not even in SportsWorld. The
questions are getting more complicated. In a finite world with
limited resources how can we justify the thousands of private
planes that fly in fans for the Super Bowl? The America's Cup
yacht races, lasting weeks off Newport, R.I., usually draw thousands of private boats. Coast Guard cutters serve as ushers for
the spectator fleet, and the public, the nonseagoing public, too,
keeps the Coast Guard afloat.

How can we justify the Indianapolis 500, the fuel and metals it
consumes, the engineering skill it diverts? Once, I thought every
person had the right to risk his or her life in worthless derring-do.

Now, I'm not so sure. If race car drivers disappeared to lick their own burns and wounds, perhaps, but they continually tie up doctors and hospital facilities, and use up blood better saved for all the highway casualties their industrial pseudo-sport has helped promote.

And the answers are often more bewildering than the questions. When Muhammad Ali was made a freedman in 1971 by the Supreme Court, one of his lawyers, Robert Arum, said, "This case proves that our justice system works—if you have the money and the influence to go all the way." Three years later Arum stage-managed—with the shameless cooperation of the mass media—the Evel Knievel Snake River Canyon jump, which lost its front-page headlines that September Sunday to Ford's pardoning of Nixon.

Later, talking to an Arum associate, closed-circuit television promoter Michael Malitz, I wasn't absolutely sure which pseudo-event he was referring to when he said, "We really provided a realistic insight into American society. Most people thought he'd either kill himself or make it and be a hero millionaire. Well, that would have been unrealistic, life isn't that clear-cut anymore. What's realistic in America today is a minor mechanical failure that prevents you from reaching your goal."

Yet for all the cynicism and oppression and betrayal, the rhythms of sport, the sensations, and the emotions, are often the most intense and pleasurable ever experienced. They are universal. Billie Jean King describes how she feels after a perfect shot: "My heart pounds, my eyes get damp, and my ears feel like they're wiggling, but it's also just totally peaceful. It's almost like having an orgasm—it's exactly like that."

Yuri Vlasov, the great Soviet weightlifter, once sat in a Moscow gym and tried to explain to me why he was struggling to compete although he was past his prime. "At the peak of tremendous and victorious effort," he said through an interpreter, "while the blood is pounding in your head, all suddenly becomes quiet within you. Everything seems clearer and whiter than ever before, as if great spotlights had been turned on.

"At that moment you have the conviction that you contain all the power in the world, that you are capable of everything, that you have wings. There is no more precious moment in life than this, the white moment, and you will work very hard for years just to taste it again."

Great games, championship seasons, lie cool and sweet in memory forever. Jacques Plante, the goalie, exults, "And there are those nights I go home and tell my wife I don't know how they could score; I filled the net tonight, I blocked it all, and every time they shot I scooped up the puck and laughed, 'Aha, look what I found.'"

Bill Bradley rhapsodizes about the Knicks: "There's a great deal of exhilaration and contentment quick on its heels. After a good first quarter we can step back and look at it. There are not too many aspects of life where contentment follows so quickly the exhilaration of a total coordinated effort."

Dr. Benjamin Spock, author of a book that sold more copies than any other book except the Bible, cherished friend in need to millions of strangers with sick children, antiwar hero, a man of principle and daring, admitted in his seventy-second year that, secretly, he is most proud—of all his life's achievements—of the gold medal he won rowing for Yale in the 1924 Olympics.

The joy of sport is as real and accessible as the joy of sex; and both have been distorted and commercialized to make us consume and conform.

A million Little Leaguers stand for hours while a criminally obese "coach" drills the joy of sport out of their souls, makes them self-conscious and fearful, teaches them technique over movement, emphasizes dedication, sacrifice, and obedience instead of accomplishment and fun. And their mothers and fathers "Jog for Health" and "Swim for Your Life" in grim and dogged programs without ever sighing in ecstasy at the wind touching the sweaty roots of their hair, without moaning at the water's stroke on their gliding bodies.

Alvin Toffler's definition of Future Shock—novelty, transience, and diversity—also sounds like coming attractions for next season in SportsWorld: There will be even more sports, leagues, teams, contests, athletes to choose from, on so many channels of network, cable, and theater television that we will be even more fragmented and factionalized and alienated by staged events than we are now.

The millions who now define themselves as Football Fans will separate as new violent games capture their attention. Lacrosse. Power Volleyball. Karate Battle Royal. All the old sports will retreat into cults, splintered further by ideologies, sexual preferences, age, money. Regard the graffiti of tomorrow:

Support Gay Jousting!

Frisbee Uber Alles!

I Love Nude Polo!

Register Women, Not Steel Shuttlecocks!

There will even be institutionalized dissidents. People will actually play games that have no conclusions, inventing art-form athletic exhibitions in which no one wins or loses, performing tennis with stringless rackets, swinging imaginary bats at yo-yo balls, learning to breast-stroke in a manner that may not be "correct" but will be *you.*

And we will surely gamble on everything. The athlete will be a glorified betting object, like a racehorse. His skills, moods, habits, and urine will be under microscopic scrutiny by sportswriters now serving as investment advisers. Will they be any more professional or honest than the reporters who now cover horse racing? Except for those who actually ride, own, breed, or train horses, racing is no sport.

I once told Howard Samuels, then launching New York's Off-track Betting Corporation, that I thought government-encouraged gambling was just another diversion for the poor, a slice of pie in the sky to keep people from going after what they really needed. It was a counterrevolutionary tactic. Samuels dismissed my theory as patronizing and elitist. Since it is not often that a millionaire calls a sportswriter elitist, I did not argue with him. Thinking it over since, I am amazed at his gall. The alternative to false hope may be madness, rage, or revolution, but it is also meaningful change.

I am no hater of athletes and my book is not antisports, although these will be the reflex charges. I have watched more games than most people, and enjoyed them. I begrudge no one entertainment, only oblivion. Turn down the volume for a moment and think: Why should you be sitting there, where an M. Donald Grant wants you, flesh sodden, head filled with gibberish and numbers, past anger, past moving, past caring, when there is still light in the sky and time left in the day to hear the pounding of your heart and taste salt in your mouth and feel cool air caress the dampness of your skin?

We won't say that it's good for your eternal soul, or that it beats watching No. 12 get it off for you, or that you'll live longer. Just that it feels nice. "For starters," writes the Canadian distance runner, Bruce Kidd, "we should stop preaching about sport's moral values. Sport, after all, isn't Lent. It's a pleasure of the flesh."

Write that on your locker-room wall.

Index

Aaron, Hank, 8–10, 68, 195, 230–232

Abdul-Jabbar, Kareem, 37, 150–157, 160, 162, 167, 168, 270

Abernathy, Ralph, 195

Agee, Tommie, 47

Agnew, Spiro, 205, 232, 267

Alcindor, Lew (*see* Abdul-Jabbar, Kareem)

Ali, John, 120–121

Ali, Muhammad, 8, 36–37, 75–100, 104–108, 110–127, 131–132, 135, 136, 165, 182, 191, 194–199, 238–265, 274, 280

Allen, George, 11, 15–19

Allen, Mel, 3

Always on the Run, 17

Amdur, Neil, 138

Ameer, Leon 4 X, 92–93, 95, 97–102, 121

Anderson, Dave, 17, 70, 192, 196, 230

Angell, Roger, 31–32

Ardrey, Robert, 53

Arum, Robert, 280

Ashburn, Richie, 33

Ashe, Arthur, 79

Athletic Revolution, The (Scott), 268

Athletics for Athletes (Scott), 268, 272

Atkins, C. B., 247, 253, 259, 263

Atlanta Braves, 231

Auto racing, *x*, 8, 84, 209, 279–280

Axthelm, Pete, 138, 183

Bacon, Mary, 274

Ball Four (Bouton), 42, 234

Baltimore Orioles, 35, 47

Barnett, Dick, 163, 167

Baseball, *xii*, 3–4, 23–49, 230–237
  Black Sox scandal (1919), 170
  Hall of Fame, 48, 235–237

Basketball, *xiii*, 8, 23, 24, 140–169
  Boston College, 155
  college scandals, 147, 158
  UCLA, 153, 155

Baltimore Cardinals, 12, 35, 45, 46, 231

Baltimore Colts, 62

Baugh, Sammy, 59

Beatles, the, 81, 82, 198, 251

Belinsky, Bo, 179

Berkow, Ira, 37, 183

Berra, Yogi, 9, 38, 42–43, 82, 106, 277, 278

Bingham, Howard, 247, 259, 263, 265

Black Muslims, 85–95, 97–102, 105, 106, 108, 110, 111, 113–116, 120–122, 125, 135–136, 156, 247, 258

Black Sox scandal, 170

Blaik, Earl, 57

Bond, Julian, 120, 195

Boorstin, Daniel J., 59

285

Boslooper, Thomas, 220
Boston Braves, 23, 232
Boston Celtics, 145, 148
Bouton, Jim, 37, 42, 179, 234
Boys of the Summer, The (Kahn),
   45
Bradbury, Will, 196
Bradley, Bill, 37, 159–167, 169,
   281
Branca, Ralph, 19
Breslin, Jimmy, 27, 176
Brock, Lou, 46, 49
Brooklyn Dodgers, *see* Dodgers
Broun, Heywood, 171
Brown, Bundini, 90
Brown, H. Rap, 128
Brown, Jim, *xi*, 8, 98, 113, 205
Brown, Paul, 233–234
Bruce, Lenny, 111
Brundage, Avery, 28, 127, 138
Bunche, Ralph, 109, 151, 155
Burgin, Dave, 37
Busch, August A., 45

Cable television, *xiii–xiv*
Cady, Steve, 200–201
Cannon, Jimmy, 7, 25, 75, 76, 105,
   175–179, 181
Carbo, Frankie, 103, 113
Carlos, John, 139
Caro, Robert A., 26
Carpenter, Bill, 50
Castro, Fidel, 273
Catledge, Turner, 133
Chafee, Hope, 209–211
Chamberlain, Wilt, 8, 14, 148, 155,
   167, 168
Charles, Ed, 47
Chavez, Cesar, 270
Chevigny, Jack, 174
Chicago Bears, 12
Chicago Cubs, 45
Chicago White Sox, 35
Chuvalo, George, 101, 117, 119
Cincinnati Reds, 230
Cincinnati Royals, 148
Clay, Cassius (*see* Ali, Muhammad)

Clay, Cassius Marcellus, Sr., 77, 99
Clay, Henry, 77
Clay, Sonji (Roi), 94, 95, 114
Cleaver, Eldridge, 13, 108
Clemente, Roberto, 47
Clendenon, Donn, 47
Cleveland Indians, 235, 237
Cobb, Ty, 237
Cohen, Joel H., 48
Cohn, Roy, 104
Conn, Billy, 19, 233
Connors, Jimmy, 241
Conrad, Harold, 94, 105, 108
Cooper, Henry, 118, 119
Corcoran, Fred, 219
Cosby, Bill, 195, 255
Cosell, Howard, 37, 61, 72, 119,
   241, 242, 246, 249, 253
Cousy, Bob, 148, 155
Cowens, Dave, 168
Cox, Ella, 209–211
Crowley, Jim, 171
Csonka, Larry, 17, 63

Daley, Arthur, 45, 60, 129, 132,
   137, 175, 176, 181–184, 196,
   230
Daley, Robert, 184
D'Amato, Cus, 103, 109–110
Danzig, Allison, 227, 228
Dash, Sam, 19
Davis, Al, 234
Davis, Willie, 272–273
DeBusschere, Dave, 167
Decline of the Wasp, The (Schrag),
   55
Deford, Frank, 228
DeGaulle, Charles, 12, 13
Dempsey, Jack, 74–76, 233, 251
DePaula, Frankie, 190, 191
Detroit Tigers, 46
Devlin, Bernadette, 197
Didrikson, Babe, 217–220
DiMaggio, Joe, 4, 9, 38, 47, 178,
   184
DiTrani, Vinny, 21
Doby, Larry, *x*, 35, 236–237

Dodgers, 3–4, 23, 24, 31, 32, 35, 36, 46, 47, 232

Donohue, Jack, 152–155

Dundee, Angelo, 80, 107, 131–132, 134, 240–243, 245, 247, 251, 254, 263, 264

Dundee, Chris, 241, 251

Durslag, Mel, 42

Eckert, William D., 25–26

Edwards, Harry, 39, 127–128, 130, 131, 137–139, 154

Eisenhower, Dwight D., 14, 75

Ellsberg, Daniel, 272

Ellis, Jimmy, 131–132, 134–137, 240, 251–252, 254

Eskenazi, Gerald, 278

Face in the Crowd, A, 85

Farewell to Sport (Gallico), 219

Feminine Mystique, The (Friedan), 84

Femininity Game, The (Boslooper), 220

Fetchit, Stepin, 94, 95

Fimrite, Ron, 48

Finley, Charles O., 35, 48–49, 237

Fire Next Time, The (Baldwin), 84

Fisher, Mickey, 141–144, 148–149

Flood, Curt, 37, 42, 46, 278

Florence, Wally, 221–222

Foley, Zora, 119, 122, 240

Football, *xiii*, 50–73
    Army-Notre Dame games, 170–171, 174
    college, 69–70
    Four Horsemen, the, 170, 171, 173, 174
    Nixon and, 11–17, 19–21, 40, 51, 71
    Super Bowl games, *x*, 12, 18, 46, 59, 61–63, 71, 72, 84

Ford, Gerald, 14, 16, 20, 21, 230, 232, 274, 280

Foreman, George, 239, 241–245, 251, 261

Forte, Levi, 240, 242, 244, 245, 253, 264

Foster, Bob, 189–190

Foster, Phil, 44

Four Horsemen, the, 170, 171, 173, 174

Frazier, Joe, 131, 196–197, 240, 257, 261

Frazier, Walt, 157, 160, 163

Friedan, Betty, 84

Gallico, Paul, 171, 219

Gambling, sports, government-regulated, *xiii–xiv*, 282

Garagiola, Joe, 42

Gehrig, Lou, 47

Gehrig, Mrs. Lou, 233

Gent, Pete, 21

Gertz, Elmer, 114

Giants, 3–4, 23, 24, 27, 32, 36

Giardello, Joey, 187–188, 190

Gibson, Althea, 205–208, 225

Gibson, Bob, 46

Gibson, Josh, 237

Gifford, Frank, 60, 233–234

Gill, Clarence X, 92, 97, 101

Gipp, George, 174

Glenn, John, 36

Glickman, Bernie, 113

Golf, 8, 204, 205, 219–222

Gonzalez, Pancho, 208, 225, 226

Green Bay Packers, 12, 53–58, 272–273

Grant, M. Donald, 27, 277–278, 282

Gray, Barry, 98

Gregory, Dick, 75, 83, 89, 96, 130, 270

Griffin, Albert P., 240

Griffith, Emile, 188, 194

Grimes, Burleigh, 13

Gross, Lou, 249–250

Gross, Milton, 109, 154, 195–196

Halas, George, 15

Hamill, Pete, 176

Hamilton, Steve, 278

Harder They Fall, The (Schulberg), 85

Harness racing, 8

Harlem Globetrotters, 151

Hawkins, Connie, 140–148, 151, 160, 168

Hayes, Woody, 272

Haywood, Spencer, 162–163

Hecht, Ben, 176

Hefner, Hugh, 197

Hoch, Paul, 220, 268

Hockey, *vii, xiii,* 23, 77–78, 157, 168–169

Hodges, Gil, 43, 46

Hoffman, Abbie, 197

Holtzman, Jerome, 173, 180

Holy Cross, 155

Hornsby, Rogers, 48

Hornung, Paul, 53, 56–57

Horse racing, 8, 24–25, 282
  Kentucky Derby, *x,* 84, 209

Horton, Willie, 46

Houk, Ralph, 39

Howell, Jim Lee, 57

Huey, Lynda, 270

Huff, Sam, 60

Humphrey, Hubert H., 13, 46

Hunt, H. L., 97

Hunt, Lamar, 59, 226

Hunter, Catfish, 237

Indianapolis 500, *x,* 84, 209, 279–280

Inside Corner (Seaver), 48

Instant Replay (Kramer), 55

Isaacs, Stan, 32, 37, 179, 183

Izenberg, Jerry, 183

Jackson, Cass, 269

Jackson, Jesse, 195, 230

Jock chic, 20

Jock Lib, 70

Jocks, The (Shecter), 234

Johansson, Ingemar, 76

Johnson, Jack, 76, 80

Johnson, John L., 240, 242, 245, 248, 249, 264

Johnson, Lyndon B., 13, 20–21, 116

Jones, Angela, 277

Jones, Cleon, 47, 277–278

Jones, Perry T., 224

Jordan, Pat, 48

Kahn, Roger, 45, 160, 232–233

Kaine, Elinor, 222

Kansas City Chiefs, 12

Kelly, King, 47

Kemp, Jackie, 14, 274

Kempton, Murray, 167

Kennedy, Ethel, 197, 205, 208

Kennedy, John F., *xiii,* 15, 86, 232

Kennedy, Robert F., 14–15, 40, 93, 97, 205, 208, 232

Kentucky Derby, *x,* 84, 209

Kidd, Bruce, 283

Kiernan, John, 181

Kiick, Jim, 17, 63

Kilmer, Billy, 17

Kindig, Howard, 18

Kiner, Ralph, 47

King, Billie Jean, *xi–xii,* 37, 222–226, 228–230, 274, 280

King, Coretta, 195

King, Martin Luther, Jr., 117, 120, 125, 127, 128, 195, 230, 232

Kissinger, Henry, 272, 274

Klem, Bill, 182

Knievel, Evel, 86, 280

Koosman, Jerry, 46

Koppett, Leonard, 177, 235

Kramer, Jack, 226

Kramer, Jerry, 54–55

Kranepool, Ed, 34

Kremenko, Barney, 25–26

Krout, John A., 170

Kuhn, Bowie, 37, 41–42, 47, 48, 230, 235

Kunstler, William, 272

Laird, Mel, 12–13
Landis, Kenesaw Mountain, 170
Lang, Jack, 31
Lardner, Ring, 171
LaSalle Corporation, 231
Laury, Linda, 208–211, 213
Laver, Rod, 223
Layden, Elmer, 171
Lefcourt, Gerald, 272
Lenglen, Suzanne, 225
Lennon, John, 81, 192
Leopold, Nathan, 114
Liberty Two (Lipsyte), 206, 232
Liebling, A. J., 187
Lindberg, Charles, 233
Lindsay, John V., 39–40, 46–49, 205
Lipsyte, Marjorie, 100–102
Lipton, Ben, 210, 211
Liston, Sonny, 8, 36–37, 75, 76, 82–87, 90–94, 96, 97, 104–106, 109, 196, 198, 238, 241, 243
Lois, George, 159
Lombardi, Vince, 16, 37, 52–59, 106, 223, 234
London, Brian, 119
Lorenz, Konrad, 53
Los Angeles Dodgers, *see* Dodgers
Los Angeles Lakers, 167
Los Angeles Rams, 15
Louis, Joe, 19, 74–76, 84, 103, 107, 178, 197, 233, 251, 252
Love Story (Segal), 215
Lyle, Ron, 248–249

McCarthy, Eugene, 13, 138
McClinton, Harold, 18
McGee, Max, 56–57
McGee, Micki, 267–271, 275
McGeehan, W. O., 175, 181
McGraw, John, 47
Machen, Eddie, 102
Mack, Connie, 42
McKissick, Floyd, 127, 128
McLain, Denny, 37, 41

McMurtry, John, 50
McNamara, Robert, 272
McPhee, John, 164–165
McTier, Solomon, 245, 263
Maidenberg, Hy, 37
Mailer, Norman, 85, 197
Main Bout, Inc., 113, 114, 131
Malcolm X, 85, 86, 89, 92, 95, 97, 100–102, 105, 232, 261
Malitz, Michael, 280
Malone, Martha, 83–84
Mann, Carol, 220–222
Mann, Jack, 37
Mantle, Mickey, 8–9, 33, 34, 182
Mara family, 60–61
Maravich, Pete, 168
Marciano, Rocky, 74–76, 251
Maris, Roger, 9–10
Martin, Joe, 78
Massachusetts Boxing Commission, 93
Mastroianni, Marcello, 197
Mathias, Bob, 274
Mathis, Buster, 131
Mays, Willie, 27, 47
Mead, Margaret, 32
Meat on the Hoof (Shaw), 268
Meggyesy, Dave, 12, 17–18, 37, 51, 133–134, 234, 268
Merchant, Larry, 37, 179
Meredith, Dandy Don, 62
Miami Dolphins, 17, 18
Mildenberger, Karl, 119
Miller, Don, 171
Miller, Bozo, 134–135
Miller, Henry, 114
Milwaukee Braves, 23, 231
Milwaukee Bucks, 156, 167
Mitchell, John, 53
Moffitt, Betty, 224
Moffitt, Bill, 224, 225
Moffitt, Randy, 225
Molinas, Jack, 147
Molineaux, Zachary, 80
Moody, Helen Wills, 225
Moses, Robert, 26

Muhammad, Elijah, 86, 88–89, 91–93, 97, 98, 100, 118, 120–122, 125, 136, 247, 255, 257, 261

Muhammad, Herbert, 120–121

Muhammad, Wallace, 257, 261

Murray, Jim, 252

Musial, Stan, 6, 47, 231

Nagurski, Bronko, 182

Namath, Joe, 15, 37, 46, 52, 53, 59, 61–66, 68–73, 106, 114, 158, 223

National Wheelchair Games, 208–213

Negro Economic Union, 113

New York Athletic Club boycott, 45, 127–130

New York Athletic Commission, 131

New York Times Sports Department, 3–9, 25, 38, 180–182

Newcombe, John, 241

New York Giants, 60, 222

New York Giants (baseball), *see* Giants

New York Jets, 24, 46, 51, 61, 62, 68, 73, 158, 222

New York Knicks, 156–161, 163–167, 281

New York Mets, 26–36, 39–40, 42–49, 82, 106, 158, 233, 277–278

New York Titans, 59–61

New York Yankees, 3–4, 8–10, 27, 33–35, 38, 42, 232, 237, 278

Nicklaus, Jack, 204–205, 263

Nigger (Lipsyte), 83

Nitschke, Ray, 53

Nixon, Richard M., 11–17, 19–21, 40, 42, 51, 53, 71, 229, 232, 237, 272, 280

No Cheering in the Pressbox (Holtzman), 173, 180

Norris, James, 103

North Dallas Forty (Gent), 21

Norton, Ken, 257

Novak, Michael, 51

Oakland A's, 35

Oakland Raiders, 12

O'Brien, Johnny (One-Play), 174

Octopus, Inc., 103

Off-track betting, 282

Olsen, Jack, 77, 138, 152

Olympic Games, xv, 78–79, 128, 129, 154, 163, 218–219, 281
  Israeli athletes, massacre of, xv
  in Mexico City, 45, 127, 138–139
  women's participation in, beginning of, 218

O'Malley, Walter, 47

On the Pad (Shecter), 234

Orcutt, Maureen, 221

Out of Their League (Meggyesy), 133–134, 268

Owens, Jesse, 182

Padwe, Sandy, 37, 138, 183

Paige, Satchel, 235–237

Palinkas, Pat, 221, 222

Palmer, Arnold, 204, 263

Palmer, Joe, 7

Paper Lion (Plimpton), 55

Parrish, Bernie, 62

Parseghian, Ara, 53–54

Pastrano, Willie, 240, 249, 250

Paterno, Joe, 19

Patterson, Floyd, 75, 76, 84–86, 91, 101, 103, 104, 106–112, 120, 197

Patty Hearst case, 267, 271, 272

Payson, Mrs. Joan Whitney, 27–31, 277, 278

Pegler, Westbrook, 171, 176, 181

Pepe, Phil, 179, 196

Peretz, Martin, 21

Perez, Anthony, Jr., 239

Periot, Paul, 12

Perry, Lincoln (Stepin Fetchit), 94, 95

Philadelphia A's, 35
Phoenix Suns, 148
Pittsburgh Steelers, 62
Plante, Jacques, 281
Plimpton, George, 9, 55, 194, 196
Poitier, Sidney, 195
Powell, Adam Clayton, 120
Powell, Charlie, 90
Powers, Francis Gary, 10

Quarry, Jerry, 131, 134–137, 194, 195

Rafferty, Max, 267
Reagan, Ronald, 267
Reasoner, Harry, 233
Reed, Willis, 160, 167
Reston, James, 230
Rice, Grantland, 170–175, 181, 219
Richards, Bob, 225
Rickard, Tex, 170
Rickey, Branch, 28
Riggs, Bobby, 229
Rip Off the Big Game (Hoch), 220, 268
Rise of the Unmeltable Ethnics, The (Novak), 51
Rivera, Geraldo, 273
Rizzuto, Phil, 6
Roach, James, 25, 38
Robertson, Oscar, 148, 157, 166, 167
Robinson, Frank, *xi*, 234, 235, 237
Robinson, Jackie, *x*, *xii*, 35, 151, 235–237
Robinson, Sugar Ray, 76, 197
Rockefeller, David, 274
Rockefeller, Nelson, *xii*, 65, 274
Rockne, Knute, 172–174
Rodriquez, Luis, 240
Rogers, Mel, 276
Rogers, Tom, 171
Roland, Gilbert, 205
Rooney, Art, 62
Roosevelt, Franklin D., 13

Rosenthal, Harold, 182
Ross, Diana, 195, 255
Rozelle, Pete, *xiii*, 52, 59, 234
Rubin, Jerry, 272
Ruby, Jack, 114
Runyon, Damon, 7, 171, 176, 181
Russell, Bill, *xi*, 8, 155, 168
Ruth, Babe, *xii*, 9, 182, 217, 220, 230, 232–233, 237
Ruth, Claire, 233
Ryan, Cornelius, 63

Samuels, Howard, 282
Sanders, Doug, 220–222
San Francisco Giants, *see* Giants
Sarria, Luis, 238, 252, 253
Sauer, George, Jr., 51
Sayre, Nora, *xv*
Sayres, Gale, 12
Schaap, Dick, 55, 70, 80
Schrag, Peter, 55
Schulberg, Budd, 85, 197
Scott, Jack, 234, 265–275
Seaver, Nancy, 44–45
Seaver, Tom, 39–40, 43–45, 47–49
Segal, Erich, 215
Sense of Where You Are, A (McPhee), 164
Shaw, Gary, 268
Shecter, Len, 32, 37, 42, 138, 183, 194, 234
Sheehan, George A., 214–216
Shinnick, Phil, 275
Shore, Dinah, 205
Shula, Don, 17, 18
Simpson, O. J., *xi*, 61–62, 72–73, 222
Sinatra, Frank, 177, 197
Sixties Going on Seventies (Sayre), *xv*
Smith, Red, 7, 36, 171, 175, 176, 179–181
Smith, Stan, 205
Smith, Tommie, 139, 269

Sommer, Elke, 205
Soviet Union, *xiv*
Spitz, Mark, 273
Spock, Benjamin, 281
Sportswriters, 25–34, 36–39, 42,
    43, 45–47, 170–199
Stade, George, 50
Stanton, Elizabeth Cady, 217
Starr, Bart, 12, 69
Starr, Ringo, 81
Steinbrenner, George, 237
Stengel, Casey, 27–30, 42, 43
Strickler, George, 173
Stuhldreher, Harry, 171, 173
Suitors of Spring, The (Jordan),
    48
Sunni Moslems, 156
Super Bowl, *x*, 12, 18, 46, 59, 61–
    63, 71, 72, 84
Susann, Jacqueline, 63
Sweet Science, The (Liebling), 187
Swoboda, Ron, 233
Symbionese Liberation Army, 272

Talese, Gay, 8, 137
Tarkenton, Fran, 132
Tennis, *xiii*, 3, 8, 24–25, 200–208,
    223–230
Terrell, Ernie, 102, 112–114, 118–
    121
They Call It a Game (Parrish), 62
This Life I've Led (Zaharias), 219
Thomson, Bobby, 19
Thorpe, Jim, 217
Throneberry, Marv, 32–34, 42
Tiger, Dick, 184–194, 199
Tiger, Lionel, 53
Tittle, Y. A., 60
Toffler, Alvin, 281
Torres, Jose, 105, 111, 189
Tuckner, Howard, 8
Tumult and the Shouting, The
    (Rice), 174, 219
Tunis, John R., 171
Tunney, Gene, 75, 175, 233
Twombly, Wells, 37

Van Breda Kolff, Butch, 164
Vaughn, Sarah, 259
Vlasov, Yuri, 280–281
Von Hoffman, Nicholas, 123

Wagner, Honus, 47
Wallace, George, 232
Walton, Bill, 168, 270–271, 274
Warner Communications, 278
Warren, Earl, 23
Washington Redskins, 15–18
Weiner, Jay, 275
Weiss, George, 27–29
Weissmuller, Johnny, 20
Wepner, Chuck, 240, 248
Werblin, David A. (Sonny), 61,
    68, 69, 71
What Makes Sammy Run? (Schul-
    berg), 85
Wheelchair Games, 208–213
White, Gordon, 154
Whittier College, 11, 15
Wieland, Bob, 211–213
Wilkinson, Bud, 53–54
Williams, Cleveland, 119
Williams, Ted, 237
Wills, Maury, 49
Wilson, Flip, 255
Wilson, Harold, 13
Wismer, Harry, 59–61
Wolf, Dave, 138, 143, 145–147
Wooden, John, 142, 154, 156, 270
Woodward, Stanley, 25, 179, 180
World Boxing Association, 93, 102,
    131
Wrigley, Philip, 45

Young, Andrew, 195
Young, Dick, 26, 31, 36
Yuman, Bernie, 252–253

Zaharias, Babe, 217–220
Zaharias, George, 217, 219, 220
Zimmerman, Paul, 18

ABOUT THE AUTHOR

ROBERT LIPSYTE, a graduate of Columbia College and the Columbia Graduate School of Journalism, was on the staff of *The New York Times* from 1957 through 1971. He is the author of seven books, including Dick Gregory's autobiography, *Nigger*, and the novels *Liberty Two* and *The Contender*.

QUADRANGLE BOOKS

HISTORY

E. Digby Baltzell	PHILADELPHIA GENTLEMEN	3.45
Roger Burlingame	HENRY FORD	2.95
Gerald M. Capers	JOHN C. CALHOUN: OPPORTUNIST	2.95
Leroy D. Clark	THE GRAND JURY	2.95
Elisha P. Douglass	REBELS AND DEMOCRATS	4.50
Melvyn Dubofsky	WE SHALL BE ALL	4.95
Stewart Edwards	THE PARIS COMMUNE 1871	4.95
Arthur A. Ekrich, Jr.	IDEOLOGIES AND UTOPIAS	2.95
Edwin Scott Gaustad	THE GREAT AWAKENING IN NEW ENGLAND	2.25
Gerald N. Grob	WORKERS AND UTOPIA	3.95
W. O. Henderson	THE INDUSTRIAL REVOLUTION IN EUROPE	2.95
Richard N. Hunt	GERMAN SOCIAL DEMOCRACY	2.95
Edward Chase Kirkland	INDUSTRY COMES OF AGE	2.95
Walter LaFeber	JOHN QUINCY ADAMS AND AMERICAN CONTINENTAL EMPIRE	2.25
Leonard W. Levy	JEFFERSON AND CIVIL LIBERTIES	2.95
Huey P. Long	EVERY MAN A KING	2.95
George E. Mowry	THE CALIFORNIA PROGRESSIVES	4.95

William O'Neill	COMING APART	4.95
William O'Neill	EVERYONE WAS BRAVE	4.95
William O'Neill	WOMEN AT WORK	4.50
Frank L. Owsley	PLAIN FOLK OF THE OLD SOUTH	2.65
Julius W. Pratt	EXPANSIONISTS OF 1898	2.95
June Sochen	MOVERS AND SHAKERS	3.95
June Sochen	THE NEW WOMAN IN GREENWICH VILLAGE: 1910-1920	3.50
Bernard Sternsher	HITTING HOME	2.95
Athan Theoharis	SEEDS OF REPRESSION	2.95
Willard M. Wallace	APPEAL TO ARMS	3.50
Norman Ware	THE INDUSTRIAL WORKER: 1840-1860	2.65
Bernard A. Weisberger	THEY GATHERED AT THE RIVER	2.95
Robert H. Wiebe	BUSINESSMEN AND REFORM	2.65

POLITICAL SCIENCE

Leroy D. Clark	THE GRAND JURY	2.95
Melvyn Dubofsky	WE SHALL BE ALL	2.65
James P. Comer, M.D.	BEYOND BLACK AND WHITE	2.95
Gerald N. Grob	WORKERS AND UTOPIA	3.95
Frederic C. Howe	CONFESSIONS OF A REFORMER	3.95
Edward Chase Kirkland	INDUSTRY COMES OF AGE	2.95
Anne Koedt, Ellen Levine, Anita Rapone	RADICAL FEMINISM	4.95
Huey P. Long	EVERY MAN A KING	2.95
Neil McCaulay	THE SANDINO AFFAIR	2.95
Martin Oppenheimer	THE URBAN GUERRILLA	2.45
Yaacov Shimoni, et al.	POLITICAL DICTIONARY OF THE MIDDLE EAST IN THE TWEN-TIETH CENTURY	6.95
Norman Ware	THE INDUSTRIAL WORKER: 1840-1860	2.65
Alan F. Westin and Michael A. Baker	DATABANKS IN A FREE SOCIETY	4.95

SOCIOLOGY

Lewis Atherton	MAIN STREET ON THE MIDDLE BORDER	4.50
E. Digby Baltzell	PHILADELPHIA GENTLEMEN	3.45
Andrew Greeley	THAT MOST DIS-TRESSFUL NATION	2.95
Irving Howe, ed.	THE WORLD OF THE BLUE-COLLAR WORKER	2.95
Kurt Lang and Gladys Engel Lang	POLITICS AND TELEVISION	2.95
Robert Lipsyte	SPORTSWORLD	3.45
William O'Neill	COMING APART	4.95
Martin Oppenheimer	THE URBAN GUERRILLA	2.45
Arthur L. Stinchcombe	REBELLION IN HIGH SCHOOL	2.65
Telford Taylor	NUREMBERG AND VIETNAM	1.95
Peter Wilsher and Rosemary Righter	THE EXPLODING CITIES	3.45

PSYCHOLOGY

Sol Gordon with Roger Conant	YOU	7.95
Janet and Paul Gotkin	TOO MUCH ANGER, TOO MANY TEARS	4.95
Florence R. Miale and Michael Selzer	THE NUREMBERG MIND	3.95
Patricia O'Brien	THE WOMAN ALONE	3.95
Edward Rosenfeld	THE BOOK OF HIGHS	4.95
Charles W. Socarides	BEYOND SEXUAL FREEDOM	2.95
Paul Tibbetts	PERCEPTION	4.95

WOMEN'S STUDIES

Judith Hole and Ellen Levine	REBIRTH OF FEMINISM	4.50
Anne Koedt, Ellen Levine, Anita Rapone	RADICAL FEMINISM	4.95
Aileen S. Kraditor	UP FROM THE PEDESTAL	4.50
Patricia O'Brien	THE WOMAN ALONE	3.95
William O'Neill	EVERYONE WAS BRAVE	4.95
June Sochen	MOVERS AND SHAKERS	3.95
June Sochen	THE NEW WOMAN IN GREENWICH VILLAGE: 1910-1920	3.50
Tess Slesinger	ON BEING TOLD THAT HER SECOND HUSBAND HAS TAKEN HIS FIRST LOVER	4.50

HOME ECONOMICS

Ruth Amiel and Happy Gerhard	FINALLY IT FITS	6.95
Judith and Bernard Rabb	GOOD SHELTER	7.95
Rita Reif	HOME: IT TAKES MORE THAN MONEY	5.95
Louis Szathmary	THE CHEF'S SECRET COOKBOOK	6.95

GENERAL & REFERENCE

John Bailey	INTENT ON LAUGHTER	2.95
Claude A. Frazier	COPING WITH FOOD ALLERGY	3.95
Mike Jahn	ROCK	4.95
Arnold and Connie Krochmal	A GUIDE TO THE MEDICINAL PLANTS OF THE UNITED STATES	4.95
Muriel Lederer	THE GUIDE TO CAREER EDUCATION	6.95
Miriam Makeba	THE WORLD OF AFRICAN SONG	3.95
Nancy M. Page and Richard E. Weaver, Jr.	WILD PLANTS IN THE CITY	3.95
Dr. John J. Reynolds and Dr. Thomas D. Houchin	A DIRECTORY FOR SPANISH-SPEAKING NEW YORK	3.95
Richard F. Shepard	GOING OUT IN NEW YORK	4.50
Arthur Vineberg, M.D.	HOW TO LIVE WITH YOUR HEART	2.95